D1161628

APPROACHES
TO
SEMIOTICS

edited by

THOMAS A. SEBEOK

Research Center for the Language Sciences
Indiana University

54

G. H. MEAD'S CONCEPT OF RATIONALITY:

A STUDY OF THE USE OF SYMBOLS AND OTHER IMPLEMENTS

by

W. KANG

1976
MOUTON
THE HAGUE - PARIS

© Copyright 1976
Mouton & Co. B.V., Publishers, The Hague

No part of this book may be translated or reproduced in any form, by print, photo-print, microfilm, or any other means, without written permission from the publishers

ISBN 90 279 3165 8

Printed in The Netherlands

CONTENTS

6

It is the province of philosophy to work out the implication
of the fact that reason has arisen in the process of social evolution.

G. H. Mead, The Philosophy of the Act (c. 1916–31)

ABBREVIATIONS

The following abbreviations are adapted for Mead's posthumously published works. The number after these abbreviations in parentheses or footnotes is the page number of the noted book. The complete bibliographical information is given at the end of this work.

ES for George Herbert Mead: Essays on His Social Philosophy
MS ,, Mind, Self, and Society
MT ,, Movements of Thought in the Nineteenth Century
PA ,, The Philosophy of the Act
PP ,, The Philosophy of the Present
SP ,, The Social Psychology of George Herbert Mead
SW ,, Selected Writings

INTRODUCTION

The present work is an attempt to reconstruct an anthropological concept of rationality. It is an introduction to what one may, in a historical
perspective of Western philosophy, call the Critique of Impure Reason.

In a logically reconstructed perspective of the works of George
Herbert Mead (1864-1931), it is shown that the main concern and aspect of his psychological and philosophical works is a reinterpretation
of "reason" or "rationality". This reinterpretation is, on one hand,
what Mead draws as an anthropological implication of the contemporary
view of "evolutionary teleology" in biology and that of "relative objectivity" in physics. On the other hand, it is what he presents to the
sciences of man as a basic theory of man's "social act", which unifies
its pervasive mediation criteria: 1) the appropriateness or functionality
of ends and means, and 2) the functionality of symbolic process.

This concept of rationality is more inclusive in understanding man's
act or experience than the traditional concepts of "reason", "truth",
"good" or "right", and "beauty" - inclusive in the sense that it allows
us to discriminate man's acts more pervasively in their diverse contexts in terms of a set of polar concepts, rationality and irrationality.
This concept is distinguished: 1) from teleology and intelligence in the
biological sense; 2) from reason as the "faculty" of assertive discourse
or the truth function of assertive statement in the traditional or present
exclusive sense of epistemology; and 3) from reason as the "innate
faculty" or "a priori structure" of individual mind in the traditional
sense of metaphysics and epistemology. Furthermore, the concept of
rationality is given in a language which contemporary psychology and
other sciences can apply to their fields without much modification.

The purpose of the work as a whole is philosophical and anthropological.
At the same time, it is a study of the works of Mead, who is regarded
as the father of symbolic interactionism in the American setting and who
shares with C. S. Peirce the task of providing the "foundations of the
theory of signs" as Professor Charles Morris construes. From a point
of view of semiotics, the import of the work lies in: 1) its reconstruction
of Mead's theory of "significant symbols" not in the narrow traditional
sense of assertive statements (or statements of truth) but in the broader,
more inclusive sense of man's diverse processes of "signification", what
is termed in this work as "symbolic process", and 2) its analysis of and
emphasis on the function of symbolic process in the activity of man as
homo faber.

In the present work, the anthropological and philosophical thesis of
man's rationality is presented on the basis of a study of man's use of
symbols as well as that of his use of implements (or tools): 1) symbols

as implements and 2) implements as symbols - and 3) implements as
implements. If one reads the present work from a semiotic point of
view, he will see an attempt to explain the fundamental place and function
of symbolic process in the broad setting of man's rationality, namely,
the condition of the proper mediation of his social acts. (In the basic
sense as construed in this work, man's rationality amounts to the proper
use of symbols in the social contexts of using implements.)

Thus, the present work is a contribution to semiotics in the new tradition of behavioral sciences as much as a contribution to the critique
of reason in the old tradition of philosophy.

The present work suggests that rationality is construed as the
"vocation of man". It presents a view of human life which should be
clearly reformulated and emphasized in the contemporary scene in
which various views of human life - such as the fashionably dressed-up
theology of sin, the Freudian view of libidinous animal, and existential-
ism - still prevail to de-emphasize the "stronger", guiding part of man's
powers and the "better" phase of his life and to accentuate the "weaker"
part of his powers and the "miserable" phase of his life. The present
work gives, in the words of Professor Charles Frankel, a "case for
modern man" in terms of a basic study of man, his "nature" in evolution.

I would like to dedicate the present work to the great teachers I had in
my graduate and undergraduate years, whose teachings I hope it reflects:
Professors John Herman Randall, Jr., Justus Buchler, Ernest Nagel,
Charles Frankel, and Sidney Morgenbesser of Columbia University, and
Professors David Bidney, Joseph Schneider, Alfred Lindesmith, Herbert
Muller, and Frank Doan of Indiana University. A number of scholars of
Mead's works, Professors Charles Morris, Van Meter Ames, David
Miller, Frank Doan, and Darnell Rucker, kindly read an early draft of
the present work and gave me very helpful, critical comments from
which I hope the present work has benefited. My colleagues, Professors
Peter Sylvester, Paul Brockelman, Howard Press, and Val Dusek of
the University of New Hampshire, and Professors Eugene Dyche, Gary
Foulk, Imad Shouery, Don Geels, and John Van Ingen of Indiana State
University, have been very helpful in various stages of my progress
with the present work. I would also like to thank Saul Rosenthal, Anne
Parrella, Charles Wiseman, Richard Brook, Fred Newman, Michael
O'Brien, John Crawford, Jane Hayman, Robert Moskowitz, and Nancy
Milner, who have been helpful in various ways for preparing the present
work.

The Research Committee of Indiana State University provided a
research grant for the preparation of the present work.

I would like to acknowledge the following publishers for permission
to quote from their publications: The University of Chicago Press,
Columbia University Press, Bobbs-Merrill Co., and Open Court
Publishing Co.

I remain grateful to Professors Charles Morris and Thomas A. Sebeok
without whose kind guidance the present work would not have been published.

FOREWORD

I am happy to see Dr. W. Kang's fine book on George Herbert Mead included in the Approaches to Semiotics series. And this for several reasons.

First, Charles S. Peirce is already dealt with in the series, and my volume, Writings on the General Theory of Signs, also appears. Mead forms the third member of an American trilogy. All of these writers have a behavioristically based theory of signs - all of them view the interpretant (or "content") of a sign (the "idea" or "meaning" of other semioticians) in terms of a disposition set up by the sign for the organism to respond in a certain kind of way to a certain kind of object or situation. But Mead, in contrast to Peirce, develops this position in terms of a theory of social action. Mead is one of the founders of American sociology and social psychology, but his treatment of signs in this context should be of interest to anyone concerned with a general theory of signs.

Secondly, Mead contributes in a major way to that branch of semiotics often called pragmatics (in distinction to syntactics and semantics). I have characterized pragmatics as "the study of the origin, uses, and effects of signs". Mead applies his analysis of social action to the origin of linguistic signs ("significant symbols" in his terminology). He has little to say about syntactics, and he has no extended analysis of the different ways signs are used (a problem which is central in my treatment of "types of discourse"); Mead's greatest contribution to pragmatics is his theory of the effect of signs in the development of the human self and in the organization or human society.

Thirdly, Mead utilizes his behavioral (or "actional") approach to man in the analysis of such terms as "mind", "self", "self-observation", "consciousness", "subjectivity", "privacy", and "rationality". The resulting whole is a rich and complex one. Man is not "dehumanized". It is the full, complete human being that is Mead's concern, the human being that is both an actor and an object to itself.

Dr. Kang's book focuses on rationality. But since in Mead rationality is explicated in terms of symbols, Dr. Kang's book includes a careful and penetrating analysis of Mead's semiotics. That is why it is justly included in the series Approaches to Semiotics.

I may add that the interest in Mead is very much alive today. An increasing number of articles, dissertations, and books are being written about his ideas. Several international seminars have been devoted to Mead in the last few years, and will soon appear in print. A book by Professor David L. Miller entitled George Herbert Mead: Self, Language and the World was published in 1973 (by the University of Texas Press,

14

Austin, Texas); it includes many aspects of Mead's thought not included in Dr. Kang's book.

A paperback edition of Mead's <u>Mind, Self, and Society</u> (which plays a central role in Dr. Kang's work), published by the University of Chicago Press in 1962, went through seventeen printings by 1970.

Some years ago I wrote: "Mead, I believe, will come to be seen as the pivotal figure in the development of an adequate behavioral psychology and philosophy." This I still believe. And I welcome Dr. Kang's detailed contribution toward the implementation of this belief.

Charles Morris

1

RATIONALITY AS AN ANTHROPOLOGICAL PROBLEM

> What is Experience and what is Reason, Mind? . . .
> Is a Reason outside experience and above it needed
> to supply assured principles to science and conduct?
> In one sense, these questions suggest technical
> problems of abstruse philosophy; in another sense,
> they contain the deepest possible questionings
> regarding the career of man.
>
> John Dewey, Reconstruction in Philosophy (1919)

1. 0 The Questions

In this first chapter, we will consider the following questions:
1.1) How have the traditional problems of reason or rationality been
transformed under the implication of the Darwinian view of evolution?
Namely, what are the traditional, pre-Darwinian problems of reason,
and how have they been, or could they be, transformed under the
general view of evolution applied to it?
1.2) How or in what sense is Mead's philosophy an attempt to solve
these post-Darwinian problems of rationality?

1.1 Problems of Rationality in a Historical Perspective

In the history of Western philosophy, reason - what is known under
various concepts of nous, logos, reason, rationality, vernunft, and
intelligence - has been the fundamental problem in anthropology,
cosmology, epistemology, and ethics. The import and complexity of
the problem can be seen in that reason has been construed in contrast
or opposition to various entities or processes such as 1) chaos,
2) chance, 3) superstition (or myth), 4) madness, 5) necessity,
6) revelation, 7) faith, 8) authority, 9) force, 10) anarchy, 11) un-
reality (or non-being), 12) intuition, 13) instinct (or impulse),
14) passion (or emotion), 15) experience, 16) individuality, and
17) contingency.
  On the import and scope of reason, Whitehead wrote:

Various phrases suggest themselves, which recall the special
controversies depending upon the determination of the true
function of Reason:
  Faith and Reason: Reason and Authority: Reason and Intuition:

Criticism and Imagination: Reason, Agency, Purpose:
Scientific Methodology: Philosophy and the Sciences:
Rationalism, Scepticism, Dogmatism: Reason and
Empiricism: Pragmatism.

Each of these phrases suggests the scope of Reason,
and the limitation of that scope. Also the variety of
topics included in them shows that we shall not exhaust
our subject by the help of a neat little verbal phrase. (1)

In the works of traditional Western philosophers from Plato to Mill, we
may, at least, distinguish three different "positive" conceptions of what
has been referred to in the name of reason: 1) reason as cosmic - and
man's - creativity and its emerged order; 2) reason as man's discovery
and application of universal laws - namely, as the universal order of
reality, on one hand, and as man's "innate" faculty of knowing and following it, on the other; and 3) reason as man's faculty and work of
calculation, the estimation of the efficacy of means for ends. (2) The
first was suggested by Plato in Timaeus and strongly revived by Hegel
in his "historicistic" version; the second was emphasized, among others,
by Aristotle, Thomas Aquinas, Descartes and Kant; and the third was
emphasized by Hobbes and the British utilitarians.

In spite of these different concepts, the problem of reason has, until
the middle of nineteenth century, largely consisted of a combination of
common questions on: 1) its nature (or "form"), place, and division as
one of the faculties of man; 2) its place in the world; 3) its place and
limitation in the order or process of knowledge; and 4) its "content" or
structure.

As for the last question - namely, 4) What is the content or structure
of reason? - the answers have been changed through the historical
advancement of knowledge, though each of them has been always pro-
nounced as the veritas eternitas. As for the third, epistemological
question and the second, cosmological and anthropological question -
namely, 3) What is the function and limitation of reason in the process
of knowledge? and 2) What is the place of reason in the structure of the
world? - there had been various answers; in the traditional modern
philosophy since Descartes, there were two main types, the Continental

---

(1) A. N. Whitehead, The Function of Reason (Boston: Beacon Press,
1958 [orig. 1929]), pp. 3-4. Cf. M. R. Cohen, Reason and Nature
(New York: Free Press, 1964 [orig. 1931]), Bk. I; K. Jaspers, Reason
and Existenz, trans. by W. Earle (New York: Noonday Press, 1957
[orig. 1935]), pp. 20 ff.; J. Buchler, Toward a General Theory of
Human Judgment and Nature and Judgment (New York: Columbia Univ.
Press, 1951 & 1955), pp. 167-8 & pp. 94-5.
(2) Cf. P. Diesing, Reason in Society: Five Types of Decisions and
their Social Conditions (Urbana: Univ. of Illinois Press, 1962), Ch. 6.
This distinction of the three conceptions as a historical generalization
of Western philosophy is admittedly a suggestive simplification which
can be qualified in various ways.

rationalists' and the British empiricists'. But as for the first question – namely, 1) What is the nature, place, and division of reason as one of man's faculties? – reason had been generally taken as 1.a) a type of assertive discourse, exercised by 1.b) the essential, separate, independent, and substantial faculty of man, which is divided into 1.c) two parts, theoretical and practical reason.

On the problems of reason, primarily in reference to the first question, Prof. Buchler wrote:

> Traditionally the tendency has been to identify the processes of reason with the processes of assertive query. This tendency applies equally to champions of discourse, to methodological pessimists, and to irrationalists. And it is not in the least corrected by the various historical recognitions of the role of practical wisdom, practical reason, or practical "judgment" as distinguished from the theoretical capacities of man. For practical or moral judgment in these usages is simply assertive judgment about matters of practice and conduct . . . . Thus the problem of reason has been taken too often as the problem of the limits and forms of [assertive] discourse. (3)

Since Darwin's publication of The Origin of Species in 1859, attempts have been made to introduce the implication of his biological theory of evolution into the problems of reason. In these attempts, as Mead says, "to bring reason within the scope of evolution", (4) problems of reason have been radically transformed from the traditional versions. The new, contemporary questions are on: 1) the phylogenic and ontogenic development of reason as a bio-social process of man; 2) its functional (or efficacious) conditions; 3) its common basis, not merely as a cognitive process of assertive discourse, but as a pervasive "task" of man (or, its unification as a pervasive method of human activities); and 4) its structure as a set of working, provisional, and hypothetical rules.

It cannot be denied that there is even today a complete lack of concern among certain philosophers – to name a few of them, Husserl, Jaspers, Tillich, and, in a different camp, Morris R. Cohen – to investigate the problems of reason in a perspective of evolution. In an examination of Tillich's ontology, of which his theory of reason is a part, Prof. Randall wrote:

> One of the striking features of Tillich's thought to Americans who have inherited the fruits of the evolutionary preoccupations of the last generations, is the complete absence in his intellectual background of any serious concern for the implication for metaphysics of biological evolution. (5)

---

(3) J. Buchler, Nature and Judgment, pp. 96-7. Cf. G. Ryle, A Rational Animal (London: Athelona Press [Univ. of London], 1962). For a critical consideration of the exclusive emphasis on assertive discourse for rationality, see 3.33 and 4.2.
(4) MS 348. Cf. PA 518 ff.
(5) J. H. Randall, Jr., "The Ontology of Paul Tillich", in The Theology

It is in terms of the works of Mead, an American philosopher of "the last generations", that we will see how the full implication of the new dimension of evolution has been brought to the reconstruction of problems of reason. First of all, Mead presents an anthropological concept of reason or rationality free from the traditional views of reason as an innate, substantial entity or faculty, on one hand, and as an eternal structure, on the other. Second, it is not based on a post-Darwinian view of man which stresses his biological factors to the extent of over-shadowing his social, rational phase; and it is not exclusively limited to the common preoccupation of philosophers to answer the epistemological and logical problems of assertive discourse (or those of "visual", "linear" typographic media). Third, Mead presents his concept of rationality in a language which contemporary scientists of psychology and the other sciences can apply to their fields without much modification.

Like Dewey and some other contemporary philosophers, Mead avoids the terms "reason" and "rationality" in certain contexts for their historical association with the rationalists' usage, and he substitutes the new term "intelligence" or "reflective intelligence". But he commonly uses "reason" and "rationality"; he finds these terms useful especially in the context where certain teleological, intelligent activities of man are distinguished from those of other organisms. As the "key" term for the subject matter of our study, we will use "rationality" for its adjectival and adverbial connotation, while we will avoid "reason" for its substantial connotation, and "reasonableness" for its moral or sentimental connotation. Our choice is in accordance with the fact that in contemporary works of psychology and the other sciences the term "rational" is commonly used and the term "reason" (in the substantial and faculty sense) is largely eliminated. Our usage of "rationality" suggests that the present study is a reinterpretation of the old, traditional problems of reason and that the related or common aspects of 1) rational behavior, 2) internalized reasoning, and 3) rational institution are explicated in terms of the concept of rationality.

1.2 Rationality as the Basic Problem of Mead's Philosophy

Dewey wrote soon after Mead died:(6)

When I first came to know Mr. Mead well over forty years ago, the dominant problem in his mind concerned the nature of consciousness as personal and private. In the 'eighties and 'nineties, idealism prevailed in Anglo-American thought. It had a solution of the problem of consciousness ready to offer. Mind as consciousness was at once the very stuff of the universe and the structural forms of this stuff: human consciousness in its intimate

of Paul Tillich, ed. by C. W. Kegley & R. W. Bretall (New York: Macmillan Co., 1964), p. 153.
(6) George Herbert Mead, 1863-1931.

and seemingly exclusively personal aspect was at most but a
variant, faithful or errant, of the universal mind . . . . He took
the ground that it did not touch the problem in which he was
interested . . ., it did not explain how states of mind peculiar
to an individual, like the first hypotheses of a discoverer which
throw into doubt beliefs previously entertained and which deny
objectivity to things that have been universally accepted as real
objects, can function as the sources of objects which instead of
being private and personal, instead of being merely "subjective",
belong to the common and objective universe . . . .

I fancy that if one had a sufficiently consecutive knowledge of
Mr. Mead's intellectual biography during the intervening years,
one could discover how practically all his inquiries and problems
developed out of his original haunting question. His sense of the
role of subjective consciousness in the construction of objects
as experienced and in the production of new customs and institutions was surely the thing which led him to his extraordinarily
broad and accurate knowledge of the historical development of
the sciences - a knowledge which did not stop with details of
discoveries but which included changes of underlying attitudes
toward nature. (7)

As Dewey clearly implies, Mead's "haunting", "dominant" problem is
the nature of human consciousness or mind in view of the evolutionary
process of modern science which the traditional substantial concepts of
mind had not been able to explain. Educated in the late 19th century and
working in the early 20th century under the spreading influence of the
Darwinian theory of evolution, Mead has been able to attempt to replace
the dualistic or idealistic theories of mind by an evolutionary, naturalistic theory. As a part of this theory, he explains science, an important
phase of mind, in terms of the evolutionary, functional relations of bio-
social factors of man in his transactions within his environment. So he
restores both mind and science on a common basis to their natural conditions within the scope of evolution. "It is . . . the task of philosophy",
Mead says, "to restore to the world the stolen goods" (PA 658).
  In The Philosophy of the Act and Movements of Thought in the Nineteenth Century, Mead points out that the significant development in the
modern period since the end of the Middle Ages is the efficacy of scientific method and the primacy of individual experience. "Since the period
of the Renaissance", Mead says, "modern thought has been ceaselessly
rebuilding the structure of the philosophy of the old world . . . with
[these two] architectural motifs . . ., that of the experimental method
of modern science and that of the primacy of the individual's experience"
(PA 513). These two prevailing "motifs" have evolved together in a
reciprocal relation, but appear to be in conflict for certain aspects of
their consequences as well as for their general functional conditions.
Science is realized in terms of individual experience as the locus where

(7) John Dewey, "Prefatory Remarks" in PP, pp. xxxvi-viii. Italics
added.

problems appear and solutions are discovered and ultimately verified, while the field of experience is reconstructed by the advance of science. But the nature of science requires universal statements in spite of the conditions of individual experience which is always particular, limited to measurable samples. Under its methodological requirements such as exactness and determinateness, science has resulted in certain theories of objects which are beyond or incompatible with the general conditions of individual experience. Those problematic aspects of the relation of "universal, determinate science" and "particular, contingent experience" as the two phases of the process of mind within nature, present to Mead what he regards as the primary task of philosophy:

> It is the office of philosophy to envisage a universe in which both the methods of experimental science and science's own interpretations, as well as those of everyday experience, are at home (PA 516).

> It is the task of the philosophy of today to bring into congruence with each other this universality of determination which is the text of modern science, and the emergence of the novel which belongs not only to the experience of human social organisms, but is found also in a nature which science and the philosophy that has followed it have separated from human nature (PP 14).

> This is the philosophical problem that faces the community at the present time: How are we to get the universality involved, the general statement which must go with any interpretation of the world, and still make use of the differences which belong to the individual as an individual? (MT 417).

Here Mead realized that not only the process of mind in general but the enterprise of science in particular must be properly understood to account for the reciprocal relation of individual experience and universal science and for the apparent conflict between the conditions of experience and the requirements and products of science. Thus the large part of his "original" attempt to understand the nature of mind in view of the practice of science turns out for Mead to be a proper reinterpretation of science itself. In a logically reconstructed perspective of Mead's remaining works, therefore, the basic problem of his philosophy is a reinterpretation of science, its method and product, as the important phase of the evolutionary process of mind within nature. (8)

The thesis of the present study is that Mead's attempt to solve this problem on the basis of the social process of man results in a theory of rationality, what one may call a theory of "impure" or social reason. As we will see, rationality is a condition or characteristic of mediation

---

(8) It is noted that the basic concern of Mead is well expressed by the original title of The Journal of Philosophy, under which most of his published articles are printed: The Journal of Philosophy, Psychology, and Scientific Methods. See Bibliography.

(the process of adjusting means and ends) in man's social activities. This condition of mediation is realized by the functional or appropriate use of implements (mainly tools and symbols) in a "reflexive" (role-taking) and "regulative" (rule-assuming) way. And these social activities are generally "internalized" (individually assimilated) and institutionalized.

Mead says:

I have reserved for my last paragraphs an aspect of this identification of reflective intelligence with the world within which it has arisen, which is profound in its import and in its emotional resonance, and that is the implication of the social character of what we call "reason" . . . . It is society that through the mechanism of cooperative activity has endowed man with reason (PA 518).

What by the slow process of hundreds and thousands of years has taken place in the origin and development of species of plants and animals proceeds with astounding rapidity when the process of evolution has passed under the control of social reason. As a set of means it takes on the forms of the various physical, biological, and social sciences. As a philosophy it enables us to formulate the new values which at each transition determine what changes we will seek to bring about (PA 508).

The rationality of man and his world is not "pure" or "absolute", nor is it divided neatly into two parts: the theoretical and the practical. The concept of eternal or transcendental reason is either an autistic, though brave, dream of the pre-Darwinian ages, or a stubborn defense of logicism, if not a methodological exercise of it. Such a concept is blind to the very social, historical constitution of man's living conditions and products. And man has neither merely simple perception of experience, nor completely undefinable, free existence - as a man, a member of his society. His rationality, as well as his existence and experience, is very impure: socially, historically evolved. It is selected, transformed, and organized in terms of, and as a determinant perspective of, the conditions given in his present society.

When Mead speaks of the primary task of philosophy in another larger perspective, he has the following concluding statements which support the thesis of the present study:

It is the technical function of philosophy so to state the universe that what we call our conscious life can be recognized as a phase of its creative evolution (PA 515).

Philosophy is concerned, then, with the import of the appearance and presence in the universe of human reflective intelligence - that intelligence which transforms causes and effects into means and consequences, reactions into responses, and termini of natural processes into ends-in-view (PA 517).

It is the province of philosophy to work out the implications of
the fact that reason has arisen in the process of social evolution
(PA 519).

Mead is concerned with a number of important topics in philosophy and
psychology in various problematic contexts. We can see, however, that
these topics are, in an important way, derived from and interrelated to
his basic concern with solving the problem of rationality in terms of
the pervasive activities of man: social processes of making and using
implements as media of his activities. On understanding this basic
orientation in Mead's works, it is not very difficult to see his various
interrelated, though not systematized, theories of evolution, relativity,
society, impulse, mediation, implement, symbol, self, mind, science,
history, reality, and so forth, in a unified perspective.
  Prof. Morris wrote:

Mead endeavored to carry out a major problem posed by
evolutionary conceptions: the problem of how to bridge the
gap between impulse and rationality, of showing how certain
biological organisms acquire the capacity of self-consciousness, of thinking, of abstract reasoning, of purposive behavior,
of moral devotion; the problem in short of how man, the
rational animal, arose. (9)

Prof. Strauss wrote:

The Romantic writers had a profound influence on Mead, as
upon Dewey, insofar as they stressed social evolution and
made the environment in some subtle sense dependent upon
the acting organism. But since Mead lived after Darwin, the
Romantic treatment becomes in Mead's hands divested of its
mysticism and is given biological and scientific twists. Most
important, the role of reason again is raised in high service
to human action, where rationalists and political liberals had
placed it, rather than made subordinate to faith and intuition
. . . .

The corpus of biological writing [under the influence of Darwin]
allows the pragmatist to challenge mechanical conceptions of
action and the world and to restate problems of autonomy,
freedom, and innovation in evolutionary and social rather than
mechanistic and individualistic terms. Mead's pragmatic devotion to reason prevents him from going the way of certain
descendents of Darwin - Freud, MacDougal, Veblen, and Le Bon
among others - who stressed irrational and non-rational deter-
minants of human behavior. (10)

---

(9) C. W. Morris, "Introduction" in MS, p. xvi.
(10) A. Strauss, "Introduction" in SP, p. viii.

MEAD'S APPROACH TO THE PROBLEM OF RATIONALITY

> In the beginning was the Act.
>
> Goethe, <u>Faust</u> (c. 1790)

2.0 <u>The Preliminary Remarks and Questions</u>

In this second chapter, we consider the pervasive emphases or theses of Mead's philosophy as a necessary basis of its main phase, his theory of rationality. They are considered in three parts: 2.1) scientific method, 2.2) actual situation, and 2.3) social behaviorism.

These three emphases or theses are interrelated to and implicated by each other. If scientific method is emphasized by Mead in terms of a critical, contextual consideration of the development of science and its import in man's social evolution, his emphasis on actual situation, the contextual criteria of problems and solutions, is a philosophical development to rectify certain dogmatic or absolute interpretations - pro or con - of science and its production. And this contextualistic emphasis turns out to be required by the scientific method under a proper interpretation. His social behaviorism is a logical application of the methodological requirements of science as well as the logical implication of the emphasis on actual situation for the problems of mind. In turn, the thesis of social behaviorism requires and justifies the contextual attempt to find the locus of the methodic process of science in the actual situation of man's social life.

The question asked is how these three interrelated emphases or theses of Mead provide an approach to the problems of rationality. It will be seen that his theory of rationality is a logical conclusion from these three theses. Furthermore, it will be seen that it is a justification of them - provided, of course, that it (his theory of rationality) is confirmed on some extrinsic grounds of evidence.

In 2.4), we will consider a basic implication of the three theses that rationality as an anthropological concept has its locus in the context of social act. We will find out how the criteria of rationality for man's activities, ranging from the private to the public, can be considered only in reference to the social acts which these activites (concretely) constitute, or (abstractly) presuppose or anticipate. That is, such questions as whether an idea is rational or whether an institution is rational can be answered only in reference to the context of some social act in which this idea is applied, or in which this institution is lived, by men as members of a society. Thus, a theory of rationality is derived from a theory of man's social act.

In a logically reconstructed perspective of Mead's works, which we
will follow, the above mentioned three theses are the bases, the
"methodological" or "presuppositional" theses, for Mead's theory of
rationality. In a biographical perspective or other perspective of some
other problem, they may be considered and presented differently.

2.1 Mead's Emphasis on Scientific Method

2.11 His Philosophy as a Philosophy of Science

Mead's philosophy has been commonly characterized as "pragmatism"
or, with emphasis on his psychological phase, as "social behaviorism".
For various reasons, it has been interpreted under different names –
to mention only some of them found in published works and not to
mention the others in unpublished dissertations:

1) "instrumentalism"
2) "constructive pragmatism"
3) "social pragmatism"
4) "pragmatic empiricism"
5) "radical empiricism"
6) "empirical realism"
7) "critical common-sensism"
8) "contexturalism"
9) "objective relativism"
10) "radical relativism"
11) "temporal relationism"
12) "temporalism"
13) "emergent naturalism"
14) "evolutionary biologism"
15) "biological empiricism"
16) "biological positivism"
17) "romantic evolutionism"
18) "functionalism"
19) "situational behaviorism"
20) "phenomenological behaviorism"
21) "phenomenology of social reality"
22) "socialized individualism"
23) "symbolic interactionism"
24) "medieval conceptualism"
25) "social positivism"
26) "positivistic culturalism"
27) "dialectical empiricism"
28) "social idealism"
29) "naturalized Hegelian idealism"
30) "inverted naturalism" (vs. "reductive naturalism")
31) "irrationalism" (à la Bergson), etc. (1)

---

(1) 1) C. W. Morris, "Introduction" in MS, p. xxv;
     2) A. E. Murphy, "Introduction" in PP, p. xiii;

These various interpretations to which Mead's unfinished, unsystematized works lend themselves are undermined by the central effort in his philosophy to take science seriously and to understand its process properly and critically - not in a narrow, rigid interpretation à la Newtonian mechanism, but in a broad perspective in which it is construed as an evolutionary process that is pervasive in various stages in the biological and bio-social world. In his Carus Lectures, Mead regards his philosophy as "an evolutionary philosophy of science" (PP 51).

"After all", Mead says, "the world is essentially a scientific world; and any philosophy which fails to express, to make use of scientific method, is a philosophy that is out of place" (MT 144). If philosophy is distinguished from specialized disciplines of science for the general scope of its concern or for some other factor, it is no exception to them,

3) H. S. Thayer, Meaning and Action: A Critical History of Pragmatism (Indianapolis: Bobbs-Merrill, 1968), p. 264;
4) B. W. Brotherston, "The Genius of Pragmatic Empiricism", Journal of Philosophy, 1943 (40:1), p. 14;
5) H. W. Schneider, A History of American Philosophy (New York: Columbia Univ. Press, 1946), p. 50: P. E. Pfuetze, Self, Society, Existence (New York: Harper, 1961 [orig. 1954]), p. 354;
6) Murhpy, op. cit., see p. viii and the title given to one of Mead's untitled essays, p. 93.
7) C. W. Morris, "George H. Mead: A Pragmatist's Philosophy of Science", in Scientific Psychology, ed. by B. Wolman & E. Nagel (New York: Basic Books, 1965), p. 404;
8) W. C. Tremmel, The Social Concepts of G. H. Mead (Emporia: Kansas State Teachers College, 1957), p. 6;
9) Morris, "Introduction" in MS, p. xxviii; A. Reck, "Introduction" in SW, p. xliv;
10) Schneider, op. cit., p. 552;
11) M. Natanson, "George H. Mead's Metaphysic of Time", Journal of Philosophy, 1953 (50:25), p. 778;
12) Murphy, op. cit., p. xi; Reck, op. cit., p. lxii;
13) C. W. Morris, Logical Positivism, Pragmatism, and Scientific Empiricism (Paris: Hermann et Cie, 1937), p. 45;
14) J. Blau, Men and Movements in American Philosophy (New York: Prentice-Hall, 1952), p. 267;
15) R. Bierstedt, "A Great Pragmatist", Saturday Review, July 2, 1938 (18:10), p. 16;
16) Morris, Logical Positivism, Pragmatism, and Scientific Empiricism, p. 46;
17) Pfuetze, op. cit., p. 353;
18) Reck, op. cit., p. xvi;
19) Brotherston, op. cit., p. 29;
20) Morris, "George H. Mead: A Pragmatist's Philosophy of Science", pp. 403-4;
21) M. Natanson, The Social Dynamics of George H. Mead (Washington: Public Affairs Press, 1956), pp. 4 & 94;
22) A. Strauss, "Introduction" in SP, p. xxiv;

for it shares the common method of science. If Mead's philosophy is taken as pragmatism, pragmatism is itself "a logical generalization of scientific method" (SW 334). In the course of a historical review of Western "Thought", Mead says: "It is this scientific method, which finds the test of the truth of a hypothesis in its working, that has got its philosophical expression in the pragmatic doctrine. This doctrine is nothing but an expression of the scientific method" (MT 354).

Within the tradition of pragmatism Mead is not induced by the Jamesian emphasis on "immediate experience" to undermine the proper function and import of scientific method for the social, rational phase of man's life and world. (2) "Mead, far more than other pragmatists", Prof. Morris wrote, "has tried in detail to show the place of science, its method and concepts, within a general theory of human action."(3) "Throughout his mature life", another student of Mead wrote, "he formulated all philosophical problems in the same way: viz., How does a proper understanding of the method of science enable us to handle problems traditionally called metaphysical without appealing to principle transcending experience?"(4) In the perspective of the present study, Mead is seen to have attempted to understand the "scientific method" not only as man's method of knowing, but also as the evolutionary process of living, while pointing out its unique place, in its critical, refined form, in the modern history of man.

23) A. M. Rose, "A Systematic Summary of Symbolic Interaction Theory" in Human Behavior and Social Processes, ed. by A. M. Rose (Boston: Houghton Mifflin, 1962), p. 3;
24) Morris, "Introduction" in MS, p. xxvii;
25) Morris, Logical Positivism, Pragmatism, and Scientific Empiricism, p. 34; Pfuetze, op. cit., p. 352;
26) D. Bidney, Theoretical Anthropology (New York: Columbia Univ. Press, 1953), p. 154;
27) R. Burke, "G. H. Mead and the Problem of Metaphysics", Philo. & Pheno. Research, 1962 (23:1), p. 84;
28) Pfuetze, op. cit., p. 353;
29) M. R. Cohen, American Thought, ed. by F. S. Cohen (New York: Free Press, 1954), p. 302;
30) G. C. Lee, George Herbert Mead: Philosopher of the Social Individual (New York: King's Crown Press, 1945), p. 302;
31) Lee, op. cit., p. 89.
(2) Cf. "Bergson, seeing how thoroughly shot through with rationalistic considerations are our daily practical affairs, keeps away from social philosophy by insisting that the interests of practical life and those of philosophic insight are entirely foreign to each other. James, as a pragmatist, might have been expected to recoil from such a complete separation. But being bent on finding all salvation in the immediate, the demands of practical guidance as well as rational science are eluded by a leap into the mystical seas of pure experience" - M. R. Cohen, Reason and Nature (New York: Free Press, 1964 [orig. 1931]), p. 46.
(3) Morris, "George H. Mead: A Pragmatist's Philosophy of Science", p. 403.
(4) Burke, "G. H. Mead and the Problem of Metaphysics", p. 86.

2.12 Scientific Method and the Process of Living

The evolution of life is generally understood as a complex of natural processes in which organisms have emerged, and developed in their adaptation to their environments. Mead, in another perspective, takes this evolution as the complex which has resulted in a variation of new forms, not only of the organisms themselves but also of the environments as their means of adaptation. At the core of the evolutionary processes, Mead sees the activities of organisms which have overcome obstacles or solved problems in their attempt to survive in their changing environments. "Evolutionary advance means the solving of problems", Mead says. "The problem is put up to the individuals, to plant or animal, in terms of life and death; and the solution has come in the appearance of some new form, a variant that springs from the older form. And with the new form comes another environment, an environment that is dependent upon the new form itself" (MT 140):

> If we look upon the conduct of the animal form as continual meeting and solving of problems, we can find in this intelligence, even in its lowest expression, an instance of what we call "scientific method" when this has been developed into the technique of the most elaborate science. The animal is doing the same thing the scientist is doing. It is facing a problem, selecting some element in the situation which may enable it to carry its act through to completion. There is inhibition there. It tends to go in one direction, then another direction: it tends to seek this thing and avoid that. These different tendencies are in conflict; and until they can be reconstructed, the action cannot go on. The only test the animal can bring to a reconstruction of its habit is the ongoing of its activity. This is the experimental test (MT 346).

> That is the way in which evolution is taking place in the appearance of problems in life. Living forms have found themselves up against problematic situations: their food gone, the climate changed, new enemies coming in. The method which nature has followed, if we may speak so anthropomorphically, has been the production of variations until finally some one variation has arisen which has survived. Well, what science is doing is making this method of trial and error a conscious method (MT 366-7).

In Mead's perspective, evolution is the "method" of life, and the theory of evolution is a statement on the "scientific" process in reference to the development of organic forms. His analogical comparison between science and evolution does not reduce science to evolution, except to point out its genesis or emergence in evolution and its evolutionary nature; nor does the analogy "anthropomorphize" evolution. Once science has emerged, evolution can be explained in analogy to it. But the emergence of science in its modern critical form out of the general process of evolution might or could not have been anticipated prior to its emergence. And the "anthropomorphism" of the analogy from science to evolution, if it is "naive", is not constitutive in the sense of "meta-physical realism", but is a matter of explicatory perspective.

Mead construes scientific method to be pervasive in various phases of human life which have, in their core, developed through problems and solutions. In certain contexts, however, he is emphatic in pointing out that man in history - and, for certain areas, even in the present - has indulged in certain misuses and abuses of his intelligence as it has developed into a critical, refined method of science. And yet he sees the method to be imbedded in all the problem-solving situations of man from the games of children and the creation of myths to the development of social institutions and the discovery of new theories in modern sciences

The experimental method is imbedded in the simplest process of perception of a physical thing (PA 25).

The research method is, after all, nothing but the elaboration of the simplest processes of perceiving and conceiving the world, elaborated in such a way that it can be applied to the complex and subtle problems of the physicist, the geologist, the biologist, etc. (SW 62).

There is no difficulty in showing that . . . it [scientific method] is implicated in all intelligent conduct and that it has been involved in knowing the world at all times. It can be found in the absurdest conclusions of children and primitive communities. That the inferences are improperly drawn does but disguise the fact that these minds were with varying degrees of carefulness or inexact-ness trying to explain something, to solve some problem, by some idea or hypothesis, testing the idea by its fitting into their ex-perience so that it can become a part of this world. A child's explanation of the conduct of others and the savage's appeal to magic are uncritical uses of a method which requires only analysis and recognition of the implications of its techniques to become scientific (PA 90-1).

Take any institution as such and look at it from the standpoint of evolution, the way in which that is determined in society, and then you can see the development in society itself of a technique which we call the "scientific technique", but it is a technique which is simply doing consciously what takes place naturally in the evolution of forms (MT 371).

The scientific character of the method is evidently found in the careful exactness with which the problem is defined, the data gathered, the hypothesis formulated, and the experiment carried out, but these are merely the elaboration of the simple processes of everyday inference by which we meet our constantly recurring difficulties (PA 83). (5)

_____

(5) In different contexts Mead uses various terms such as "scientific

Since the development of science in its critical, elaborated form, we are able to see the structure of all the problem-solving situations of man by analogy to that of modern science. But in face of the development of science as what Mead calls "an expression of the highest type of intelligence" (MT 290), men as intelligent beings are not free to revert to the crude or uncritical prototypes of the scientific method without "dismissing the intelligence itself". Today we try to apply the scientific method in its critical, elaborated form to all problematic situations as long as their given conditions practically permit. "Scientific method is", Mead says, "not an agent foreign to the mind, that may be called in and dismissed at will. It is an integral part of human intelligence, and when it has once been set at work it can only be dismissed by dismissing the intelligence itself" (SW 255).(6)

In view of the large part of the present life of mankind which is still dominated by the traditional dogmas of religions or by the partisan ideologies of politics, Mead's emphasis on scientific method is yet to prevail as the "guiding principle" of man's social life. And even in philosophy, it is still a large statement and criticism in view of certain attitudes of contemporary philosophers such as Bergson, Heidegger, and Gilson. "Some philosophers feel", Mead says, "that philosophy goes further and can criticize the propositions, the presuppositions of science. But as a general rule it can be said that what philosophy has been doing, especially since the time of the Renaissance, is to interpret the results of science" (MT 343). As suggested earlier, philosophy is not distinguished from the other sciences or enterprises of man by reason of its own distinct method, though it may be for other factors.

Mead's emphasis on scientific method prescribes the methodological conditions under which man's problems can be solved. Most of the traditional problems of philosophy - such as the metaphysical question of "Reality and Appearance", the ontological argument of the existence of the "Perfect Being", and the problem of the substantial dualism of "Mind and Matter" - are dissolved under methodological considerations because they are impossible, at least as they have been formulated, to be answered in one way or another. As for the traditional problems of reason or rationality, Mead has to reformulate them as suggested in 1.1, and has to answer them under the methodological conditions of science which are prescribed for solutions of problems in general. The following 2.2 and 2.3 amount, in a way, to a consideration of some specific, important methodological conditions for philosophy in general and for the present study of rationality in particular. On the other hand, as we will see by the end of 3.23 the explication of rationality which we find in Mead's works is a generalized version of the scientific method itself.

---

method", "experimental method", "research method", "scientific technique", etc. in referring to the same method. For an explanation, see 3.232.

(6) In 3.232, we will further consider Mead's view of scientific method.

2.2 Mead's Emphasis on Actual Situation

2.21 Science and the Philosophy of the Act

In the logical perspective of Mead's works which we have followed, he
does not begin his philosophy with a theory of "act" or any other primary
unit of reality or analysis; rather, he begins where science has reached -
namely, with a study of the nature of scientific process and the implications of scientific theories. It is generally accepted, on the other hand,
that his philosophy is represented by the volume, The Philosophy of the
Act, as its editors suggested when they wrote that "they [his papers
posthumously edited into this volume] do represent Mr. Mead's thought
in the last ten or fifteen years of his life". (7) Here we may note that
"all titles, including that of the volume itself, are due to the editors". (8)
In the perspective we have followed, the meaning of Mead's "philosophy
of the act" can be properly understood when it is seen as a logical implication of his emphasis on science.

Mead's concern with scientific method leads to his emphasis on the
act, or the actual situation, in which science is carried out: in which its
problems emerge and are solved, and to which its data and theories refer
for their meaning and validity. By analogy to the process of science - to
be understood in the sense of the previously explained "analogy" between
science and evolution - the act is, in general, construed by Mead as the
unit of social or transactional context in which men begin and end a task,
or face and solve a problem. In the terms we will use, the act as an
anthropological concept refers to the social context in which men in their
relation(s) - at least, an individual man in the role of another or a generalized other(9) - undertake their selected or problematically (or "extrinsically") presented task and consummate their end(s). And so it is
the act in which is found the reality of man's experiences, including
problems and solutions.

The act as the basic unit of analysis is not the metaphysical substantial,
atomic unit like "monad" or "sense datum", but in a way like such contextually more limited concepts as "cycle", "game", "laboratory condition",
"semester", "fiscal year", etc. (10) Nor is the act the locus of ultimate,

---

(7) PA, p. v. To this volume, MS may be regarded as a psychological
or anthropological introduction; PP, as a "cosmological" or ontological
conclusion; and MT, as a historical appendix.
(8) Ibid.
(9) See 3.33.
(10) Mead has been subject to criticism for his "philosophy of the act"
as it is taken as the ultimate metaphysical unit of reality. In an article
on Mead, A. E. Murphy wrote: "'The act' . . . is as dubious a pretender
to philosophical ultimacy as its traditional metaphysical rivals [such as
'sense data']" ("Concerning Mead's The Philosophy of the Act", Journal
of Philosophy, 1939 [36:4], p. 86).
Also consider: "The first question to be raised in criticism of Mead's
theory of the act is a definitional one . . . . We shall argue that there
are at least two quite different concepts in Mead and that these variant

total Reality in a metaphysical holistic sense, because an act presupposes the "reality" of "the world-which-is-there", over which the act is undertaken. (11) In the on-going process of life, man is not confronted with the question of "Reality and Appearance" in general. If the question of reality arises, it is always in an actual situation in reference to some of its phases. In this sense, the act as "the unit of reality" is a methodological concept generalized from the process of science.

2.22 Phases of Act: Their Contextual, Gestaltic, & Functional Criteria

In his emphasis on actual situation, Mead recognizes a number of theses commonly known today under the names of "contextualism", "gestaltism", and "functionalism". The general point of these theses is that objects or processes, (12) and their concepts and theories, are to be taken as parts of a whole, related in a certain structure of their functions, in their actual contexts. This general point is basically a methodological requirement of Mead's philosophy of science. And so his concept of "act" or "actual situation" itself must also be taken and used under the same requirement.

The following statements of Mead suggest the main theses of his emphasis on act in their important contexts. And these quotations, highly selective and edited, illustrate his usages of some basic terms:
1) "act", "experience", "behavior", "social act", "social process";
2) "act", "situation", "context", "field", "universe of discourse";
3) "actuality", "existence", "reality", "objectivity"; etc. They are, respectively in each numbered group, the "sibling" terms which, though slightly different in emphasis and nuance, refer to the same "family" in terms of different contexts:

---

concepts are confused and intertwined . . . . The first concept is that of the act as a biological function built up out of stimulus and response patterns. The second concept is that of the act as the selective, constitutive function of subjectivity" (M. Natanson, The Social Dynamics of George H. Mead, pp. 68-9).

Murphy's and Natanson's criticisms suggested here are based, though respectively in their different ways, on a misunderstanding of Mead's works, especially his contextualism (which is explained further in the following 2.22 and 2.3).

(11) PA 280, SW 268, etc. Cf. D. Rucker, The Chicago Pragmatists (Minneapolis: Univ. of Minnesota Press, 1969), pp. 37 ff.

(12) "Object" (or, "thing", "entity", or "form") and "process" (or "event") are the generic terms Mead uses in various contexts to refer in general to all phases of reality or nature. Each of them contextually corresponds to what Prof. Buchler calls "complex" or "natural complex". As Prof. Buchler explains, terms such as Mead's suffer in their generic designation for their "associations which interfere with the desirable level of generality" (J. Buchler, Metaphysics of Natural Complexes [New York: Columbia Univ. Press, 1966], p. 5). The terms "complex" and "natural complexes" suffer in a similar way under the traditional and common contrast of "complex" to "simple" or "atomic" and under

a. 1) The unit of <u>existence</u> is the <u>act</u>, not the moment (PA 65). (13)

a. 2) The unit of <u>existence</u> in human <u>experience</u> is the <u>act</u>, within which nothing is there that does not involve successive phases (PA 60).

a. 3) <u>Things</u> . . . find their perceptual <u>reality</u> in manipulatory <u>experiences</u> which lead on to consummations. They involve the stoppage of the <u>act</u> and an appearance of a <u>field</u> that is irrelevant to passage in which alternative completions of the <u>act</u> may take place. The <u>act</u>, then, is antecedent to the appearance of <u>things</u> and of the organisms as <u>objects</u> . . . . The theory of the subjectivity of secondary qualities exactly reverses the <u>actual situation</u> (PA 147-8). (14)

b. 1) Any <u>object</u> is . . . always an expression of a peculiar relation between itself and the individual, but it is an <u>objective relation</u> (PA 7).

b. 2) Science . . . recognizes <u>objects</u> as <u>existing</u>, and arising in <u>situations</u>, and a <u>situation</u> may be defined as <u>things</u> in such a relationship with one another that they maintain or tend to maintain that relationship (PA 77).

b. 3) These <u>situations</u> are the <u>reality</u> . . . . The comparison of different <u>situations</u> and the recognition of identities and differences within them imply the constitution of the different <u>situations</u> in the <u>experience</u> of the same individual. However abstractly and symbolically this may be carried out, the abstraction and the symbolization can only take place over against an <u>experience</u> within which in some extent the compared <u>situations actually exist</u> (PA 215-6).

---

the Freudian use of "complex". These generic terms have to be used and understood in their contexts in terms of their intended designation. (13) In this and the following quotations all italics are added. (14) This quotation begins with "Physical". This term is not in contrast to "non-physical" in the common sense. Nor is it used exclusively in reference to objects of physics in the scientific or technical sense. "Physical things" (or "physical objects") refer to various objects from stones and quanta to buildings and governments, symbolically discriminated or abstracted as implements, separable in a logical sense from on-going acts of men. Mead commonly uses "physical object" in contrast to "social object". In this context "physical object" refers to a special class of social objects, which can be "desocialized" or "depersonalized" - that is, they are separable from their functions in man's social acts to the extent that they are not "self-conscious" themselves. Cf. PA 190 ff. & MS 184 ff.

c. 1) <u>Meaning</u> involves . . . [a] relation among phases of the <u>social act</u> as the <u>context</u> in which it arises and develops (MS 76).

c. 2) The significant . . . <u>symbol</u> always presupposes for its significance the <u>social process</u> of <u>experience</u> and behavior in which it arises; or . . . a <u>universe of discourse</u> is always implied as the <u>context</u> in which, or as the <u>field</u> within which, significant . . . <u>symbols</u> do in fact have significance (MS 89). (15)

c. 3) The inclusion of the matrix or complex of attitudes and responses constituting any given <u>situation</u> or <u>act</u>, within the experience of any one of the individuals implicated in that <u>situation</u> or <u>act</u> . . . is all that an <u>idea</u> amounts to (MS 72 fn.). (16)

First, the emphasis on act as "the unit of reality" recognizes that man's living, his experience, is carried out in a context, in transactional relation to various factors in the given context; and that problems are solved in terms of the actual context in which its objects or values emerged can be meaningfully explained as parts of the whole context.

The act is 1) "limited" to a certain extent, in terms of the nature of the problem(s) involved which requires a tentative solution "here and now". And it is, on the other hand, 2) "unlimited" in the long run, in view of the nature of its solution which is open in its implication to a "larger, more complete" context in terms of the future. That is to say, when a solution is found for a problem in an actual situation, it is regarded as a solution in the given limited situation, and it is regarded as provisional and hypothetical, as the practically delimited situation is open to be implicated into other "larger" contexts. The act is, as Mead would say, "short and long enough" and "small and large enough" to enable its objects to be what they are. (17)

The actual situation in the present is of a "passage", not of a "moment". The objects emerged in the act "re-define" its present which implicates a past and a future. Every act is a re-presentation of the past and a presentation of the future. "The pasts and the futures", Mead says, "are implications of what is being undertaken and carried out in our laboratories" (PP 89).

Here Mead may appear to do violence to the common "realistic" view

---

(15) Cf. e.g., "Mind arises . . . in a social process or context of experience" (MS 50); or: "Only through the taking by individuals of the attitude or attitudes of the generalized other toward themselves is the existence of a universe of discourse, as that system of common or social meanings which thinking presupposes at its context, rendered possible" (MS 156).
(16) Cf. e.g., ". . . in any given social act or situation" (MS 37); ". . . in any given social situation or act" (MS 156).
(17) Cf. e.g., PP 23-4.

of contextualism. For example, when we say we consider an historical problem in its context, we tend to think we go back in some sense of imagination or reduction to its "real" historical period or society in which the problem has its referential locus. If any aspect of Pericles' speech, for example, is a problem in our present, the Meadean emphasis on actual context gives a choice between 1) a reconstruction of the present (discovery of new records, reinterpretation of other evidences we have, etc.) and 2) the present in which the problem remains. It does not give a choice to "go back" to the period of Pericles for which the present (the remaining records, etc.) was only a future. It would not be denied by Mead that we talk in reference to its past locus in the context of solving problems.

Or, consider the case of A. E. Murphy's example in his criticism of Mead's "philosophy of the act". (18) Mead would not deny that a man who committed murder several days before his arrest was a murderer before the public identification. In a perspective of the public - i.e., in terms of the investigation and arrest and their announcement in the mass media - the murderer does not emerge as the man who has murdered at the moment of arrest but as the murderer who had committed the crime several days before. The present perspective of the investigation and mass media reconstructs the past as a part of the present situation. Furthermore, in the perspective of the murderer he is the murderer from the original act of killing, not from the moment of arrest. And we also make the distinction between the "murderer loose" and the "murderer arrested". The act as a problematic context is the present, "here and now", but a present in which a past is implicated and a future is foreseen.

Secondly, in his emphasis on act Mead recognizes the Kohlerian thesis of "gestalt psychology"(19) that various aspects of experience are realized only as the related parts of a whole and must be understood not in isolation but in their interrelation: and that the whole, its configurational or gestaltic structure, is found in the actual situation and is not construed as an association or organization of intrinsically separate elements or parts (20) "Experience . . .", Mead says, "must start with some whole. It must involve some whole in order that we may get the elements we are after" (MS 37-8). In another context, he says: "What the behaviorist does, or ought to do, is to take the complete act, the whole process of conduct, as the unit of his account" (MS 111). The emergence of objects in an actual situation means that they belong to the given situation as a whole, and that they cannot be taken apart from the situation within which they are realized. Our inhibited response to, or symbolic analysis of, objects presupposes that they are "out there" in the actual world as parts of the whole.

---

(18) Op. cit., p. 93.
(19) MS 37. Cf. W. Kohler, Gestalt Psychology (New York: Liveright, 1947 [orig. 1929]); and Dynamics in Psychology (New York: Grove Press, 1960 [orig. 1940]).
(20) For Mead's application of this gestaltic thesis as a criticism of the traditional "atomistic" empiricism, particularly Hume's, see PA 629-30.

Mead construes the "successive" phases of act in various ways:
1) disposition, stimulus, inhibition, and response; 2) impulse, perception,
manipulation, and consummation; 3) distant, contact, and consummatory
experiences (or objects); etc. (21) The prototype of act is the selective
process of responding, on the basis of impulses or dispositions, to
perceptual, distant objects, and of manipulating or reconstructing them
as or into contact objects for consummation and assimilation. As a
paradigm, consider a "sexual act" which is regarded in a certain tradition as a "cognitive" act: "carnal knowledge".

These phases of act are not reducible to any one phase which could be
taken as a metaphysically substantial atomic unit; nor is there any object
or value which is justified as a metaphysically transcendent, absolute
principle apart from some actual situation. The actual situation presents
itself as a whole, a gestaltic structure or relation, in terms of which
its phases can be explained. All objects and values are accepted for or
confirmed by their place or function as phases of their actual situations.

Thirdly, as suggested by the contextual and gestaltic explication of
act, Mead recognizes that objects (or processes) are construed to have
been formed by their functions in actual situations, and that man's symbolization (and valuation) of them is required to be based on its function
in its actual situations. "The object", Mead says, "is clearly a function
of the whole situation, whose perspective is determined by the individual"
(PA 224). The analysis and abstraction of situations are based on the
functional relations of their phases. It is implied that man's symbolic
process is functional for the purpose of the on-going activity of his life
in the situations. "The abstraction", Mead says, "is functional in conduct
and belongs to the experience of individuals in whose conduct there
appears the world of relatively permanent objects" (PA 382). (22)

The objects man discriminated, or the objects symbolically presented,
have their "locus" in, or their reference to, their actual situations.
They are relative to the situations. They are there as functional relations
and so objective insofar as their situations are concerned. Consider the
example of a "dragon" in the context of story-telling, not in that of sea-
faring or skin-diving. "Science always tries", Mead says, "to state an
organized system of relations, but it never states the character of [an]
object in itself apart from its relations" (PA 80). If an object is found
functional(23) in a large number of situations with no exceptional case,

---

(21) These phases of act, insofar as they are pertinent to the present
study of rationality, are further considered in Ch. 3.
(22) Here "function" and "functional" are in contrast to "non-functional"
in the sense of being "substantial" or "being-in-itself". This concept
of 1) "functional" is distinguished from 2) "functional" in the sense of
being "efficacious" or "successfully working" in contrast to
"dysfunctional", and from 3) "functional" in the sense of "presently
functioning" in contrast to "genetic". These three different concepts
are used by Mead under the same term "functional" in various contexts,
and they can be discriminated in terms of the contexts of his usage. See
3.0 and 3.31.
(23) See 3.233.

it is considered a "universal" under the methodological assumption of induction (or under the conditions of functional implementation). And it is taken to be objectively in each of the situations, not necessarily transcendent to them in a Platonic sense. The universality of objects lies in their pervasiveness and/or endurance, or what Mead calls their "irrelevance to passage".

In science and other specialized disciplines, we undertake to select the common recurrent relations of various situations in an extensive, systematic way. The symbolic process of generalization is based upon the emergence of various new situations, of which functionally related phases can be selected or abstracted as a common structure over their diverse, peculiar features. We do not undertake to formulate or translate the involved situations in every aspect; we attempt to get hold of the significant, enduring phases of the situations in reference to problems involved, so as to control them for our required purposes or anticipated ends.

We may note the three corollaries of the above three theses which constitute Mead's emphasis on act.

First, Mead's emphasis on act as a generalized attitude of scientific process does not present any definite identical "basic activity" or its situation as the "philosophical ultimacy" to which all meanings of objects are reduced or translated; it recognizes and requires the condition that various dimensions of man's experience (impulses, perceptions, attitudes, values, habits, satisfactions, institutions, etc.), or their objects or processes, are explained as functionally related parts in their actual contexts.

Second, Mead's gestaltic concept of "a whole" does not presuppose any Hegelian concept of the whole as the whole universe or as the totality of experience, or any Quinian concept of a whole as the totality of assertive symbolic structures. (24) The functional criteria of objects, especially problems and solutions, determine their acts as limited contexts, and the given actual situations are respectively taken as a whole as long as they result in the completion of an experience or task, or in the solution of a problem, for the on-going life of those individual men who are involved and (abstractly) implicated in the situations.

Third, the emphasis on the functional dimension of act is not based upon the "primacy" of any biological or other function as Malinowski and other social scientists tend to present in their "functionalism". (25) For certain situations of man, one must take into consideration his biological functions for their basis, but its primacy or pertinence in the consideration of given situations is entirely contingent upon the nature

---

(24) W. V. O. Quine, From a Logical Point of View (Cambridge, Mass.: Harvard Univ. Press, 1953); and A. Hofstadter, "The Myth of the Whole: A Consideration of Quine's View of Knowledge", Journal of Philosophy, 1954 (50:14), pp. 397-417.

(25) Cf. B. Malinowski, A Scientific Theory of Culture and Other Essays (Chapel Hill: Univ. of N. Carolina Press, 1944). As for the critical implication of this Meadean view against the Freudian and Marxian views of human life, see 3.12.

of their problems involved. In construing the function within the contextual, gestaltic emphasis on act, Mead is able to recognize and require only the condition that objects or values are construed in terms of their proper functions in their situations as determined by the problems involved. Of course, these problems contextually vary from one situation to another. "There is only one field", Mead says, "within which the estimation [of values or objects] can be made, and that is within the actual problem" (SW 262).

In our perspective, Mead's emphasis on actual situation is basically a methodological requirement of science. Under this emphasis, man's symbolic process and its productions in general, and science and its theories in particular, are seen to be based on actual situations and their objects. The symbols - rules, theories, arts, etc. - are the "knowledge" or mediation of the actual, real world under the conditions of the evolved method, the critical, refined method of science, which may be taken, as we will see, as the method of man's "life of reason".

2.3 Mead's Social Behaviorism

2.30 The Preliminary Remarks

In a biographical perspective, Mead's "social behaviorism" as his attempt to solve what is the traditional problem of mind results in the general realization that objects or processes must be considered functionally as related parts of a whole in their problematic situations. In the logically reconstructed perspective of his works, his social behaviorism is the application of the emphasis on actual situation - as the generalized attitude of scientific process - to the problem of mind.

In approaching the problem of mind, Mead takes the presently common view that the traditional substantial dualism of mind and body is a mistake. He rejects the concept of substance applied both to mind and body - that is, to objects in general - if "substance" refers, as it does for Descartes and others, to some entity which exists and is knowable unrelated to other entities. Secondly, Mead rejects any theory of "innate" and/or "transcendental" faculty of mind or reason. He explains that the origin and application of its contents, i.e., ideas, etc., are derived from and based upon social conditions and processes.

Mead accepts the data or states of consciousness - sensations, emotions, memories, images, etc. What he rejects here is the substantial theory that the relation of these phenomena to the external, physiological, and/or behavior processes is intrinsically such that it must be justified or explained on some metaphysical principle such as "substantial parallelism", "pre-established harmony", "idealism" or "materialism" in extreme, "nothingness", etc. Mead finds that these phenomena are intrinsically unisolated but functionally related to and contingent on external, physiological, behavioral processes as a part of the on-going processes in actual situations, and that the former are variable and can be controlled in terms of the latter on the basis of the correlation of the two.

Mead does not reduce mind, the phenomena of consciousness or mental processes, to body and its behavior. He proposes for the methodological consideration of science to approach the psychological study of the functions of human organism through its objectively observable behavior. This proposal is, furthermore, justified by the social, behavioral nature of symbolic process which constitutes mind – the way perception, imagination, judgment, etc. function – as well as by the nature of consciousness as a dynamic, functional process which presents the mental processes only as a related phase of the organism's transactions in its situations. (26)

Mead proposes the thesis of social behaviorism – a methodic approach to psychological problems on the basis of social, behavioral criteria – in consideration of the methodological requirements of science as well as of the nature of consciousness. The following factors of import are considered to justify the social behaviorism: 2.31) the nature of psychology as a science; 2.32) the import of behavior as the criterion of psychology under its methodological requirements as a science; 2.33) the import of behavior in the functional, dynamic correlationalistic interpretation of consciousness; and 2.34) the import of the social conditions for self-consciousness in general and for behavior in particular.

2.31 Psychology as a Science of Control

Mead construes science in general as a "technique of control", a methodic attempt to reconstruct the problematic aspects of our living world for the purpose of the control of the conditions under which we are able, in the well known words of Whitehead, "(i) to live, (ii) to live well, (iii) to live better". (27) Psychology as a science, as long as it is concerned with the "practical" problems of the control of experience of man, can properly limit itself to the problems of correlations between the experiences of individuals and the conditions under which they take place. As we have suggested in 2.2 and will see further, the nature of these experiences and conditions justifies Mead's thesis for social behaviorism that the required correlations can be established in terms of the relation of transactional experiences, or behavioral responses, and their social conditions. (28)

Mead says:

Psychology does undertake to work out the technique which will enable it to deal with these experiences which any individual may have at any moment in his life, and which are peculiar to that individual. And the method of dealing with such an experience is

(26) See Appendix A: Mead's Social, Functional Concept of Consciousness, of which the above paragraphs are a summary and which comes in an original outline of the present work before the following 2.31.
(27) Whitehead, The Function of Reason, p. 8. Mead's concept of science and its method is further considered in 3.232 and 3.233.
(28) Also see Appendix A. especially A.5 Transactional Correlationism.

in getting the conditions under which that experience of the individual takes place. We should undertake to state the experience
of the individual just as far as we can in terms of the conditions
under which it arises. It is essentially a control problem to
which the psychologist is turning. It has, of course, its aspect
of research for knowledge . . . . There is back of that an
attempt to get control through the knowledge which we obtain
. . . .

Our modern psychology is going farther and farther into those
fields within which control can be so realized. It is successful
in so far as it can work out correlations which can be tested.
We want to get hold of those factors in the nature of the individual
which can be recognized in the nature of all members of
society but which can be identified in the particular individual.
Those are problems which are forcing themselves more and
more to the front (MS 37).

The problems of psychology turn out to be largely the problems of discovering the correlations in universal terms - statistically if necessary -
which will be useful in relating particular experiences to particular conditions. Under the established correlations, the experiences of individuals can be explained and predicted in terms of the criteria of the
conditions of actual situations.

As long as psychology is interested in the problems of the control of
transactional experiences in terms of their social conditions, its
research and application can be carried out, as we will see, on the
basis of the criteria of behavioral responses as the transactional
experiences, and of the social conditions as their stimuli. In a sense,
psychology as a science of control may be regarded as a development
out of the motive of social behaviorism; on the other hand, it provides
the ground for the development of social behaviorism as a proper
approach of psychology.

2.32 Behavior as the Objective Criterion of Psychology

In the contemporary history of psychology, the development of behaviorism has been stimulated, on one hand, by the dismal failure of traditional
psychology rooted in the introspective approach to the "subjective states
of consciousness", and, on the other hand, by the fruitful inauguration
of animal psychology in the works of Pavlov(29) and others, which are,
with no choice of turning to the introspective approach, based upon the
relations of the behaviors of animals as responses and the environmental
conditions as stimuli. (30) The appeal of behaviorism is the unique nature

---

(29) I. P. Pavlov, Conditioned Reflexes: An Investigation of the
Physiological Activity of the Cerebral Cortex, trans. and ed. by
G. V. Anrep (London: Oxford Univ. Press, 1927).
(30) Cf. MT 190-1.

of behavior as a subject matter of psychology in view of the methodological requirements of science. Behavior is open to public investigation
and so it can be objectively controlled - especially so in comparison to
the "states of consciousness" which are supposedly "subjective" and
difficult to investigate objectively. (31)

Therefore, behaviorism as an approach to the psychology of man was
first presented in consideration of the methodological requirements of
psychology as a science. It was a program of psychological investigations
which had to overcome the difficulty of explaining certain "internalized"
(or "subjective"), private phases of man. These phases are obviously
a part of the subject matter of psychology, and yet are not readily
"reducible" to behavioristic concepts. As the program of behaviorism
was first carried out by Watson(32) and others, it tended to present an
"ontological" thesis in a negative way in the field of psychology, specifically, that those phases of man which are difficult to subject to a
behavioristic program were denied to exist.

Mead says:

Watson insists that objectively observable behavior completely
and exclusively constitutes the field of scientific psychology,
individual and social. He pushes aside as erroneous the idea
of "mind" or "consciousness", and attempts to reduce all
"mental" phenomena to conditioned reflexes and similar
physiological mechanisms - in short, to purely behavioristic
terms. This attempt, of course, is misguided and unsuccessful,
for the existence as such of mind or consciousness, in some
sense or other, must be admitted - the denial of it leads inevitably to obvious absurdities. But though it is impossible to
reduce mind or consciousness to purely behavioristic terms -
in the sense of thus explaining it away, or denying its existence
as such entirely - yet it is not impossible to explain it in these
terms, and to do so without explaining it away, or denying its
existence as such, in the least. Watson apparently assumes
that to deny the existence of mind or consciousness as a
psychical stuff, substance, or entity is to deny its existence
altogether and that a naturalistic or behavioristic account of
it as such is out of the question. But, on the contrary, we may
deny its existence as a psychical entity without denying its
existence in some other sense at all; and if we then conceive it
functionally, and as a natural rather than a transcendental phenomenon, it becomes possible to deal with it in behavioristic terms
(MS 10). (33)

---

(31) See Appendix A. 4 The "Subjective" as a Functional Phase of Act.
(32) J. B. Watson, Behavior, an Introduction to Comparative Psychology.
(New York: Holt, 1914); Psychology from the Standpoint of a Behaviorist
(Philadelphia: Lippincott, 1919); and Behaviorism (New York: Norton,
1925).
(33) In a present perspective, Watson is a historical figure who had his
role of dramatizing the import of behaviorism in its early stage, and

Mead makes it clear that behaviorism as a methodological thesis does not require any "ontological" thesis which denies or ignores any psychic phase of man. "Behaviorism in [a] wider sense", Mead says, "is simply an approach to the study of the experience of the individual from the point of view of his conduct, particularly, but not exclusively, the conduct as it is observable by others" (MS 2). "But it is not behavioristic", he goes on to say, "in the sense of ignoring the inner experience of the individual - the inner phase of that process or activity. On the contrary, it is particularly concerned with the rise of such experience within the process as a whole" (MS 7-8):

A behavioristic psychology represents a definite tendency rather than a system, a tendency to state as far as possible the conditions under which the experience of the individual arises (MS 38).

The psychologist is interested in finding that sort of condition which can be correlated with the experience of the individual. We are trying to state the experience of the individual and situations in just as common terms as we can, and it is this which gives the importance to what we call behavioristic psychology (MS 39).

Behaviorism is not to be regarded as legitimate up to a certain point and as then breaking down. Behavioristic psychology only undertakes to get a common statement that is significant and makes our correlation successful (MS 40).

It is Mead's suggestion that the development of methodological behaviorism has been closely related to that of modern psychology construed as a technique of control, as the former fulfills all the required conditions of the latter. Insofar as psychology is interested in the control of the responses of individuals, it can be carried out under a correlation between the behavioral responses of individuals and the common conditions which are taken as their stimuli.

2.33 Behavior as the Dynamic Determinant of Consciousness

Mead's behaviorism is not merely based on a consideration of the required conditions of the scientific solutions of psychological problems. More fundamentally, it is based on a consideration of the nature of psychic processes as implied by his interpretation of the present scientific theories of evolution and relativity. (34) The psychic processes as a phase of the evolution of man are the processes of man which emerge and function in his relation to the actual situation of the environment. "In

---

who renders himself now as a nice scapegoat of behaviorism in the narrow, dogmatic sense for certain critics of today like H. B. Veatch. (Cf. his work, Rational Man: A Modern Interpretation of Aristotelian Ethics [Bloomington: Indiana Univ. Press, 1962].)
(34) See Appendix A.3 Consciousness as a Social Perspective.

other words", Mead says, "the doctrine is behavioristic not only in a
psychological sense but also in a metaphysical sense - using metaphysics
as Professor Dewey has undertaken to present it in Experience and Natur
(35) This implies in particular . . . that nature exists in varied aspects i
its relation to the organisms of which it is patient" (SW 340). Mead's
behaviorism is more than a methodological requirement; it is a thesis
which emphasizes man's transaction, his activity of relating, as the
determining factor of his consciousness as well as of his world of nature.

In one sense, consciousness is the very process of an individual's
relating or responding to his environment, a transactional experience.
In another sense, consciousness as "certain contents" is basically
determined and structured by the nature of the individual's act of relating
his behavioral response.(36) Thus, the criterion of behavior provides the
determining factor of the individual's consciousness, his transactional
experiences, which is variable from individual to individual, from contex
to context.

The contents of consciousness are the objects of the environmental
world which exist or prevail in relation to the individual. The relations
of objects (or the objects as relations) are not established in terms of
some general principles of mental association on the basis of disparate,
atomistic data or objects. They are found, intrinsically related, in
nature in terms of the way the individual attends to, is interested in,
selects, manipulates, and/or reconstructs them. And it is this dynamic,
active character in the (contextual, gestaltic, and functional) transactions
of individual men that determines the related objects of consciousness
and those of the world of reality. Accordingly, the processes of consciou
ness can be investigated behavioristically in terms of the common conditions of the world and the ways the individuals transact in the world.
Mead says:

If one approaches the problem of psychology simply from the
standpoint of trying to find out what takes place in the experience
of the individual as an individual, you get a surer clue if you
take the man's action than if you take certain static contents and
say these are the consciousness of the man and that these have
to be approached by introspection to be reached. If you want to
find out what the man is doing, what he is, you will get it a good
deal better if you will get into his conduct, into his action. And
you come back there to certain of his impulses, those impulses
which become desires, plus his mental images, which from one
standpoint are his own but from another standpoint represent
certain of his past experiences, or part of his future experience
. . . . Behavioristic psychology undertakes to examine the acts
of the man from outside without trying to get them by introspection as such, although introspection . . . has a certain
definite meaning even for behavioristic psychology (MT 399).

---

(35) J. Dewey, Experience and Nature (New York: Dover, 1958 [orig.
1925]), pp. 51 ff.
(36) See Appendix A.2 Three Senses of "Consciousness".

Psychology itself cannot very well be made a study of the field
of consciousness alone; it is necessarily a study of a more
extensive field. It is, however, that science which does make
use of introspection, in the sense that it looks within the
experience of the individual for phenomena not dealt with in
any other sciences - phenomena to which only the individual
himself has experiential access . . . . Even when we come
to the discussion of such "inner" experience, we can approach
it from the point of view of the behaviorist, provided that we
do not too narrowly conceive this point of view. What one must
insist upon is that objectively observable behavior finds expression within the individual, not in the sense of being in
another world, a subjective world, but in the sense of being
within his organism. Something of this behavior appears in
what we may term "attitudes", the beginnings of acts. Now,
if we come back to such attitudes we find them giving rise to
all sorts of responses . . . . Now, if our behavioristic point
of view takes these attitudes into account we find that it can
very well cover the field of psychology (MS 4-6).

Behavioristic psychology, if carried out consistently enough,
can cover the field of psychology without bringing in the dubious
conception of consciousness. There are matters which are
accessible only to the individual, but even these cannot be
identified with consciousness as such because we find we are
continually utilizing them as making up our world. What we
can do is to get at the organism as something that you can
study . . . . What is of importance about this psychology is
that it carries us back . . . to the act as such. It considers
the organism as active (MT 404).

In the previous 2.32, we have explained that 1) behaviorism is an
emphasis on the public or objective criteria of psychological data. This
emphasis, which no philosopher of science can deny, must be distinguished from the thesis of "observation terms", though they have
been commonly associated. Behaviorism is not necessarily based on
the distinction of theoretical and observational terms, and on the
requirement of the reduction of the former to the latter. In this 2.33,
we have just explained that 2) behaviorism is an emphasis on the
dynamic, active, and relational nature of man's psychic processes.
Both of these Meadean emphases are especially significant in an historical perspective of the earlier work in psychology (e. g., intro-
spectionism of the nineteenth century) and in philosophy (e. g., British
empiricism from Locke to G. E. Moore).
    In the recent literature of philosophy we notice the rise of critical
reaction against certain developments of behaviorism. Prof. Chomsky's
critical review of Skinner's Verbal Behavior(37) clearly points out the

---

(37) B. F. Skinner, Verbal Behavior (New York: Appleton-Century-
Crofts, 1957).

difficulty of applying to human situations the Skinnerian concepts developed to explain animals other than man in laboratory situations. (38) However, the present defensive exposition of Mead's behaviorism constitutes a basic argument for the behavioristic approach of Skinner and other contemporary psychologists (though not for their specific concepts and formulations) and certainly against the Chomskyan "theory of innate ideas" as an approach in psychology. (39) In another recent article, (40) Prof. Nelson concludes that "behaviorism is false", because not only the complexity of human activities but also that of "animal behaviors" as "automaton behaviors" cannot be fully explained without requiring "descriptions using internal state terms" which "cannot be introduced by reduction sentences even in a certain broadened sense". (41) Prof. Nelson's negative conclusion basically follows if we accept a certain conception of psychology as a science which he assumes but does not explicitly state. The difficulty of behaviorism in a "reductive" sense is not a problem in the works of Pavlov and other psychologists as well as in Mead's conception of psychology as a "science of control", as explained in the previous 2.22 . Prof. Nelson draws certain implications from his negative conclusion, specifically: 1) "conjoined with the proposition that an automaton (hence an animal) is or embodies a formal system", his conclusion "suggests a functional theory of mind"; and 2) "it also shows the irreducibility of psychology to physics in any philosophically interesting sense". These implications are entirely in support of Mead's functional concept of mind. (42)

2.34 Social Conditions of Behavior and Consciousness

"Our behaviorism is a social behaviorism", Mead says (MS 6). Here he recognizes that behaviorism as an approach to the psychology of man is based on and justified by the fact that the conditions of man's consciousness in general and his behavior in particular are social. When we turn to consciousness in the sense of symbolic (self-conscious) process, (43) it is not merely that it can be explained in terms of behavior, but that

---

(38) N. Chomsky, "Verbal Behavior. By B. F. Skinner . . .", Language, 1959 (35:1), pp. 26-58.
(39) N. Chomsky, Cartesian Linguistics (New York: Harper & Row, 1966); "Recent Contributions to the Theory of Innate Ideas", Synthese, 1967 (17:1), pp. 2-11; and "Language and the Mind", I & II, Columbia Forum, 1968 (11:1 & 3), pp. 5-10 & 23-25. Cf. H. Putnam, "The 'Innateness Hypothesis' and Explanatory Models in Linguistics", Synthese, 1967 (17:1), pp. 12-22; and N. Goodman, "The Epistemological Argument", Synthese, 1967 (17:1), pp. 23-8.
(40) R. J. Nelson, "Behaviorism is False", Journal of Philosophy, 1969 (66:14), pp. 417-52.
(41) These quotations are from an abstract of the above cited article, given by Prof. Nelson (Review of Metaphysics, 1969 [22:2], p. 377).
(42) Cf. Appendix A.
(43) See Appendix A.2.

self-consciousness, or consciousness as a social, symbolic process, cannot be explained except in terms of the criterion of behavior as the transaction in social situations in which it emerges and functions. And so the psychology of man as the "counterpart" of the physiology of man is social psychology in the fundamental sense, and this social psychology is behaviorism. (44)

As suggested in 2.22, it is Mead's view that the meanings or objects of individual minds are derived from or presuppose the common meanings or objects in social situations. (45) In an actual situation, the perspectively different experiences of individuals presuppose their common perspective. Individual minds or selves emerge from the social process of relations as parts of the situations. As Mead's theory of perspective carries the evolutionary or genetic dimension, the order of emergence, derivation, and presupposition, is not only logical but temporal, biological, and historical. "What I want to particularly emphasize", Mead says, "is the temporal and logical pre-existence of the social process to the self-conscious individual that arises in it" (MS 186).

The differences between the type of social psychology [A] which derives the selves of individuals from the social process in which they are implicated and in which they empirically interact with one another, and the type of social psychology [B] which instead derives that process from the selves of the individuals involved in it, are clear. The first type [A] assumes a social process or social order as the logical and biological precondition of the appearance of the selves of the individual organisms involved in that process or belonging to that order. The other type [B], on the contrary, assumes individual selves as the presuppositions, logically and biologically, of the social process or order within which they interact . . . .

The latter theory [B] takes individuals and their individual experiencing - individual minds and selves - as logically prior to the social process in which they are involved, and explains the existence of that social process in terms of them; whereas the former [A] takes the social process of experience or behavior as logically prior to the individuals and their individual experiencing which are involved in it, and explains their existence in terms of that social process. But the latter type of theory [B] cannot explain that which is taken as logically prior at all, cannot explain the existence of minds and selves; whereas the former type of theory [A] can explain that which it takes as logically prior, namely, the existence of social process of behavior, in terms of such fundamental biological or physio-

---

(44) The way psychology is labeled "individual psychology" in reference to the study of the basic processes of experience is in a strict sense absurd. And on the other hand, what is called "social psychology" in reference to the study of the "collective behavior" of mob, crowd, rumor, mass movements, etc. is another matter, a part of sociology.
(45) Also see Appendix A.3.

logical relations and interactions as reproduction, or the
co-operation of individuals for mutual protection or the
securing of food. (46)

Our contention is that mind can never find expression, and
could never have come into existence at all, except in terms
of a social environment; that an organized set or pattern of
social relations and interactions (especially those of communication by means of gestures functioning as significant symbols
and thus creating a universe of discourse) is necessarily
presupposed by it and involved in its nature (MS 222-3).

The human being's physiological capacity for developing
mind or intelligence is a product of the process of biological
evolution, just as is his whole organism; but the actual
development of his mind or intelligence itself, given that
capacity, must proceed in terms of the social situations
wherein it gets its expression and import; and hence it itself
is a product of the process of social evolution, the process of
social experience and behavior (MS 226 fn).

It is true, of course, that once mind has arisen in the social
process it makes possible the development of that process into
much more complex forms of social interaction among the
component individuals than was possible before it had arisen.
But there is nothing odd about a product of a given process
contributing to, or becoming an essential factor in, the further
development of that process. The social process, then, does
not depend for its origin or initial existence upon the existence
and interactions of selves; though it does depend upon the latter
for the higher stages of complexity and organization which it
reaches after selves have arisen within it (MS 226).

It is Mead's contention that the import of social behaviorism is obviously
evident when we turn to the basic problems of self-consciousness, those
of symbolic and rational process. That symbols are common or universal
as well as private or internal to individuals in certain contexts can be
explained in terms of social behaviorism without introduction of the
traditional principles of transcendent forms or eternal objects.
Mead says:

Much subtlety has been wasted on the problem of the meaning
of meaning. It is not necessary, in attempting to solve this
problem, to have recourse to psychical states, for the nature
of meaning . . . is found to be implicit in the structure of the
social act, implicit in the relations among its three basic
individual components: namely, in the triadic relation of a
gesture of one individual, a response to that gesture by a

---

(46) The notations [A] and [B] are added to the original.

second individual, and completion of the given social act initiated by the gesture of the first individual. And the fact that the nature of meaning is thus found to be implicit in the structure of the social act provides additional emphasis upon the necessity, in social psychology, of starting with the initial assumption of an ongoing social process of experience and behavior in which any given group of human individuals is involved, and upon which the existence and development of their minds, selves, and self-consciousness depend (MS 81-2).

Are selves psychical, or do they belong to an objective phase of experience which we set off against a psychical phase? I think it can be shown that selves do belong to that objective experience, which, for example, we use to test all scientific hypotheses, and which we distinguish from our imaginations and our ideas, that is, from what we term psychical. The evidence for this is found in the fact that the human organism, in advance of the psychical experiences . . ., assumes the attitude of another which it addresses by vocal [or other reflexive] gesture, and in this attitude addresses itself, thus giving rise to its own self and to the other. In the process of communication there appears a social world of selves standing on the same level of immediate reality as that of the physical world that surrounds us. It is out of this social world that the inner experiences arise which we term psychical, and they serve largely in interpretation of this social world as psychical sensations and percepts serve to interpret the physical objects of our environment. If this is true, social groups are not psychical but are immediately given, though inner experiences are essential for their interpretation. The locus of society is not in the mind . . ., and the approach to it is not by introspection (SP 304-5).

If we can carry back the social behavior within which selves and others arise to a situation that antedates the appearance of the psychical as distinguished from an outer world, it will be this primitive behavior [of assuming the attitudes or roles of others in terms of reflexive gestures] that we can trace back the origins of the social patterns which are responsible not only for the structure of society but also for the criticism of that structure and for its evolution. The social pattern is always larger than the group that it makes possible. It includes the enemy and the guest . . . . Its mechanism of communication carries with it the possibility of conversation with others who are not members of the group. It has in it the implication of the logical universe of discourse. If symbolization can be stated in terms of the behavior of primitive communication, then every distinctively human being belongs to a possibly larger society than that within which he actually finds himself. It is this, indeed, which is implied in the rational character of human animal. And these larger patterns afford a basis for the

48

criticism of existing conditions and in an even unconscious way
tend to realize themselves in social conduct (SP 306).

The meaning or significance of gestures or symbols lies in the triadic
structure of social act. A symbol of an individual man is 1) a response
to 2) others (persons and/or objects) in anticipation of 3) the completion
of their common social act. Mind, as the consciousness of the meaning
or significance, is a social process of assuming the attitudes or roles
of others. In certain contexts, this process is internalized or taken as
inner (or inaccessible-to-other) experiences. Self, as the social
development of a human organism by means of symbolic process, is
the individualized structure of a set of roles, in reference to which the
individual self can function in distinction from some members of society
and in identification with the others in terms of the situations he is
placed in. Rationality lies in the social process in which self-conscious
individuals take themselves as related parts of their social situation in
responding to its role of "generalized other". In a non-problematic or
ongoing situation, this "generalized other" prevails as its common
structure of roles in symbolic forms to be assumed and observed; in a
problematic or delayed situation, this role is introduced by the individuals involved as the situation is reconstructed by them in terms of
the methodic process, the role (of generalized other) of the society of
science. (47)
    The psychological attempt to explain man's individuation as well as
his rationality does not, then, presuppose the "pre-existence" of mind
which expresses the subjective states or inner meanings of individual
men, and that of the structure of meanings in communication such as
language and other symbolic forms as the collective sum or product of
the intrinsically subjective expressions. Otherwise, it would be inevitably involved with the traditional philosophical problems of
"solipsism" and "other minds". On the contrary, it presupposes the
ongoing social process of communication in which various aspects of
the individuals are related to those of the others in their social situation.
In this process some aspects are selected by the individuals as the
relation of themselves to the others for their own structure of meanings.
    Mead's social behaviorism requires, therefore, that we must approach
the function of mind - as well as its genetic formation - as the social,
symbolic process of role-taking, not in terms of the subjective states
or meanings to be expressed and socialized but in terms of the large
social context of transactions in which the inner meanings are an
internalized functional phase. The process of mind or self-consciousness as the functional symbolic relation - of which its world of reality
or universe of discourse can be contextually distinguished between its
private internalized phase and its public environmental phase - can be
explained by a behavioristic analysis of the transactional relation of
the individuals and the social condition of which they are a part.

-----

(47) This paragraph is stated in a summary form in anticipation of the
following, main chapter, 3.3.

2.4 Social Act as the Context of Rationality

In conjunction with Mead's emphases on scientific method and on actual
situation, his social behaviorism suggests that rationality as a psychological, or anthropological, concept can and should be explained in
terms of the criteria of social behavior, or in terms of the context of
social act. "Reason", Mead says, "is a function of behavior in an
evolving society of human individuals" (PA 519).

By a logically "primitive" or prototypical case of social act, Mead
refers, as explained earlier in 2.2, to the situation in which an individual
man is in a transactional relation with the other members of a society -
at least, concretely with another member or abstractly with the whole
society as a "generalized other". This relation develops to complete
his act to an end in reference to certain selected conditions of the situation. In the context of social act as such lies the locus of rationality
as an anthropological concept. Rationality is a type of man's activities
in which the individual involves or implicates himself in the role of
others, and anticipates the others' responses to his own role. The
rationality of man's activities, ranging from the "private", "internal",
to the public, institutional, can be determined in reference to the context
of some social act in which these activities are functional. In this sense,
rationality is basically a problem of human sociality.

In traditional philosophy, the problems of rationality have been considered, as noted in 1.1, primarily in reference to the process of
"reasoning"; that is to say, the problems have been mainly those of the
forms and conditions of assertive discourse for reasoning, of which the
logical and the psychological criteria have not been clearly delineated.
Yet, rationality in this traditional perspective refers to the context of
social act in the following sense: when an individual is self-conscious
in the process of reasoning (perceptual judgment, etc.), that is, when
he takes himself to be an object (to himself), his process is an
internalized (or internal) process of certain social, symbolic acts. In
these acts he has been, and/or is, able to take himself as an object (to
himself) by assuming the role of others (who take him as an object). The
individual's judgment or idea has a social import in terms of its effect
on the other members of a society, and this effect is realized in the
context of some social acts. Under the present conditions of human life,
there is no activity of man so private or isolated that it has no effect on
others directly or indirectly.

In contemporary works of anthropology and sociology, we speak of the
rationality of certain social customs and institutions. Insofar as they
are the working, effective parts of man's social life, their rationality
is determined in reference to the context of social acts in which they
are applied - because they function and have effects on individual men
only in the context of certain social acts.

Mead says:

> The other conception [of consciousness] that I have brought out
> concerns the particular sort of intelligence that we ascribe to
> the human animal, so called "rational intelligence", or conscious-
> ness in another sense of the term. If consciousness is a substance,

it can be said that this consciousness is rational per se; and just
by definition the problem of the appearance of what we call
rationality is avoided. What I have attempted to do is to bring
rationality back to a certain type of conduct, the type of conduct
in which the individual puts himself in the attitude of the whole
group to which he belongs (MS 334). (48)

Here Mead makes clear how he approaches the basic problem of the
rational phase of human consciousness or mind: he construes it on the
basis of "conduct" and "a certain type of conduct". In this context, as
noted in 2.33 and 2.34, he distinguishes 1) one conception of consciousness, self-consciousness, as the social act in which self appears - from
the other conceptions of consciousness as 2) the "private content" of
human organism in his transaction within nature, and as 3) the very
process of the transaction in reference to the "private content". (49) In
his works on psychology, (50) Mead is largely concerned with the first
conception, and within this concern, his various theories of gesture,
attitude, symbol, role, and self are aimed at the explanation of a certain
type of self-conscious conduct which constitutes rationality. There is no
doubt, though it has not been fully pointed out by most of the students of
Mead, that in the large part of his psychological works on the social,
symbolic process of role-taking, Mead is mainly concerned with this
rational type of conduct and its social conditions.

It is needless to say that rational act is not the only type of social act
which appears in man's various situations, and with which the sciences
of man are concerned. And it is not the case that Mead is unaware of
other types of man's social acts and their import. It is the case, for a
historically well known reason in philosophy, that in the name of a
general theory of human conduct Mead inquires into the very conditions
of human life, the type of human activity without which man's "human"
life - or, in other, loose terms, his social, civilized life, is not possible
Quite in accordance with the attitude of traditional philosophy in this
matter, Mead's answer is his theory of rationality.

In a perspective of social act, Mead investigates various problems of
the functions and conditions of man's impulses, attitudes, habits, tools,
methods, symbols, institutions, etc. as its phases. And his works result
in a theory of man's rationality with emphasis on social act as the basic
context of rationality. It is one of his major contributions to philosophy
and the other sciences of man. The re-interpretation of his works given

---

(48) Cf. PA 508-9 & MS 347 ff.
(49) See Appendix A.2.
(50) His articles on psychology published in his life, most of which are
presently reprinted in SW; and his lectures for the course, "Social
Psychology", which were stenographed (mostly in 1927) and edited
(after his death) by others as MS. (SP is a selection of parts from MS,
PT, PA and PP - with the exception of an article, "Cooley's Contribution to American Social Thought", which is not reprinted in SW.)
See Bibliography.

in this study shows that 3.3) his theory of symbolic process in terms of the concept of "generalized other" explains what may be regarded as the "necessary" condition of rationality, while 3.2) his theory of implemental process in terms of the generalized concept of scientific method explains what may be regarded as its "sufficient" condition.

As suggested in 1.2, Mead re-interprets the traditional concept of "reasoning" in terms of contextual, behavioral criteria as the internalization of the symbolic process of rational, social acts; he interprets the sociological concept of rational organization as the habituation or institutionalization of rational acts. The problem of whether an idea or institution is rational or irrational does not arise properly unless it is asked in reference to the context of certain social acts in which it is applied or used.

CONDITIONS OF RATIONALITY

> The evolution of Reason from below has been entirely
> pragmatic, with a short range of forecast.
>
> A. N. Whitehead, The Function of Reason (1929)

3.0 The Preliminary Remarks and Questions

In this third chapter, we will, in the perspective of social act as explained in the previous chapter, consider the three basic factors involved in rationality as an anthropological problem: 3.1) man's physiological impulses - their social, inhibitable, and variable nature as the
precondition of rationality; 3.2) man's teleological, implemental process
its methodic phase as the "sufficient" condition; and 3.3) man's symbolic
process - its reflexive, regulative function as the "necessary" condition.
In 3.4, the given explication of Mead's concept of rationality is considered
and justified in terms of an interpretation of some recent experimental
studies done on his theories of social psychology.

The following three statements of Mead could be regarded, respectively
as the conclusions of the first three sections in this chapter: 3.1) "Human
nature is . . . social through and through" (MS 229). 3.2) "Man is an
implemental animal" (SW 314). 3.3) "Man lives in a world of Meaning"
(SW 234). These statements are ordered so as to suggest that the explication of 3.1) "sociality" in terms of 3.2) "implementality" and 3.3)
"meaning" constitutes an explication of the conclusion of the chapter:
"Man is a rational being because he is a social being" (MS 379).

In view of the above quotations, certain questions may be raised; they
are the basic questions asked in this chapter. They are formulated and
will be answered in view of the problems which are explained in 1.1 to
be the problems of rationality in a perspective of the biological and social
evolution of man. 1) How or in what sense is man's rationality derived
from his sociality? 2) Under what biological and other conditions is man
(i.e., his act) social? 3) Under what conditions is a social act required
to be mediated by an implemental, "meaningful" (or symbolic) process?
And 4) under what implemental, symbolic conditions of mediation is a
social act regarded to be rational? The answers to these questions will
be our attempt to deal with the general questions of this study: (a) What
is rationality? (What do we refer to by rationality? Or, what do we
understand in regarding something as rational?) (b) How can a man be
rational in his act? (c) What is the import of rationality in a perspective
of human life?

The questions 1) and 2) are considered in the previous chapter, especially in 2.4; but they are reconsidered in 3.1 in terms of the "nature" of man's impulses. The answers to them will suggest how to answer the questions 3) and 4) which are considered in 3.2 and 3.3.

The Meadean perspective of social act, which we follow in this chapter, can be characterized as that of "functional genesis" or "genetic function- ality". (1) If it appears in certain context that Mead considers factors or phases of the act in a (genetic) perspective of the growth of children or of the evolution of mankind, it is certainly not his aim (and not ours) to give a systematic genetic account of the given problem of rationality in the ontogenic or phylogenic sense. We are mainly concerned with the functional conditions of implemental and symbolic processes which, as phases of the act, constitute the conditions of rationality. Mead has a motif of speculating on the conditions in which these processes have been generated. But he speculates on them in terms of the functional conditions of these processes, without which they could not and cannot be generated and function.

As explained in 2.22 (fn. 22), the term "functional" (or "function") is used by Mead in the three related, yet distinct, senses which can be clearly indicated by its contrasting terms. 1) "Functional" in the sense of being "dynamically relational" is in contrast (contradictory) to "non- functional" in the sense of being "substantial" or "essential" (or a "thing-in-itself"); 2) "functional" in the sense of "presently functioning" or "presently dynamically relational" is in contrast (not necessarily contradictory) to "genetic" in the sense of being "originated" or "going back to the original context"; and 3) "functional" in the sense of being "efficacious" or "successfully working" is in contrast (contradictory) to "dysfunctional" in the sense of "malfunctioning" or being "ineffective" or "unsuccessfully working". These different senses of "functional" can be distinguished by the contexts the term is used in. In 2.2 (and Appendix A), we have used "functional" in the first sense. In this chapter, "functional" is mainly used in the second and third senses.

3.1 Impulses and Social Mediation

3.11 Impulses and Sociality

In The Philosophy of the Present, Mead speaks of "sociality" as a basic concept which is not exclusively limited to the social relations of men or organisms. "The social character of the universe", Mead says, "we find in the situation in which the novel event is in both the old order and the new which its advent heralds. Sociality is the capacity of being several things at once" (PP 49). In terms of contexts, the concept of sociality in the broad sense as "relationality" in reference to 1) the relation of natural objects in general can be distinguished from those of sociality in reference to 2) the "life-dependent" relation of organisms

---

(1) The question on the nature of Mead's "genetic" theories does not arise until we turn to his theory of symbolic process. It is considered in 3.31.

or 3) the "self-conscious" relation of men. They are clearly different concepts which Mead distinguishes in most of his works except in The Philosophy of the Present. (2)

All organisms from cells to men require an interaction with their environment, certain selected elements of a given surrounding for the preservation of life and welfare. In this sense the living process of organisms is social. They cannot exist except by being functionally related to their environment. Furthermore, to the extent that organisms have developed certain physiological needs or impulses which cannot be fulfilled without cooperation with members of their own species, these organisms are social in a sense which comes close to the anthropological case. These physiological impulses provide an important functional basis for the social or communal relations of organisms, including men, among their own species located in an environment of limited space and time.

Mead says:

The behavior of all living organisms has a basically social aspect: the fundamental biological or physiological impulses and needs which lie at the basis of all such behavior - especially those of hunger and sex, those connected with nutrition and reproduction - are impulses and needs which, in the broadest sense, are social in character or have social implications, since they involve or require social situations or relations for their satisfaction by any given individual organism; and they thus constitute the foundation of all types or forms of social behavior, however simple or complex, crude or highly organized, rudimentary or well developed. The experience and behavior of the individual organisms are always components of a large social whole or process of experience and behavior in which the individual organism - by virtue of the social character of the fundamental physiological impulses and needs which motivate and are expressed in its experience and behavior - is necessarily implicated, even at the lowest evolutionary levels. There is no living organism of any kind whose nature or constitution is such that it could exist or maintain itself in complete isolation from all other living organisms, or such that certain relations to other living organisms (whether of its own or of

---

(2) In the present work, the term "social" or "sociality" is used after MS and SW in the biological or anthropological sense which can be distinguished in terms of contexts. The problem of Mead's "metaphysical" or "cosmological" category of sociality is not a question in this present work. (Cf. F. M. Doan, "Notations on G. H. Mead's Principle of Sociality with Special Reference to Transformations", Journal of Philosophy, 1956 (53:20), pp. 607-15, and Emergence and Organized Perspectives: A Study in the Philosophy of George Herbert Mead, Ph. D. Dissert, Toronto: Univ. of Toronto, 1952; and P. H. Hare, "G. H. Mead's Metaphysics of Sociality", Ph. D. Dissert. New York: Columbia Univ., 1965.

other species) - relations which in the strict sense are social -
do not play a necessary and indispensable part in its life. All
living organisms are bound up in a general social environment
or situation, in a complex of social interrelations upon which
their continued existence depends (MS 227-8).

Mead thinks, in accordance with a common view in biology, that the
social life of organisms other than men can be explained in terms of
physiological impulses and functions responsive to them. All the complex
social behaviors of organisms other than men, from the communicative
process of bees to the herd movement of mammals, can be seen as
functions of their evolved physiological plasticity and differentiation.
We realize, on the other hand, that the differentiation and complexity
of man's social life cannot be fully explained in terms of our respectively
corresponding impulses and functions which are biologically explicable.
Still, the diverse, complex social relations of human life - from those
of family and school to those of political parties and television communication - can be shown to be rooted genetically and functionally in
these common or similar biological aspects of man which require us
"by nature" to be social. "These socio-physiological impulses", Mead
says, " . . . are the essential physiological materials from which
human nature is socially formed; so that human nature is something
social through and through, and always presupposes the truly social
individual" (MS 229).
   In one context Mead lists ten or eleven common "primitive" impulses
of man, ranging from those of organic balance and response organization
to those of sex and "herding" (MS 348-9). For certain (obviously social)
impulses or needs such as sex and reproduction, men are social in a
narrow sense of cooperative relations among a group of the species. The
other (comparatively "a-social") impulses such as sleeping and breathing
are transformed in the social evolution of man into social impulses in the
narrow sense, as clearly suggested by the extreme cases of overcrowded
transportation and polluted air.
   In another context Mead finds two opposing types of classes of "fundamental" impulses of men, "social" and "anti-social", or "social cooperation" and "social antagonism" (MS 303-4). "In the broadest and
strictest sense", both of them are social. Even in the case of the "anti-
social", the impulse or behavior tendency is social in the sense that if
it is against one society in a given situation, at the same time it implies,
or is for, another society. And this "destructive" impulse of antagonism
can be and often is re-directed as a "constructive" social principle within
a limited society, as suggested by the example of the emergence of
solidarity before a common enemy. But such impulses generally divert
the involved society from a genuine, long-range development of common
interests, and "could not, alone, constitute the basis of any organized
human society" (MS 304). On the other hand, the impulses of "social
co-operation" such as the sexual or the parental impulses can function
as the bases of social division and disorganization. Under proper social,
institutional arrangements, these aspects of division and disorganization
"can be given a function under social control" (SW 238), and can be the
dynamic forces in a society. If we accept, following the insight of

Buddha, that man's desires or impulses are the root of all evil or
misery, we must also realize that they are the root of all good, the good
or valuable things man produces and enjoys.

In consideration of the problem of rationality, the import of these
impulses as a basis of man's sociality is evident in view of the conclusion of 2.4 that social act is the context of rationality.

3.12 Inhibited Impulses and Process of Mediation

In the evolutionary process of life, the functions of organisms have
developed in relation to conditions of their "natural" habitats so as to
be fulfilled "immediately" (i.e., without prolonged delay) and "directly"
(i.e., without extended modification of their objects). Otherwise, they
become extinct through the evolution of their organic bases. Man's
organic functions may be regarded, in one sense, to remain under such
a condition. No doubt, a large part of them do. Through the history of
civilization, on the other hand, man's impulses as his organic functions
are known to have been determined and controlled in a large variety of
ways which commonly require that the impulses are physiologically
inhibited and delayed for their fulfillment. And it appears to be theoretically possible under the advancement of science and its technological
application that most of man's organic functions can be, as some of
them have already been, replaced, extended and/or modified by socially
implemented functions. (3)

In a perspective of man's sociality, his impulses cannot be construed
as the physiological functions which are immediately and directly expressed and satisfied. They largely function in terms of their inhibition
and control - if not in terms of their being blocked and in conflict - and
in terms of their openness to various social modifications and extensions
To the extent that variations of their expressions are pervasive and
extensive, man's impulses are distinguished from the "instincts" of
other organisms, which are limited to their fixed variations determined
by their given organic bases and environmental conditions and which
fulfill their functions immediately and directly.

Mead says:

Human behavior, or conduct, like the behavior of lower animal
forms, springs from impulses. An impulse is a congenital
tendency to react in a specific manner to a certain sort of
stimulus, under certain organic conditions. Hunger and anger
are illustrations of such impulses. They are best termed
"impulses", and not "instincts", because they are subject to
extensive modifications in the life-history of individuals, and
these modifications are so much more extensive than those to
which the instincts of lower animal forms are subject that the
use of the term "instinct" in describing the behavior of normal
adult human individuals is seriously inexact (MS 337).

_____

(3) See 3.22.

Many of the acts of these [organisms other than man] are as highly complex as many human acts which are reflectively controlled. The distinction is that which I have expressed in the distinction between the instinct and the impulse. The instinct may be highly complex, e.g., the preparation of the wasp for the larval life that will come from the egg which is laid in its fabricated cell; but the different elements of the whole complex process are so firmly organized together that a check at any point frustrates the whole undertaking. It does not leave the parts of the whole free for recombination in other [ways]. Human impulses, however, are generally susceptible to just such analysis and recombination in the presence of obstacles and inhibitions (MS 362).

The evolutionary transformation of man's impulses into socially variable or modifiable processes requires two conditions of social act: 1) that the impulses can be inhibited – and responses to them can be delayed – provisionally, as physiological functions; and 2) that the inhibited impulses are not "fatal", or causal to organic extinction, but are causal, catalytic, and receptive to the process of mediation. (One may consider these conditions in reference to cases of domestic animals and other organisms controlled by man, to which the conditions apply as an "extension" of his own case.) These two conditions refer (in the sense of "origination" or in that of "anticipation") to the situation in which impulses, as the incipient phase of the act, come into conflict or break down in the absence of immediate consummatory objects or in the presence of diverse stimuli or obstacles. Such a situation (confronted or anticipated) under these two conditions is "problematic" in the paradigmatic, anthropological sense; and it is the situation in which rational conduct appears.
Mead says:

It has been impossible to avoid the attempt to bring reason within the scope of evolution; and if this attempt is successful, rational conduct must grow out of impulsive conduct. My own attempt will be to show that it is in the social behavior of the human animal that this evolution takes place. On the other hand, it is true that reasoning conduct appears where impulsive conduct breaks down. Where the act does not bring its function, when the impulsive effort to get food does not bring the food – and, more especially, where conflicting impulses thwart and inhibit each other – here reasoning may come in with a new procedure that is not at the disposal of the biologic individual. The characteristic result of reasoning procedure is that the individual secures a different set of objects to which to respond, a different field of stimulation. There has been discrimination, analysis, and a rebuilding of the things that called out the conflicting impulses and that now call out a response in which the conflicting impulses have been adjusted to each other (MS 348).

In a social act, the intermediate phase between the incipient phase of

impulses and stimuli and the terminating phase of readjustment and
consummation appears as a reaction to – or an anticipation of –
inhibited impulses. In this mediate phase of the act, as we will consider fully in 3.2 and 3.3, certain physiological functions of man,
especially his nervous system, operate as delayed responses to
coordinate distant (perceptual) and contact (manipulative) objects,
which are fused with emotions as immediate responses to inhibited
impulses. The delayed, mediate process results in, or functions in
terms of, the objects selected, indicated, manipulated and reconstructed as social media: meanings and values; means and ends. It is
the basis of the social development of symbolic, implemental mediation.
And it is what Mead calls the "reasoning procedure", to which man's
impulses are subject in order to be analyzed and disconnected and then
to be selected and reorganized in a certain order or harmony as
socially functional processes.

    In one context, Mead says that "impulse certainly can be given a
statement in terms not only of acts but also of the organism" (MT 359).
In accordance with his social behaviorism, he gives two slightly
different versions of the definition of "impulse" in terms of social act.
First, as quoted earlier, "an impulse is a congenital tendency to react
in specific manner to a certain sort of stimuli under certain organic
conditions" (MS 337). Second, an impulse is the incipient phase of an
act, which initiates the act in the direction of certain objects as its
consummatory end.(4) If the first version is construed as a statement
in terms of the organism, it is certainly not in terms of the organism's
anatomical parts or structures. The import of statements on impulse
in terms of social act, social objects, lies in the fact that the statements
in terms of organism, especially its anatomical parts or structures, are
very limited. And impulses as congenital tendencies are not completely
efficacious to determine social processes in actual situations.

    In the context of social act, impulses are directed to certain social
objects as their consummatory ends. These objects are what we need
or desire; or what we are motivated by, interested in or disposed to.
(5) And they are significant, meaningful, and valuable. Insofar as
various implements or media are necessary for, or functional to, the
consummatory ends, these media are also the objects that we want,
desire, or are motivated by. In terms of limited contexts, these media
are the functional ends of social act. We desire or are interested in
them contextually as ends in themselves. And they are significant,
meaningful and valuable. So, we can desire or be motivated by various
social objects which appear to be remotely related to the consummatory
ends of our impulses.

    The functional "precondition" of mediation in reference to impulses
is that insofar as they persist or recur on the basis of the evolved
physiology of man, they are provided with consummatory objects and
are satisfied. That is, an act which requires mediation is dealt with by
a process of mediation, not by an attempt to eliminate or demolish the

----

(4) Cf. PA 3 ff, MS 6, MT 395, etc.
(5) Cf. MS 383, MT 396, etc.

process of mediation. The meaning of this precondition may be suggested in terms of consideration of a Buddhistic or Schopenhauerian attitude that the root of man's misery is desires or impulses and so the answer to misery is the destruction of all desires. In the perspective of this study of man's life, this "attractive" solution is not an answer to the problems of his misery or desires, because the desires or impulses are not only the root of misery but also the root of happiness. "All of our impulses", Mead says, "are possible sources of happiness" (MS 383).

Of course, under conditions of various actual situations, some impulses are terminated in frustration and disappointment. But it is not the function of social process of mediation to perpetuate these conditions. On the other hand, this functional precondition cannot be construed in the sense of the anthropological or psychological view (common in traditional philosophy and not entirely vanished from contemporary philosophy) that man has an inborn "general" impulse (or drive or motive) over and above his specific impulses (or drives or motives), and that it is directed toward the satisfaction of the specific in a certain universal way, e.g., egoistic, "sublimational", etc. To the extent that this view is not supported by the mediational conditions of impulses, especially by the fact that processes of mediation are not fully determined by impulses as physiological functions, and that they are contingent and diverse in terms of social conditions, various versions of psychological hedonism (Hobbes', J. S. Mill's, Freud's, etc.) are not justified. Nor do we have to pre-suppose, just because man acts in terms of various impulses and goes on living, that in back of various impulses there is one "general" force or drive such as Nietzsche's "will to power" or Bergson's "élan vital".

Impulses are the "original" or physiological sources of desires, motives, interests, dispositions, etc. They provide the physiological sources of value to means and ends of social acts, and those of meaning to these social media. But impulses are extensively mediated by symbolic, implemental processes. Thus, they are incomplete and inadequate in themselves, or as physiological functions, to determine social objects as their consummatory ends.

Most of man's impulses and their physiological bases are common or similar(6) - with the exceptions of age (parental and infantile) and sex (feminine and masculine); they provide no biologically determined differentiation for the organization of human society. Certain contemporary social trends indicate that the two exceptions of age and sex are, in one way, rapidly being disconnected from their physiological roots. As for the first, the parental functions are taken away from parents themselves and provided by certain social institutions such as nurseries, schools, juvenile courts, trusts, etc. As for the second, the woman's liberation movement, homosexuals' public defense, and "uni-sex" fashions, as well as the possibilities of artificial transformation of sex and reproduction, are certainly steps toward the disintegration

(6) Cf. "All human beings have fundamentally the same anatomical structure, operate through the same physiological processes, and are driven by the same biological urges" (R. Debos, "Biological Individuality", Columbia Forum, 1969 [12:1], p. 5).

of any strong sexual differentiation of humanity. Certain diverse physiological features of man such as the colour of the skin and the size of the breast are also biologically undetermined for the social functions they have in various societies. Their social functions are largely determined by the social process of mediation in these societies. The import of man's common or similar impulses is that they provide not only the pervasive basis of man's sociality but also an important basis of social equality and an "open society" in appropriate social situations. On the other hand, in the peculiar nature of man's undifferentiated, variable impulses lies the necessity and import of implemental and symbolic processes as the "mechanism" of social differentiation and organization.

At the end of 3.11, we noted Mead's list of man's ten or eleven "primitive" impulses, which corresponds to the common practice in anthropology and psychology of providing a classification of a number of impulses as the basic or primitive impulses of man. We no longer take seriously the claim that in terms of such a classification, various social media – tools, ideas, institutions, etc. – can be correlated, or causally related, to different impulses, and that such a classification does provide a theory of man's culture or social life. Various attempts have been made in anthropology, psychology and other sciences to isolate and classify man's impulses (or needs, drives or motives) into a limited number as his primitive or basic types, or to select one or two of them as the dominating, determining "force". These attempts generally turn out to be reflections of the problems to be solved in different social contexts. In view of Mead's criteria of actual situation, given in 2.22, it would be a mistake to take these common classifications or selections other than as functionally useful theories in reference to given problematic situations. Of these attempts, Mead says: "It is, of course, difficult if not impossible to isolate the fundamental impulses of our natures" (SW 394).

Whether the impulses in the basis of economic process or in that of sexual process predominate over or determine the other impulses – and so the social process of human life – is very much determined by how they are not functionally mediated by existing social media of given societies. It is needless to explain the social as well as the physiological import of impulses to eat, etc. as the impulses of economic process. The import of the impulses of sexual process is another matter; it lies at least in the following factors: 1) their consummatory objects are commonly individual men who are in the end "reduced" to physiological functions of "naked" bodies in the milieu of complex social media (conversations, letters, gifts, masks, ceremonies, fantasies, etc.) involved in situations; 2) these impulses are, for most men, their persistent, frequently intense motives under constant exposure to abundant stimuli, although these impulses are part of the physiological functions which can be "transcended" by individual men, if not by a whole society or human race; and 3) these impulses commonly present problems each individual man has to solve himself to various degrees within and in spite of the framework of institutional arrangements. The predominance of sexual problems in Freud's Europe or Kinsey's America, among other societies, indicates that the mediational arrangements provided for the impulses of sexual process are inadequate in comparison to the media provided, say, for the impulses of economic process. (When Freud discovered <u>libido</u> as the predominant, determining "force" of human life, it was a discovery of the social conditions of his society; and it is not <u>libido</u> but the process of discovery, a process of mediation, which characterizes him and his society as well as humanity.)

In a recent work in social psychology which may be regarded as an attempt to reinterpret Freudian psychology within a Meadean framework, Gerth and Mills say:

> The enormous variety of specific activities which make up the histories of biologically similar men forces us to acknowledge that the objects and goals of behavior are not biologically given, but are derived from the (social) environment in which men act . . . . Indeed, such regularities of behavior as we may observe in men are best described in terms of their goals or end-situations rather than in terms of any constant set of "urges" somehow "lying in" the organism and "back of" their conduct regularities . . . .
>
> There is usually a direct correlation between an act and its object: we act towards something when it is a goal, away from it when it is not . . . . These objects involve, as George Mead has said, a "content toward which the individual is susceptible as a stimulus". It is these objects, toward which men learn to be sensitive, that are important in explaining the diversities and regularities of the specific conduct of man. No inventory of conveniently catalogued biological elements in man's organism will enable us to predict or account for the varied and changing activities in which men in different societies engage . . . .
>
> From the biological point of view, then, man as a species and men as individuals are seen as organisms . . . who possess undefined impulses, which may be defined and specified by a wide range of social objects. (7)

It is evident in view of the "undefined" variable nature of man's impulses that the diversity and complexity of social processes could not be explained fully in terms of physiological impulses, especially if they were stated in terms of organism. Monogamy versus polygamy, or heterosexuality vs. homosexuality, could not be explained in terms of, say, "sexual-reproductive" impulses, though both of them are derived from or based on those impulses. Nor could private ownership vs. public ownership (of the means of production), or "well done" vs. "medium rare" (as preferences for steaks), be explained in terms of, say, "gastro-nutritional" impulses, though both of them are based on these

---

(7) H. Gerth & C. W. Mills, <u>Character and Social Structure: The Psychology of Social Institutions</u> (New York: Harcourt, Brace & World, 1953), pp. 9-10. The given quotation of Mead is from SW 98. Cf. J. Dewey, <u>Human Nature and Conduct</u> (New York: H. Holt & Co., 1922), Part II; and E. Cassirer, <u>An Essay on Man</u> (New Haven: Yale Univ. Press, 1944), Chap. VI.

impulses. The point made suggests <u>prima facie</u> a definite criticism of anthropological or psychological theories of "biological determinism" such as Spencer's and Sumner's "bio-sociology"(8) or such as the orthodox version of Freudian psychoanalysis and a bio-psychological interpretation of Marxian economics.

Furthermore, it is, as suggested earlier, in terms of the objects and types of social processes that we can discover what impulses man does have and how they are related. And so the sciences of <u>man as man</u>, not as organism, must be properly approached in terms of his social processes rather than in terms of his physiological functions and bases. This conclusion is a justification of Mead's social behaviorism.

3.13 Impulses and Rationality

In traditional philosophy as well as in contemporary sciences of man, the problem of man's impulses has been commonly discussed under the topic of "human nature". The (anthropological) problem of rationality can be construed to arise largely because of the peculiar conditions and functions of man's impulses, or "human nature", in contrast to those of other organisms' impulses or instincts.

In a perspective of human sociality, Mead explains that man's "socio-physiological" impulses, their processes and objects, constitute what he calls the "content" or "matter" of man's social acts. And this "content" is mediated or "formed" by implemental, symbolic processes, what he calls the "mechanism" or "form" of the social acts (PA 547). In contrast, in the cases of organisms other than man - and in the "primitive" phylogenic and ontogenic situations of man - their "socio-physiological" impulses or instincts provide both "the content and the form of . . . social objects" (SW 98). That is, these organisms carry out social processes on the strength of the biological plasticity of different instincts. The comparison suggested is supported by the fact that while these organisms generally fail to present alternative objects for an instinct when its well organized process is extrinsically disturbed or blocked in departure from its plastic routine in an unusual situation, men as members of societies have, by means of implemental, symbolic processes, presented a large variety of alternative objects for most of their impulses. (9) Some of these alternatives are so extreme that they are regarded as "perversions" to the "nature" of impulses.

In another perspective of human sociality, Mead takes these impulses

---

(8) Cf. MS 310.

(9) It is a common problem in anthropology and ethology to delineate the difference between the sociality of man and that of other organisms, particularly certain unusually communal organisms like bees, ants, and chimpanzees. Mead has written much on the problem and generally makes a distinction in terms of criteria of the function of symbolic mediation which is found exclusively in the social process of man. On this problem he says: "It is a distinction which still has to be made with reservations, because it may be that there will be some way of discovering in the

of man as "one of the two poles in the general process of social differentiation and evolution" (MS 229). It is called "the individual or physiological pole", while the other is "the institutional pole" (MS 230). Institutions, ranging from eating with chopsticks and working five days a week to the Olympic Games and the United Nations, are contextually enduring "generalized" ways of social process. They are what Mead explains as "roles of generalized others" in social acts. From the point of view of individuals, institutionalized roles are habits. Or, institutions are "embodied habits", as Dewey says. (10) These institutions, as one pole in the social process in which the impulses are the other pole, may be construed in one sense to constitute the "content" of social acts; they develop and function in terms of the "mechanism" of implemental, symbolic processes. On the other hand, insofar as institutions are implements and symbolic structures which mediate impulse-initiated social acts toward consummatory ends, institutional processes are themselves the "mechanism" of social acts.

In the previous section, 3.12, we have explained that in social acts man's impulses function largely in terms of their inhibition and catalyctic receptivity to the process of mediation. In problematic situations of inhibited impulses, implemental, symbolic processes of mediation, if they are functional, are the solutions of problems; they provide the consummatory objects for the impulses. If similar problematic situations recur, these solutions are remembered and preserved. And these assimilated, enduring solutions are the institutions of society. (On the other hand, some institutions are conserved and endure in spite of the fact that the situations to which they were the solutions have disappeared. Herein lie certain problems of irrationality.) If similar problematic situations recur, it is also possible that the processes of mediation evolve, as part of the solutions, a method, a generalized approach to similar problems, i.e., a common, systematic functional way of solving these problems. In one sense, a method, as a symbolic, implemental process, is an institution. It is Mead's interpretation, as suggested in 2.1, that the scientific method in a broad sense is the very process of mediation generalized as a method, a method of solving

---

future a language among[other organisms like] bees and ants" (MS 235). This problem remains today as in his time in spite of recent studies, including von Frisch's study of the communicative process of honeybees. (For a recent review of ethological studies, see P. Maler, "Developments in the Study of Animal Communication", in Darwin's Biological Work: Some Aspects Reconsidered, ed. by P. R. Bell (New York: J. Wiley & Sons, Inc., 1964 [orig. 1959], pp. 150-206.

(10) J. Dewey, Human Nature and Conduct, p. 108. The basic problems of habits are considered in this study in terms of those of institutions. The concept of "habit" has special problems under its association with 1) "subconscious" or "unconscious" periodic activities, 2) addicted compulsory responses, 3) individualized idiosyncracies, etc. In comparison to "institution", furthermore, "habit" is limited, at least, in one important sense which may be suggested by the following question: Whose habit is it to select or be elected as a Pope, or to reward or receive the Nobel Prizes?

problems in general. It is an institution, the special institutional process which has emerged to be the method of all other social institutions.

Here, one perspective of human sociality presents the social evolution of the "content" of acts from the physiological pole to the institutional in terms of the "mechanism" of social act, the methodic (implemental and symbolic) process of mediation. In another perspective, human sociality refers to the methodic, institutional mediation of social acts, of which impulses are their incipient phase. If this mediation of social acts is functional, the acts are rational. Man's rationality is constituted by the conditions of functional social mediation. (These conditions are the problems in the next two sections, 3.2 and 3.3.)

Mead says:

The life of the child in human society subjects . . . all the impulses with which human nature is endowed to a pressure which carries them beyond possible comparison with animal instincts, even though we have discovered that the instincts in lower animals are subject to gradual changes through long-continued experience of shifting conditions. This pressure is, of course, only possible through the rational character that finds its explanation, if I am correct, in the social behavior into which the child is able to enter (MS 349-350).

A society of men as a complex of institutional processes of mediation provides what Mead calls "the rational character" in social acts, "into which the child is able to enter". (Of course, in man's society are also the conditions in which social acts are mediated dysfunctionally or inappropriately and so turn out to be irrational.) The character of rationality is a "pressure" on man's impulses in one sense, but it is the "nature" of their naturally incomplete functions completed, as it is the condition of functional social acts.

The question of rationality and irrationality is a question directly about the process of social mediation, and only indirectly about impulses. No question of rationality arises in reference to impulses and their process if they are consummated immediately and directly in the sense explained in 3.12. Whether the impulses to eat are rational in common contexts of human life is not a proper question. The question of rationality arises in the mediate phase of social act and only in reference to the relations between alternative means and ends which are possible objects of impulses. We can properly ask, as a general question, whether the use of one's feet to pick food on a table is rational in common contexts of meals.

Rationality is in one sense the condition of social act in which its mediation is functional, or its means are appropriate to its ends. Insofar as the process of mediation is rational, the impulses which initiated the mediated act are consummated by means of implements possible in the given situation. But rationality is not merely a matter of impulses, certainly not their immediate and direct consummation, nor their harmonious relation in itself. Here we can understand a possible ground of justification for Prof. Buchler's critical statement: "To call [rationality or reason], with Santayana, 'a harmony of the

passions', is . . ., however true partially, to give it a psychologistic
flavor that is surely inadequate."(11) The "life of reason" or the
"discontents of civilization" is not a problem of impulses or passions;
it is a problem of social mediation, of which impulses are a given,
preconditional factor.

Man's social evolution of the mediational process into a complex of
methods and institutions is the development of what Mead calls the
"premediated field" of symbolic, implemental media in a society.
Insofar as this field, or a part of it, is functional in recurrent situations,
it is the basis of rationality in the society. Within this field man's impulses can be and are consummated immediately, if not directly, in
terms of premediated implements, and the acts completed are rational.
But this immediacy of social process is distinctly different from the
immediacy in the biological sense, which functions in conjunction with
the "directness" of "socio-physiological" processes. The difference lies
in the fact that the immediacy in terms of premediation is based on what
one may call the "intrinsic" inhibition of impulses as a general condition
of social acts.

In a genetic perspective, "extrinsically" inhibited impulses - inhibited
by external obstacles, etc. - are the causal precondition of the process
of mediation and so of rationality. In a present, functional perspective,
most of man's impulses are "intrinsically" preset or premediated as
inhibited impulses in anticipation of distant or possible obstacles or
breakdowns. (Consider one or two examples: "You shall eat only kosher
food"; or, "You shall marry and then fornicate.") In the society of highly,
extensively developed premediation, especially of methodic nature, the
problematic situations in terms of extrinsic obstacles or conflicts are
"secondary" as the source or mechanism of inhibition. Furthermore,
the intrinsic inhibition of impulses is not simply a causal matter based
on the common conditions of life on earth: scarcity of means and overpopulation, though it is largely justified by them. It is deeply rooted in
the conditions of human life which are social in the anthropological sense.
"In all adjustment of individuals to each other's action", Mead says,
"there must be some inhibition" (MS 362). Rationality as the condition of
functional premediation requires that problematic situations are anticipated and premediated, if possible. In present conditions of human society,
intrinsically inhibited impulses are a pervasive phase of institutional roles.

The apparent paradox of civilization in reference to impulses is that the
whole enterprise of civilization can be regarded to have evolved toward
the condition in which man's impulses are satisfied immediately, if not
directly, but in the course of civilization, the impulses have been intrinsically or premediately inhibited. The dissolution of the paradox is
logically simple, but in actual situations the apparent paradox appears
in forms of absurd feelings and tragic conflicts, which are "human, all
too human".

The functional distinctions Mead has made between the "content" and
"mechanism" of man's sociality, between the "physiological pole" and
the "institutional", and between the "impulsive" phase and the "rational"

(11) Buchler, Toward a General Theory of Human Judgement, p. 168.

appear to correspond to a common distinction in anthropology between the biological or basic impulses (or drives or needs) and the derived or institutional. (12) But Mead does not construe his dinstinctions in the sense of the latter, for it commonly implies that in present conditions of society, man has some secondary, institutional needs and their functions, in addition or in contrast to some basic, physiological needs or impulses and their functions. As explained earlier, the mediational or rational process of social acts appears where these impulses as physiological functions break down or are inhibited, not where they function independently so as to be simply "enlarged" or "supplemented". In present conditions, man lives largely in terms of institutional processes; he fulfills his impulses - rationally or irrationally - in terms of his participation in a complex combination of social institutions. "It would be a mistake", Mead says, "to assume that a man is a biological individual plus a reason, if we mean by this definition that he leads two separable lives, one of impulse or instinct, and another of reason" (MS 347).

3.2 Implemental Mediation

3.21 Teleology and Implementation

3.211 Biological Evolution: Sociality and Teleology

In a present perspective, we may speak not only of the evolution of organisms, their structures and functions, but also of that of their environments as their means or objects. In the sense that an environment can exist for an organism only insofar as it "answers to the susceptibilities of the organism", we can speak of an evolution in which organisms select and constitute their own environments.

Mead says:

A statement of evolution that was common in an earlier period assumed simply the effects of an environment on organized living protoplasm, molding it in some sense to the world in which it had to live. On this view the individual is really passive over against the influences which are affecting it all the time. But what needs now to be recognized is that the character of the organism is a determinant of its environment. We speak of bare sensitivity as existent by itself, forgetting it is always a sensitivity to certain types of stimuli. In terms of its sensitivity the form selects an environment, not selecting exactly in the sense in which a person selects a city or country or a particular climate in which to live, but selects in the sense that it finds those characteristics to which it can respond, and uses the resulting experiences to gain certain organic results that are essential to its continued life-process. In a sense, therefore, the organism states its environment in terms of means and ends (MS 214-5).

(12) Cf. B. Malinowski, A Scientific Theory of Culture and Other Essays.

The individual organism determines in some sense its own
environment by its sensitivity. The only environment to which
the organism can react is one that its sensitivity reveals . . . .
If in the development of the form there is an increase in the
diversity of sensitivity there will be an increase in the
responses of the organism to its environment. There is a
direct reaction of the organism upon the environment which
leads to some measure of control . . . . There may be, of
course, influences which affect the form as a whole which do
not answer to this type of determination, such as great
cataclysms like earthquakes, events which lift the organism
into different environments without the sensitivity of the form
itself immediately involved. Great geological changes, such
as the gradual advance and disappearance of the glacial epoch,
are just superinduced on the organism. The organism cannot
control them; they just take place. In that sense the environment
controls the form . . . . Nevertheless, in so far as the form
does respond it does so in virtue of its sensitivity. In this sense
it selects and picks out what constitutes its environment. It
selects that to which it responds and makes use of it for its own
purposes, purposes involved in its life-processes (MS 245).

Organisms live in and depend on a unique environment which they select
and determine in terms of their own physiological functions, particularly
their sensitivities which call out their social impulses or instincts under
proper stimuli. As a part of evolution, each organism has a determinate
set of these physiological functions as its ends in order to preserve and
continue its living process. It is directed by them in its selection and
determination of a limited set of objects in its environment as means to
its ends. Thus organisms are teleological in their sociality. They are
directed by their physiological plasticity and differentiation to organize
their life with other organisms for those ends which require the co-
operative responses of the others. Mead says that "the living form in
its teleological process can react, as a whole, purposively, to conditions
of its own organism" and that "the peculiar method that distinguishes
their reactions from the motions of inanimate objects is that of [teleo-
logical] selection" (PP 69 & 71). (13)
    This teleological process in terms of sociality and selectivity con-
stitutes intelligence in the biological sense. Mead regards the living
processes of organisms as intelligent in the sense that "intelligence

---

(13) "There are", Mead says, "certain problems that, like the poor, are
always with us; for example, that between the mechanical and teleological statements of the world and its physical objects" (SW 23). This
problem - in particular, the question of whether a teleological theory
can be reduced to or translated into a mechanical theory - is a problem
of abstraction or theory. It is a problem of different perspectives and
their languages in terms of emphasis on different phases of act, which
is contingent on interests and requirements of explanation or solution
of problems involved in their contexts. "The purpose [of organic pro-

finds its simplest expression in the appropriateness of the responses of a living form to the environment in the carrying-out of its living process" (PA 404). Intelligence as "appropriate response" is basically a function of teleological selectivity. In this sense, "intelligence . . . is almost coextensive with life" (PA 68).

Mead says:

> We have undertaken to consider the conduct of the organism and to locate what is termed "intelligence", and in particular, "self-conscious intelligence", within this conduct. This position implies organisms which are in relationship to environments, and environments that are in some sense determined by the selection of the sensitivity of the form of the organism. It is the sensitivity of the organism that determines what its environment shall be, and in that sense we can speak of a form as determining its environment. The stimulus as such as found in the environment is that which sets free an impulse, a tendency to act in a certain fashion. We speak of this conduct as intelligent just in so far as it maintains or advances the interests of the form or the species to which it belongs. Intelligence is, then, a function of the relation of the form and its environment (MS 328).

In pointing out intelligence as a common phase of the evolution of organisms, Mead goes so far as to assert that "it [human intelligence] is entirely the same as intelligence evidenced in the whole upward struggle of life on the earth" (SW 266). As noted earlier in 2.12 in explaining his view of the scientific method to which the "method of evolution" itself is construed by analogy, what one may regard as an "anthropomorphic" explanation of intelligence is a perspective possible only after the emergence of human intelligence. It does not necessarily imply that any distinct aspects of human intelligence are found in its "original" processes of evolution.

Because the difference between the intelligence of man and that of other organisms is extreme and irreducible in the variety and complexity of their manifestations, it is a question whether we must presuppose a mutational evolution, as Cassirer and Bidney suggest, (14) instead of a Darwinian gradual evolution. In the present condition of evolution, the possibility of the development of the intelligence of other organisms is certainly insignificant in comparison to the actuality of man's. It is Mead's attempt to explain the difference in terms of a set of basic criteria of social act or behavior. (15)

---

cess] need not be 'in view'", Mead says, "but the statement of the [biological] act includes the goal (or end) to which the act moves. This is a natural teleology, in harmony with a mechanical statement" (MS 6 fn). Cf. E. Nagel, The Structure of Science: Problems in the Logic of Scientific Explanation (New York: Harcourt, Brace & World, Inc., 1961), Chap. 12.

(14) D. Bidney, Theoretical Anthropology, p. 4.

(15) This difference could be simply explained as a matter of evolved

3.212 Man's Social Evolution: Teleology and Implementation

Man, a part of organic evolution, is teleologically selective, and, at least in this sense, intelligent. This teleology as organic process is implied by his sociality in the biological sense, particularly in terms of the socio-physiological impulses of organisms. As the peculiar nature of man's open-ended, modifiable impulses is explained earlier to distinguish his social acts from those of other organisms, it suggests a special case of teleology: what Mead calls the implemental process which is not limited to the mere selection of means but is based on the reconstruction and reformulation of means and ends. In terms of this implemental teleology, human intelligence is in one sense distinguished from that of other organisms.

In the teleological process of certain organisms, Mead finds what he regards as a reconstructive control of environments in terms of "active" or "manipulative" response. He notes its examples in the animals which dig holes or build nests, and in the insects which keep certain vegetables in their galleries to feed on. (16) These reconstructive activities of rearranging and transforming parts of their environments, as processes of teleology and intelligence, go beyond sensitive, selective control. They require manipulative responses of organisms which determine what their environments will be. "Such [manipulative] actions", Mead says, "make up a very slight part of the lives of these insects [and other animals], but they do occur . . . . The striking thing about the human organism is the elaborate extension of [this reconstructive] control" (MA 248).

In the present state of evolution, men determine our environments even to the extent that an environment required for our welfare can be reconstructed and implemented in a circumstance which is otherwise destructive or inconvenient. In this new aspect of evolution, the "causal" direction between environments and organisms is reversed. It may be regarded as the entirely new dimension of evolution which ends "evolution" as it has been.

Mead says:

We speak of Darwinian evolution, of the conflict of different forms with each other, as being the essential part of the problem of development; but if we leave some of the insects and micro-organisms, there are no living forms with which the human form in its social capacity is in basic conflict . . . . There is no longer a biological environment in the Darwinian sense to set our problem. Of course, we cannot control the geological forces, the so-called "acts of God". They come in and wipe out what man has created. Changes

physiological differences as Mead admits in one context (MS 235 fn.). But it is his attempt to explicate the difference in terms of differences in social acts. This attempt is carried out by Mead in terms of criteria of symbolic mediation. In this 3.2, the symbolic criteria are considered as those of implemental mediation.
(16) Cf. MS 237-8.

in the solar system can simply annihilate the planet on which we live; such forces lie outside our control. But if we take those forces which we look upon as important in the development of this species on the face of the globe, they are to a great extent under the control of human society . . . . It is this control of its own evolution which is the goal of the development of human society . . . .

The human situation which I have just presented does in a certain sense present an end, not, if you like, in the physiological sense, but as a determination of the process of life on the surface of the earth. The human society that can itself determine what the conditions are within which it lives is no longer in a situation of simply trying to meet the problems that the environment presents. If humanity can control its environment, it will in a certain sense stabilize itself and reach the end of a process of development, except in so far as the society goes on developing in this process of controlling its own environment. We do not have to develop a new form with hairy covering to live in cold climates . . . . We can determine the conditions under which the heat of the tropics shall be made endurable . . . . We are so far away from any actual final adjustment of this sort that we correctly say that the evolution of the social organism has a long road ahead of it. But supposing it had attained this goal, had determined the conditions within which it could live and reproduce itself, then the further changes in the human form would no longer take place in terms of the principles that have determined biological evolution. (17)

The human situation is a development of the control which all living forms exercise over their environment in selection and in organization, but the human society has reached an end which no other form has reached, that of actually determining, within certain limits, what its . . . environment will be . . . . Those forces which affect the life of the form and can conceivable change it in the Darwinian sense have come under the control of the society itself, and, in so far as they come under the exercised control of the society, human society presents an end of the process of organic evolution.

It is needless to add that, so far as the development of human society is concerned, the process itself is a long way from its goal (MS 250-2).

The elaborate development or extension of selective, reconstructive

---

(17) It may be noted that one can be critical of Mead's view here in terms of the possible evolution of human organism through some sort of genetic mutation. But his view is valid in principle, particularly on the condition that human society would be able to exercise certain control over the process of genes or DNAs as a result of increasing knowledge.

control constitutes the implemental nature of man's teleology and intelligence. It sets his sociality on principles or factors other than those of biological evolution. It denotes the transition to what Mead calls social evolution, the history of civilizations of <u>Homo Faber</u>. Civilization is, among other things, a process of enlarging and improving the enduring field of implementation.

3.22 The Physiological Basis of Implementation

3.221 Physiological Functions and Implementation

Contrary to the bias in traditional philosophy for perception, especially visual perception, as the physiological basis of man's experience and/or knowledge, Mead explains that the important physiological basis of our implemental process, inclusive of symbolic and cognitive process, is the functions of "free" hands and "reflexive" gestures in conjunction with those of the nervous system.

In 3.212, we have explained that the implemental process is based on social principles or factors other than those of biological evolution. Nevertheless, as an activity of human organisms, it is no doubt dependent on our evolved physiological functions. Furthermore, as Mead explains in anticipation of McLuhan, (18) our implements – from utensils and languages to political systems and scientific theories – can be regarded as extensions of our physiological functions.

As qualifications of the previous paragraph, we may note the following: individual men could lose some of their physiological functions, such as the visual and the manual, which are important but which can be ("naturally" or implementally) eliminated from the living process of individual men; as members of a society, they can continue to live fully, even though inconvenienced, through the social implementation provided largely by the functions of the other members. It appears to be theoretically possible, in view of the advancement of science and its technical application, that most of our physiological functions can be eliminated and replaced by those of implements, as some of them have already been. (What is the limit of surgical operation on a person is a decision which depends as much on the development of technical implements as on the conditions of their symbolic mediation, i.e., cultural values and decision

(18) M. McLuhan, <u>Understanding Media: The Extension of Man</u> (New York: New American Library, 1964). McLuhan refers by "media" not only to vehicles of communication in the ordinary sense but also vehicles of transportation and various other implemental vehicles or media of man's social acts. His view suggested here is in a way, thought not entirely, in accordance with Mead's theory of mediation given in this study. McLuhan's distinction between "media" and "message" and his view of their relation are not contextual at all. And, in particular, it is misleading to construe what he calls "media" basically as the extensions of "our human senses" (<u>op. cit</u>, p. 35), because these media have as much to do with our hands, nervous system, and reflexive gestures as with our senses.

procedures in the given society.) On the other hand, most of our social implements - such as a bomb (possibly as an extension of a fist) or a university (possibly as an extension of parental instruction) - can be hardl related to their corresponding "original" physiological functions as they now stand, having developed into complex functions in their own ways.

Nevertheless, the significant relation of implementation and physiology can be seen in that the operation and development of implements are closely connected with a few specific physiological functions, such as those of 1) hands, 2) the nervous system, and 3) vocal and other reflexive gestures. These physiological functions also suggest the definite functions and conditions of implemental process.

3.222 Hands

First of all, we may consider the implemental functions uniquely fulfilled by man's two "free" hands and their ten fairly long fingers. These functions have emerged, together with the functions of his bipedness and long arms, in the process of biological evolution. (19) The hands naturally intervene, with their "handy" usefulness in grasping and separating objects, between the incipient responses to distant stimuli and the consummations of acts such as eating and fighting. "In the human animal", Mead says, "this preliminary termination of the act in the contact of the hand is . . . the starting-point of a more complex process in which a physical thing appears as a mediation of the entire act" (PA 24). In a phylogenic perspective, we realize that the freely manipulative and comparatively reliable contact functions of the hands must have been very crucial and necessary in the development of implemental mediation. (20) At present they still are necessary in the mediational process of isolating, reconstructing, and re-evaluating parts of our environment as the implements of our social acts.

Mead says:

I refer to the contact experiences which come to man through his hands. The contact experiences of most of the vertebrate

---

(19) In a pre-Darwinian perspective of man, Aristotle states: "Standing . . . erect, man has no need of legs in front, and in their stead has been endowed by nature with arms and hands" (De Partibus Animalium, trans. by W. Ogle, in The Works of Aristotle, Vol. V, ed. by J. A. Smith & W. D. Ross [Oxford: Clarendon Press, 1912, IV 10: 687a.5]). Cf. D. G. Carroll, "Evolution of Hand Function", Maryland State Medical Journal, 1967 (16:1), p. 103.
(20) This point is beautifully suggested in the scene, "The Dawn of Man" in 2001: A Space Odyssey, a cinerama directed by S. Kubrick, based on A. C. Clark's short story The Sentinel (released by Metro-Goldwyn-Mayer in 1968). Cf. J. Agel, ed., The Making of Kubrick's 2001 (New York: New American Library, 1968). Clark's original story is reprinted in this book, pp. 15-26. In the scene the man-apes discover the use of bones as tools, and a bone, thrown into the sky by a man-ape in triumphant release after using it as a weapon, appears as a space ship.

forms lower than man represent the completion of their acts.
In . . . the food process, sex . . ., attack, flight to a place
of security, search for protection against heat and cold . . . ,
contact is coincident with the goal of the instinct; while man's
hand provides an intermediate contact that is vastly richer in
content than that of the jaws or the animal's paws . . . . The
hand, of course, includes in this consideration not only the
member itself but its indefinite co-ordination through the
central nervous system with the other parts of the organism.
This is of peculiar importance for the consideration of the
separability of the parts of the act, because our perceptions
include the imagery of the contacts which vision or some
other distance sense promises. We see things hard or soft,
rough or smooth, big or little . . . . It is this imaged contact
that makes the seen thing an actual thing. These imaged
contacts are therefore of vast import in controlling conduct.
Varied contact imagery may mean varied things, and varied
things mean varied responses . . . . This variety will exist
in experience only if there are impulses answering to this
variety of stimuli and seeking expression . . . . Man's
manual contacts, intermediate between the beginnings and
the ends of his acts, provide a multitude of different stimuli
to a multitude of different ways of doing things, and thus
invite alternative impulses to express themselves in the
accomplishment of his acts, when obstacles and hindrances
arise. Man's hands have served greatly to break up fixed
instincts by giving him a world full of a number of things
(MS 362-3).

The human animal . . . has this implemental stage that
comes between the actual consummation and the beginning
of the act, and the thing appears in that phase of the act.
Our environment as such is made up out of physical things.
Our conduct translates the objects to which we respond over
into physical things which lie beyond our actual consummation
of the immediate act. The things that we can get hold of, that
we can break up into minute parts, are the things which we
reach short of the consummation of the act, and which we can
in some sense manipulate with reference to further activity.
If we speak . . . of the animal as constituting its environment
by its sensitivity, by its movements toward the objects, by
its reactions, we can see that the human form constitutes its
environment in terms of these physical things which are in
a real sense the products of our own hands. They, of course,
have the further advantage from the point of view of intelligence
that they are implements, things we can use. They come
betwixt and between the beginning of the act and its consummation, so that we have objects in terms of which we can
express the relation of means to ends. We can analyze our ends
in terms of the means at our disposal. The human hand, backed
up, of course, by the indefinite number of actions which the

central nervous system makes possible, is of critical importance
in the development of human intelligence . . . . We thus break
up our world into physical objects, into an environment of
things that we can manipulate and can utilize for our final ends
and purposes (MS 248-9). (21)

Mead goes so far as to say that "man's implements are elaborations
and extensions of his hands" (MS 363). It would be an overstatement to
construe all the implements from dresses and vehicles to scientific
theories and political institutions as the "elaborations and extensions"
of our hands unless they are liberally interpreted. On the other hand,
Mead's suggestion is clear in the sense that the hands are unique among
men's physiological features in their biologically inherent implemental
function which is mediate to other functions. The hands are the only
"tool" given by nature to man which can make other tools. "The hand
is not", Aristotle states, "to be looked on as one organ but as many;
for it is, as it were, an instrument for further instruments."(22)
    In a pre-Darwinian perspective of "human nature", Aristotle presents
a problem of the relation between man's intelligence in general and the
functions of his hands in particular: "Now it is the opinion of Anaxagoras
that the possession of these hands is the cause of man being of all animals
the most intelligent. But it is more rational to suppose that his endowment
with hands is the consequence rather than the cause of his superior intelligence."(23) The problem as the choice between Anaxagoras' opinion
and Aristotle's cannot be simply solved in Mead's post-Darwinian perspective of man's social evolution. (24)
    No doubt, the functions of man's hands, like most of his organic and
cultural functions, is not possible without his "intelligence"(25) or the

---

(21) For Mead's use of the terms "physical thing", "object", etc., see
2.2.2, fn. 1 & 3.
(22) Op. cit., 687a.20.
(23) Op. cit., 687a.5-10.
(24) In the contemporary anthropological works on evolution, the problem has been similarly formulated, and investigated without a definite
conclusion on the basis of the latest discovery of bones and tool-like
remains. Cf. J. Napier, "The Evolution of the Hand", Scientific
American, 1962 (207:6), pp. 56-62. In this article Napier questions a
"strong" evolutionary version of the Aristotelian position. Such a
version is suggested by J. Wood Jones in his book, The Principles of
Anatomy as Seen in the Hand (Philadelphia: P. Blakiston's Son & Co.,
1920), and by D. G. Carroll in his previously cited article of 1967. "It
is a curious observation" Carroll concluded, "that the rhesus monkey
has a hand that has all the physical (muscle, nerve and bone) structures
necessary to perform all the functions performed by the human hand,
yet lacks the association areas in the brain to synthesize and coordinate
movements necessary for tool-making. It is as though the hand were
awaiting the development of the brain to be put to full use" (op. cit.,
p. 104).
(25) The Aristotelian concept of nous, man's intelligence or intellect,

functions of his highly developed nervous system. On the other hand, the development of man's implements from primitive weapons to modern computers, as the (social) evolution of his intelligence, is difficult to conceive without the functions of hands. In present conditions, however, the functions of hands can be, like those of many other physiological organs but unlike those of the nervous system, replaced, for individual men as members of a society, not merely by others' hands but by implements.

3.223 The Nervous System

We have explained in 3.12, that the implemental mediation of man's social acts is a "delayed response". Fundamentally, the implemental process as the delayed response is based on 1) the functions of the nervous system and 2) those of "reflexive" gestures which develop under appropriate conditions to constitute man's symbolic process. (26) These two constitute what one may call the basic "binary" functions of the implemental mediation. They can be logically distinguished but they are inseparable in actual situations of man.

In view of the above paragraph, the importance of the hands may be suggested in the following ways: 1) As Mead's statements quoted in the previous 3.222 explain, the functions of the nervous system are included in the consideration of those of the hands; 2) the hands, as the tactile organs, are an integral part of the nervous system like the other sensory organs; and 3) the movements of hands and fingers are gestures which, under proper conditions, can be "reflexive" in conjunction with the eyes.

The necessity of implemental process appears, as explained in 3.12, in the situations where our socio-physiological impulses (or dispositions) are, or seem likely to be, frustrated in their immediate and/or direct consummation (or expression). In these situations men are forced to inhibit their impulses and delay their responses before final adjustment and consummation in order to discriminate and evaluate alternative distant stimuli and future consequences, and to manipulate and reconstruct their sources or causes in contact and/or hypothetical experiences of the present in terms of past experiences.

This delay of an on-going act before its completion is made possible through the neural-coordinated functions of symbolic process (or, the symbol-organized functions of the nervous system). Such a delay provides an "observatory" or "laboratory" field of mediation where objects are transformed into implements we can manipulate and control. It is an innervational, symbolic perspective of simultaneity in which future or distant values of objects can be anticipated, regulated or determined,

---

certainly differs from the Meadean concept of man's intelligence (or mind), which we will consider in the following 3.223 & 3.225. Also see Appendix A, especially A.1 Problems of Consciousness in a Historical Perspective. Cf. J. H. Randall, Jr., Aristotle (New York: Columbia Univ. Press, 1960), pp. 90 ff.

(26) "Reflexive gesture" and 'symbolic process" are explained in the following 3.224 and 3.33 respectively.

in terms of a selected, reconstructed past - what Mead calls the
"permanent world which is irrelevant to passage" (PA 143). While the
selective indication and organization in the mediate phase is provided
and carried out - in the recent language of computers, "programmed
and processed" - in terms of reflexive symbolic process, its temporal
dimension of simultaneity is a function of the nervous system.
    Mead says:

> One of the peculiarities of this [central nervous] system is that
> it has, in a sense, a temporal dimension: the things we are
> going to do can be arranged in a temporal order so that the
> later processes can in their inception be present determining
> the earlier processes; what we are going to do can determine
> our immediate approach.
>   The mechanism of the central nervous system enables us to
> have now present, in terms of attitudes or implicit responses,
> the alternative possible overt completions of any given act in
> which we are involved; and this fact must be . . . recognized,
> in virtue of the . . . control which later phases of any given
> act exert over its earlier phases . . . . The higher centers
> of the central nervous system are involved in [this] type of
> behavior [delayed response], by making possible the inter-
> position, between stimulus and response in the simple stimulus-
> response arc, of a process of selecting one or another of a
> whole set of possible responses and combinations of responses
> to the given stimulus . . . .
>   The various attitudes expressible through the central nervous
> system can be organized into different types of subsequent acts;
> and the delayed . . . responses thus made possible by the
> central nervous system are the distinctive feature of . . .
> intelligent behavior (MS 117-8).

These "various attitudes . . . organized" and "different types of
subsequent acts" are selected and indicated in terms of symbols, and
differentiated and related in terms of the structures of the symbols.
In this sense, the implemental mediation of innervational delayed
response is organized and carried out in terms of symbolic process.
Thus, implementation is, in its basic sense, a symbolic process. And
the unity - organization and structure - of the neural functions of
delayed response is constituted by social act as symbolic process.
    Mead says:

> In considering the role or function of the central nervous
> system - important though it is - in intelligent human behavior,
> we must nevertheless keep in mind the fact that such behavior
> is essentially and fundamentally social; that it involves and
> presupposes an ever ongoing social life-process; and that the
> unity of this ongoing social process - or of any one of its
> component acts - is irreducible, and in particular cannot be
> adequately analyzed simply into a number of discrete nerve
> elements . . . . These discrete nerve elements lie within the

unity of this ongoing social process, or within the unity of any
one of the social acts in which this process is expressed or
embodied; and the analysis which isolates them - that analysis
of which they are the results or end-products - does not and
cannot destroy that unity (MS 118 fn). (27)

The development of implemental intelligence is largely a matter of
social symbolic process, limited by the criteria of its structures and
environmental conditions. The variety and intensity of stimuli for the
functions of intelligence lie in the conditions of social life, mediated by
symbols. "The process of communication simply puts the intelligence
of the individual at his own disposal", Mead says (MS 243). And the
structured and organized unities of implemental mediation are given
by the "generalized" and/or institutionalized unities of social, symbolic
process. (28)
No doubt, the complexity and appropriateness of man's nervous
system is a physiological prerequisite of his implemental, symbolic
sociality. And in contrast to those of other organisms, it is a biological
factor which emerged in the evolution of human organisms (MS 226 fn.).
Intelligence as the physiological function of individual men's nervous
systems is genetically variable, (29) but their common or similar
functions within a certain range of variation are a prerequisite of our
implemental, symbolic process as the "mechanism" of man's sociality -
from a given local group to the global world of mankind. "We all have
hands and speech", Mead says, "and are all, as social beings, identical,
intelligent beings. We all have what we term [self-] consciousness and

---

(27) Cf. "We still lack today a satisfactory picture of the underlying
neural mechanism [of the conditioned response]. Even the broadest
outlines of the neural events remain obscure" (R. W. Sperry, "On the
Neural Basis of the Conditioned Response", British Journal of Animal
Behavior, 1955 [3:2], p. 41). Also see: P. Laslett, ed., The Physical
Basis of Mind (Oxford: Blackwell, 1950).
  In a more recent article, Scholl concludes that "the cortex cannot be
regarded as an organization of neurons with an invariant topographic
arrangement of the perikarya" (D. A. Scholl, "A Comparative Study of
the Neural Packing Density in the Cerebral Cortex", Journal of
Anatomy, 1959 [93:2], p. 157). It is his suggestion that the arrangements or patterns of the neurons in the cerebral cortex are such that
the functions of the nervous system to react to the range of varying
stimuli "can only be specified in statistical terms and by probability
laws" (ibid.). Also see his book, The Organization of the Cerebral
Cortex (London: Methuen, 1956).
(28) The distinction and relation of the implemental process and the
symbolic is further explained in the following 3.231.
(29) For a short summary review of the last 50 years' researches on
this genetic variation of individual intelligence, see: L. Erlenmyer-
Kimling & L. F. Jarvick, "Genetics and Intelligence", Science, 1963
(142), pp. 147-9; reprinted in Intelligence and Ability, edited by
S. Wiseman (Baltimore: Penguin Books, 1967), pp. 282-6.

we all live in a world of [implemental, meaningful] things. It is in such media that human society develops, media entirely different from those within which the insect society develops" (MS 237).

In one context, Mead suggests that structures of symbolic, implemental processes, their institutionalized forms in particular - from languages and schools to transportation systems and political parties - are in one sense the extensions and elaborations of the functions of man's nervous system. "The institutions of society", Mead says, "such as libraries . . . [and] political organizations, are nothing but ways of throwing on the social screen, so to speak, in enlarged fashion the complexities existing inside of the central nervous system, and they must, of course, express functionally the operation of this system. The possibility of carrying this elaboration . . . is to be found in the development of communication" (MS 242).(30) And yet the nervous system is an important exception to the theoretical possibility of isolation and replacing our physiological functions with implements. The reason for this exception is that any serious impairment of the nervous system involves social problems for the personality of the individual, even if it does not bring about his death.

On the other hand, the implemental, mediate functions of the nervous system as delayed responses can be replaced by implements in a "logical" sense, that is, in the sense that in socially conditioned or habituated acts of men, their innervational delayed responses are not actually carried out, but they are premediated in terms of symbolic process for their immediate consummations. Consider, as a simple example, how we can smoke a cigarette at the moment of craving by carrying the cigarettes and lighter around. As we have developed a permanent mediate field in our society, a good part of our acts is ("extrinsically" and) temporarily immediate, though ("intrinsically" and) symbolically inhibited, delayed, and mediated. In this fact lies the import of implemental, symbolic process in human life, particularly for its rationality.

Of the neural basis of man's symbolic, implemental sociality, there is still a question of whether "the social development . . . of the human species" is limited, as Mead says, "theoretically at least, by the number of nerve cells or neural elements in the human brain, and by the consequent number and variety of their possible combination and interrelations with reference to their effect upon . . . individual behavior" (MS 237 fn.). The question cannot be entirely answered in terms of increasing knowledge in neurology.(31) The answer is also

---

(30) Mead lived some time before the presently prevailing use of computers and introduction of cybernetics. Still, these social institutions may be regarded as the extensions and elaborations of man's nervous system in an important sense more than computers which are commonly taken as "model" extensions and elaborations of the nervous system. In fact, these computers are more the extensions and elaborations of hands and fingers, like abacuses and slide rules.
(31) See the fn. 20 in this 3.222. Cf. R. Brain, "The Neurology of Language", Brain, 1961 (84), pp. 145–66; reprinted in Language, edited

contingent on the nature and development of implements themselves, including symbols, as social processes.

3.224 Reflexive Gestures

We have suggested that man's symbolic process is based on and extended from the physiological functions of what Mead calls "gestures": vocal sounds, facial expressions, manual motions, bodily postures, etc. In spite of the development of written, typographical, and electronic implements, these gestures, especially vocal gestures, are the basic, pervasive implements or media of symbolic process.

In a genetic perspective of social process, Mead construes gestures as physiological functions to be "prior" to gestures as symbolic media. (32) In present conditions of social life, man's gestures are "significant symbols" which denote (or designate to denote) and connote. Any unusual gesture is mediated in terms of familiar or institutionalized symbols. These gestures, strictly as physiological functions, are a contextual isolation or theoretical abstraction.

"Gestures", Mead says, "if carried back to the matrix from which they spring, are always found to inhere in or involve a large social act of which they are phases" (MS 69 fn.). In terms of this matrix, a gesture is 1) the response of an individual to the early phase of an act, and 2) his attitude or disposition to act in the next phase. This attitude is, from the point of view of others, a gesture: the phase of the individual's behavior which is a stimulus to the others to respond.

Mead says:

> The gesture is that phase of the individual act to which adjustment takes place on the part of other individuals in the social process of behavior . . . . The gesture . . . indicates some object or other within the field of social behavior, an object of common interest to all the individuals involved in the given social act thus directed toward or upon that object. The function of the gesture is to make adjustment possible among the individuals implicated in any given social act with reference to the object or objects with which that act is concerned (MS 46).

In a logical analysis, the following factors or conditions of social act, at least, are involved in the transformation of gestures into symbolic media.
1) A gesture is a transaction between members of a social act. A series of gestures as a functional unit is an interchange or "conversation" of related gestures. 2) Gestures are transactional in relation or reference to certain objects involved in social acts. They function as "signs" to indicate or designate these objects (MS 69 fn.).
3) Gestures as forms of stimuli are similar within a range of variation

by R. C. Oldfield & J. C. Marshall (Baltimore: Penguin Books, 1968), pp. 309-32.
(32) As for the problem of Mead's theory of symbolic process as a genetic theory, see 3.31.

under the similar conditions of the acts. 4) Gestures as attitudes or
dispositions are related or refer to common or similar objects - as
the gestures are based on the common impulses involved in the acts.
5) Gestures are transitional interconnecting phases in the mediational
process of the acts - providing natural orders or structures of mediation.
6) Gestures are variable to a greater or less degree - providing natural
implements of various significations for various objects.
And 7) gestures are naturally or derivatively "reflexive", that is, they
affect or stimulate, in the same way, not only the others but also the
individual who makes these gestures. Or, the individual is sensitive to
his own gestures in the same way the others are stimulated by them.
Thus, the gestures have the same or common significance for both
himself and others.

Under these conditions, gestures function as reflexive or commonly
significant media to indicate or designate common or similar objects
in the transactional relation between oneself and others. The conjunction
of these conditions is the basic, necessary condition, if not the sufficient
condition, for gestures to function as symbolic process.
    In a genetic perspective of symbolic process, Mead explains that
without an extensive development of naturally reflexive physiological
functions, symbolic process is not possible. (33) This reflexiveness is
the crucial, genetic sine qua non through which gestures are transformed to function as common stimuli for members of a society, symbols
of common meaning and identical reference. In the present perspective
of symbolic process, any use of gestures or other media can be said to
have failed or broken down as a process of communication if it is not
reflexive, that is, if the individual who makes or uses the gestures has
no disposition to respond to them in the way others respond to them.
Insofar as these gestures are used as "indications", "directions",
"orders", etc. to control or reconstruct objects in the mediate phase
of social acts, they are implements, the special implements which may
be construed to mediate other implements.
    Among man's gestures, Mead never fails to emphasize the import of
vocal gestures in the phylogenic (and ontogenic) context of symbolic
process. They are naturally reflexive in conjunction with auditory
sensitivity. In the symbolic life of man, the dominance and import of
speech based on vocal and auditory functions lies not only in 1) the
natural reflexiveness of vocal gestures but also in a number of other
factors, such as the following:
2) The variation of the vocal function, as a process of social transaction,
tends to be remarkably similar or uniform among members of a society.
(34) 3) At the same time, this variation is almost unlimited (or, its
"physiological" variations are large enough to lend themselves to an

---

(33) As for the question of whether Mead construes "reflexiveness" as
a precondition or a function of symbolic process, see 3.333.
(34) Cf. "The plausibility of Mead's contention of the social uniformity
in response to the vocal gesture is not seriously diminished by inventing
special counterinstances and caveats against it . . . . In conversations

unlimited number of combinations), while the auditory function is correspondingly sensitive to the variations of the former. Thus, the two provide an unlimited, socially common resource of implements for signification.

4) Both vocal and auditory functions are "handy", easily produced and simultaneously carried out with various other activities of man, especially with the implemental functions of hands. Thus, they are instrumental in the creation of the "world of simultaneity" necessary for the process of mediation.

5) In comparison with the media of writing, vocal gestures are not "frozen" but "fluid", flexible and improvisational; they are easily open to contextual variations and suggestive nuances. And 6) the vocal and auditory functions as natural implements are socialized and assimilated almost effortlessly in childhood through "primary" institutions (such as family, etc.) and without many other complicated implements (such as school, pencils, typewriters, etc.).

Among the other gestures, those of hands (and fingers) are naturally reflexive in conjunction with visual (or tactile) sensitivity. These gestures could have contributed to the phylogenic development of symbolic process dominated by audio-vocal functions. Certainly, their natural reflexiveness is fully utilized as symbolic media in cases of the mute. Furthermore, the import of manual gestures in the genetic and functional perspective of symbolic process is obvious in view of their implemental functions in pointing, painting, sculpting, writing, typesetting, typing, etc. This double function of hands as implemental and symbolic media suggests the close relation between these two social processes of mediation.

The evolution of symbolic process is the elaboration and extension of naturally reflexive functions, primarily vocal and auditory functions. In this development, all the other gestures, such as facial expressions, are rendered reflexive, in terms of the principles of symbolic process and only incidentally by means of certain implements such as mirrors and films, to function as symbolic media of the arts, make-up, deception, etc. In one sense, the very process of implementation, or specifically the development of the neural functions, is the extension of certain physiological functions. It is the sensitivity to one's own stimuli in the way they affect "others", other persons and things. Man's sociality, teleology, and intelligence are, in this sense, his capacity to be reflexive in various complex situations. "The field of the operation of gestures", Mead says, "is the field within which the rise and development of human intelligence has taken place through the process of symbolization of experience which gestures - especially vocal gestures - have made possible" (MS 14 fn.).

---

among persons, speech differences and variations tend shortly to become unnoticed - one thinks one's own and others' speech achieves uniformity" (H. S. Thayer, Meaning and Action, p. 247 fn.).

3.225 Intelligence and Implementation

In conjunction with teleology and implementation, the term "intelligence" has been used, largely in accordance with Mead's usage. It does not refer to "intelligence quotient", a genetically variable, congenital capacity or potentiality of individual men which various I.Q. tests are supposed to measure. Instead, it refers to a generic, dispositional characteristic of normally healthy men and women who have assimilated some specific culture or symbolic process, which the I.Q. "logically" presupposes.

In the sense of I.Q., one may say that some men are not intelligent or not very intelligent. But all men are intelligent in the sense of the dispositional characteristic, that is, insofar as they are teleological and implemental in their activities. Of course, intelligent men make - or try perversely to make - mistakes in implementation. For the Meadean view of human intelligence, unusual cases of social deprivations or cases of extreme pathological disorders are analogous to cases of blindness or colour-blindness in relation to the common notion of man's vision.

As for the "logical" sense that the I.Q. presupposes intelligence as a disposition, we may note that it is a common practice among psychologists to define "intelligence" as some "innate . . . ability"(35) of individual men's physiological functions, particularly those of their brains or nervous systems - just as it has been not uncommon among philosophers to regard perception (or reason) as some mere "innate" function or exercise of the physiological organs (or mental faculties). It is obviously an abstraction to regard man's intelligence (or perception) in its function as the mere exercise of our congenital physiological abilities or capacities.

In one sense, the above critical comment explains - and is supported by - "the impossibility of devising intelligence tests which are completely culture free".(36) It appears that "culture-free" I.Q. tests are sometimes misleadingly construed as tests which measure individual men's genetically variable physiological functions "in a way free or apart from all cultures". What is attempted properly in various "culture-free" I.Q. tests is that certain subgroup or provincial symbolic biases or advantages are eliminated or reduced to an invariant or common basis of symbols available to all of those who are taking the tests. And what is measured in terms of these "culture-invariant" tests is presumably what is genetically variable congenital capacities of individual men. Thus "culture-free" I.Q. presupposes certain invariant or common cultural or symbolic structures. After all, an I.Q. test is practice in implemental, symbolic process.

In conjunction with implementation and intelligence, the term "symbolic process" is used in accordance with Mead's usage, not exclusively

---

(35) R. Miles, "On Defining Intelligence", in Intelligence and Ability, p. 172 (orig. in British Journal of Educational Psychology, 1957 [27:3], pp. 153-65).
(36) S. Wiseman, "Introduction", in Intelligence and Ability, p. 13. Italics added.

in reference to verbal language, but inclusively in reference to all
symbolic forms, from spoken and written languages to arts and mass
communication media, and in reference to all symbolic situations, from
conversations and soliloquies to silent cinema and computer programs.

It has been recently pointed out that "the ability to acquire language
is a biological development [of man] that is relatively independent of
that elusive property called intelligence", and that "language is due to
as yet unknown species-specific biological capacities [of man]". (37)
Here it appears, though it is not clearly stated, that "language" specifically refers to verbal language, "speech and language". (38) Speech, the
physiologically inherently reflexive process of vocal gestures and
auditory functions, may be regarded, particularly from a phylogenic
perspective of man, to be the "root" of all other symbolic processes.
But it is difficult to see how symbolic process (in the inclusive sense)
can be clearly distinguished from socially actualized processes of "that
elusive property called intelligence" - from chess games and stock
exchanges to theory formulations and music compositions - as all of
them are carried out in terms of implements mediated by symbols.

3.23 Implementation and Methodic Process

3.231 Implementation and Premediation
Mead says:

> Man is an implemental animal. [An implement] is mediate to
> consummation. The hand carries the food to the mouth, or the
> child to the breast, but in the social act this mediation becomes
> indefinitely complicated, and the task arises of stating the
> consummation, or the end, in terms of means (SW 314).

Men, like other organisms, are directed by certain biologically evolved
ends in our selection of means. But as explained earlier in 3.212, we
are directed not merely in the biological sense of teleology based on
sensitive (or perceptual) selectivity. We actively implement what is
"unfinished in nature" as our means and ends. We manipulate and reconstruct the means in given situations and/or modify and readjust our
ends according to those means within certain limits without terminating
our organic functions. The basis and import of our teleological intelligence -
and of our creativity and freedom - lies in our implemental process, which
"transforms causes and effects into means and consequences, reactions

---

(37) E. H. Lenneberg, "A Biological Perspective of Language", in
Language, pp. 40 & 45 (orig. in New Directions in the Study of Language,
ed. by E. H. Lenneberg [Cambridge: M. I. T. Press, 1964], pp. 65-88).
  Cf. N. Chomsky, "Recent Contributions to the Theory of Innate Ideas".
Concerned with "the problem of acquisition of language", Prof. Chomsky
says: "We are dealing with a species-specific capacity with a largely
innate component" (p. 4). Also see 2.33, fn. 39.
(38) Lenneberg, op. cit., p. 32.

into responses, and termini of natural processes into ends-in-view"
(PA 517). (39)

In anticipation of distant consequences and future goals, we evaluate
and reconstruct means or implements. A means is justified by its end
in a given context. (40) Of course, it is another problem if the complex
of such an end and means, when it is placed in another "larger" context,
is justified by the end given in the new context. As an example, the use
of DDT is justified by its effect on insects which are harmful to man's
life and agricultural production; but in considering its effect on the
other factors of man's environment, its use has to be reconsidered.

On the other hand, in view of the functions of means, our ends and
values are contextually modified and reformulated. "It is through the
use of means", Mead says, "that we advance to the redefinition of the
ends" (PA 474). This reformulation of our ends implies the social
modification and regulation of our physiological impulses on the basis
of available means. Furthermore, these implements we use emerge as
social values or ends assimilated and preserved in a large context of
society. As an example, the development of the techniques of birth
control from rhythm method to artificial insemination has resulted in
disconnecting the impulses of sexual intercourse from reproduction.
And birth control as a value has been historically transformed, in
certain societies, from a socially censored crime or evasion of responsibility to an institutionalized policy of demographic or eugenic
control.

---

(39) In another perspective, natural processes or objects as causes and
effects – which are there without a social import for man – are abstractions from various contexts in which they are found or used and in which
their various properties have become familiar or known. Consider the
case of water. And the meaning of transforming, say, X-rays into a
means is that they are manipulated, reconstructed or controlled – in
an important part, in terms of symbolic indication and selection of
their factors – as a social, medical implement.

(40) This statement may be qualified by Prof. Danto's following statement: "If you were aware that there were alternative means to a given
end, and you chose among them, an independent justification for this
over and against that means has to be given" (A. Danto, "Student
Morality: From Skepticism to Dogmatism", Columbia Forum, 1969
[12:3], p. 36).

Here Prof. Danto's assumption is that these alternative means are
variable in their functions or effects. In the contexts where they are
not, which are not uncommon in human life, no justification is called
for. On the other hand, what Prof. Danto calls "an independent
justification" of the chosen means can be another justification of the
means in terms of another end in a different perspective of the given
context, or, as suggested above, "in another 'larger' context".

The problem of the "Machiavellian" principle that all means are
justified by its ends is that the principle is abused in its application by
the refusal to consider the implication of a given (perspective or) context in a "larger" context of which it is a part.

Men as members of a society live in the world of their implements.
It is their socialized world. In another perspective, it may be construed
as the world of atoms or quakes, or that of organisms or cells. Such a
world without (or before or in spite of) man and his implementation is
an abstraction. "The implements are social", Mead says (SW 313). In
an important perspective, gravitation and DNA are our implements as
much as fire, fruits, rules, theaters, etc. They are social because
1) they function directly or indirectly as mediate means to consummatory
ends derived from our socio-physiological impulses, and 2) the implements
are commonly discovered and/or produced in cooperative efforts, and
used and transmitted through social diffusion and preservation. Above
all, our implements are social because 3) they are generated and they
function through and as the "mechanism" of our social act, the symbolic
process of common meanings. "The symbolization of" objects (or things) -
by means of indicative gestures or other signs - is, as Mead says, "what
constitutes the mechanism that gives the implements" (MS 120). A man's
symbolic indication of an object (to himself), as will be explained in the
following 3.3, is an indication in the social process of assuming the role
of the other members of society concretely or abstractly. And the
implements as parts which constitute the social, symbolic process are
the objects of our "shared experiences". Although they are always limited
in actual situations (because of "scarcity of means", "institution of
private ownership", "lack of education", etc.), they are open to the
scope of universality abstractly presupposed by symbolic process.
Mead says:

. . . things are not only the meanings of what we see and hear;
they are also the means we employ to accomplish our ends. They
are mediate in both senses. They constitute a meaning of all that
lies between us and our most distant horizons, and they are the
means . . . of our consummations. They lie in the mediate
fashion between the distant stimuli that initiate our acts and the
enjoyments or disappointments that terminate them (SW 294). (41)

Insofar as implemental process, i.e., discovery and manipulation of
objects (or things or processes) as means, is, in general, distinguished
from symbolic process, i.e., indication and communication of meanings
in reference to them, the following may be noted: 1) Objects of social
acts are implements (or, phases of social acts are implemental) if they
are directly or indirectly mediate to consummatory ends of the acts.
2) Symbols are a special type of implements which mediate other implements. (Of course, symbolic process is largely mediated by implements such as sign-vehicles, pens, typewriters, films, etc.) 3)
Implements (or certain phases of implemental process) also function as

---

(41) This quoted part begins with "Physical" in Mead's article, but this
qualification of "things" is omitted because the point to be made is
about the relation of means and meanings in general. The general point
is no doubt Mead's. An explanation of Mead's usage of "physical things"
(vs. "social objects") was given in 2.22, fn. 12 & 14.

symbols insofar as they remain mediate to other implements (or to other phases of implemental process). And 4) in certain contexts, primarily those of aesthetic situations, symbols are implemental objects of consummation, mediated by other implements. Thus, the distinction between an implement and a symbol is only a contextual, functional distinction. In general, implemental process refers to the process of mediation, inclusive of symbolic process. And symbolic process is not limited to processes of what is commonly regarded as languages, especially not to assertive statements.

The nature and complexity of man's teleology and intelligence as implemental process of mediation has been transformed in his social evolution, as noted earlier in 3.13, by the development of an enduring field of premediational implements as institutions and/or methods.

The attempt of members of a society to observe and preserve mediate phases of acts in recurrent situations brings about the perpetuation of a mediate field in their society, in which a complex series of abstracted implements are prepared or premediated in advance of future acts. In this premediate field, the implements are pre-arranged or pre-fabricate (in common words, "pre-medicated", "pre-paid", "pre-meditated", etc while members of the society are pre-conditioned or pre-disposed to symbols (in common words, "labels", "directions", "instructions", etc. in reference to the implements. These premediate processes consist of 1) conversions of "surplus" - i.e., "something that is immediately with value" (MS 301) - into "abstract" media such as commercial products and publications, and 2) transactions of surplus through "abstract" media such as money and contracts. At the same time, they consist of habit-formations or institutionalizations of delayed (or anticipated) responses in social acts. These premediate processes are what Mead calls the "bases and stuff of social institutions" (MS 230).

One of the important developments in the premediate field based on institutions is the development of the division of labor and specialization on a communal or societal scale. A part of this development is the rise of a leisure class and the societal diffusion of leisure not simply as a surplus of time but as a "free" attitude or disposition to delay (or anticipate) responses for no specific end but for any distant end chosen.

The premediate field of institutional implements in a society is, in another perspective, the development of implemental processes as methods: assimilated and diffused functional processes of mediation, commonly improved, refined and/or systematized. Insofar as an implemental process is an institution, it is (or has been) a method. And insofar as an implemental process is a method (and insofar as its situations recur), it can be diffused and institutionalized. On the other hand, certain institutions remain actively conserved in a society in spite of the fact that the situations to which they are functional have disappeared. In a perspective of new situations, these institutions are no longer methodi but obsolete; they are museum pieces at best, if they are not obstacles to introduction of new methods.

In ordinary English, the terms "institution" and "method" are distinguished by different associations. "Institution" is commonly used in referring to "localized" establishments such as churches, schools, hospitals, etc.; and "method" is used in a special sense of "means", as suggested by "a method in his madness", "a method of beating the system", etc. In a perspective of philosophy and social science, "institution" is a concept in sociology and social philosophy, and is associated with political and other social systems and organizations; and "method" is a concept in epistemology and philosophy of science, and is associated with knowledge or "inquiry".

Mead speaks of "the institutions of society" as "organized forms of group or social activity - forms so organized that individual members of society can act adequately . . . by taking the attitudes of others toward these activities" (MS 261-2).(42) An institution "represents a common response on the part of all members of the community to a particular situation" (MS 261). From the point of view of individual men, "these institutions are . . . the habits of individuals in their interrelation with each other, the type of habit that is handed down from one generation to another" (MS 366). In the present, institutions range, to name a few examples, from the uses of shoes, arabic numbers, 24 hours in a day, money, school, and airplanes to the practices in incest taboo, war, the Olympic Games, and the Nobel Prizes.

Mead speaks of "methods" or "techniques" such as: "the method of exact measurement" (PA 516), "a new method of conserving the temperature of the body" (PA 580), "the technique which is transforming the control of scarlet fever" (PA 509), "the techniques of eugenics" (PA 510), "a method of conversation" (MS 90 fn.), "methods of [social reform or] change" (MT 362), "the technique by which . . . values are given concrete form in society" (PA 511), the "technique . . . in bringing . . . value to expression" (PA 458), etc. These methods or techniques as social processes are construed in contrast to absolute "ideals" (SW 3), fixed or eternal "structures" (SW 324), or utopian or permanent "programs" (PA 519). A method is a provisionally functional (or working) implemental process in (or process of responding to) a particular inhibited (or problematic) situation.(43) The situation is inhibited ("extrinsically") under given unmediated conditions or ("intrinsically") in terms of symbolic premediation. Consider the case of a vaccination. It can be developed and used in problematic situations where members of a society suffer under an epidemic, namely, where they are "extrinsically inhibited". On the other hand, in certain other situations, namely, those of "instrinsic inhibition", a vaccine can be developed and used in anticipation of an epidemic. And insofar as a method is functional in a situation, it is assumed that the method can be repeated in recurrent similar situations.

For a number of reasons, Mead's concept of "method" or "technique" comes close to the ancient Greek concept of techne as man's "motion", the refined teleological process of craftsmanship or artisanship (or

---

(42) For an explanation of institutions as "roles of generalized others" in terms of symbolic process, see .3.33.
(43) In one context, Mead simply speaks of "means and their relationship" as the "technique" ("The Relation of Play to Education", University Record [Univ. of Chicago], 1896 [1:8], p. 141; reprinted in ES 27).

88

artistic skill). (44) Mead understands methodic process as a type of
"generic" or pervasive process of man, not exclusively limited to the
field of visual perception and knowledge as some modern philosophers
have tended to suggest. For him, methods are typically exemplified in
the field of "making": manipulation and reconstruction.

In a work(45) in which the "universal and essential traits"(46) of method
are carefully examined, Prof. Buchler summarizes:

> A method is a power of manipulating natural complexes,
> purposively and recognizably, within a reproducible order of
> utterance; and methodic activity is the translation of such a
> power into the pursuit of an end - an end implied by the
> reproduction. (47)

Prof. Buchler's detailed explication of method in the above mentioned
work is basically in support of Mead's concept of method, a type of
purposive, "mediatory" use of "recognized means to possible ends"
(SW 80-1). (48) In Mead's perspective of social act, methods are construed
as social processes with emphasis on "social" in the various senses that
an implement was explained to be social.

Methods and institutions as Mead construes them are certain types of
social processes of implemental mediation, commonly refined, diffused
and/or passed down. He refers to an implemental process as an institution
insofar as he is interested in it as "an organization which gives unity to
the variety of the responses" of members of a society in certain specific
situations (MS 261). And he refers to the same process as a method
insofar as he is interested in it as a process of "organizing", discovering
and setting up - or "unifying" and "generalizing"(49) - the conditions of
responses in the situations (PA 508). (Consider the case involving aspirin
or traffic lights as an institution and as a method.)

"Method" and "institution" are distinct concepts in spite of certain
relations between them. An implemental process as a method does not
necessarily suggest that it is diffused widely or inherited, while an
implemental process as an institution suggests that it is commonly
diffused and passed down at least for a limited number of generations.

---

(44) Cf., J. H. Randall, Jr., Nature and Historical Experience (New
York: Columbia Univ. Press, 1958), p. 151; and Aristotle, pp. 273 ff.
(45) J. Buchler, The Concept of Method (New York: Columbia Univ.
Press, 1961).
(46) Op. cit., p. vii.
(47) Op. cit., p. 135. Among other things, the aspect of "reproducible
order of utterance" is, in the following 3.233, considered in relation
to Mead's concept of "the common method of implementation".
(48) There are prima facie certain distinct differences between their
concepts, some of which will be considered. But a comparative
examination of them is not within the scope of this study.
(49) These two quoted terms are explicated in the following 3.233 as
the main parts of Mead's concept of "the common method of implementation".

In an important sense, a process both as an institution and as a method presupposes the diffusive recurrence of the situations to which it applies. And in a society, most of the important functional implements are institutionalized methods, although certain "cherished" institutions are often not functional and methodic but obsolete in a perspective of changed situations in which they remain as parts.

It is said that man is a creature of habit. In our perspective, man lives largely in terms of the roles of the various institutions of which he is a part or a member. If it is the case, in the familiar words of Aristotle, that "moral virtue comes about as a result of habit", (50) it also follows that immorality and vice come about as a result of habit. Men as members of a society live largely in terms of the premediation of their acts, based on institutionalized, methodic implements. Men organize and individuate their personalities and careers by means of their selective participation in a large number of institutions of their society. (51) The import of novel or original methods introduced by members of a society in response to the new stimuli of changing social situations lies in their power to constitute new institutions. The great "revolutions" in the history of mankind consist of the transformation of dominant institutions of existing societies in the fields of communication, production, government, Weltanschauung, and style of imagination and expression.

"It is within this field of implemental things", Mead says, "picked out by the significant symbols . . ., not in that of physiological differentiation, that the complexities of human society have developed" (SW 315). As explained earlier in 3.12 and 3.13, man's common biologically undistinguished impulses are socialized - determined, organized, and individuated - by implements as mediate structures or values. The efficacy and variety of methods and institutions as premediate implements imply the organization and diversity of man's sociality in which his sociophysiological impulses regularly function, controlled, harmonized, and satisfied. The variety of implements not only as means but also as emerged functional or "cult" (i.e., institutionalized dysfunctional) values in the premediate field of society implies the complexity and diversity of man's social life, which may appear in contexts to be very remote from the consummatory expression of his physiological impulses. This contextual valuation of implements, as well as the implemental reformation of consummatory ends, explains the fact that men are not simply limited, as explained earlier in 3.12, to individual consummation or "subjective" pleasure as ends or values, but are open to other social values which are complex and contextually important.

The implemental mediate phase of social act raises, among many things, the problems of valuation (evaluation, calculation, knowledge, parsimony, maximization, melioration, etc.), as well as those of freedom and responsibility, because it is a condition of alternatives which, however,

---

(50) Nicomachean Ethics (trans. by W. D. Ross), in The Basic Works of Aristotle, ed. by R. Mckeon (New York: Random House, 1941), p. 952 (II, 2: 1103a.15)
(51) Of course, there are certain biological "preconditions" of human organisms, which individuate them to various degrees.

limited, is open to active expansion. In a premediate field of implemental "surplus", provided by methods and institutions, we have various social problems which characterize humanity in its two extreme versions: 1) on one hand, problems in what may be called "transcendental purities" or "endless passions" - such as "speculative" metaphysics, "basic researches", "art for art's sake", ritualistic ceremonies, professional sports, "useless" hobbies, etc.; 2) on the other hand, problems with what may be called "survival of the unfit" or "perpetuated failure" - such as dogmas, cults, perversion, insanity, etc. In this premediate field, furthermore, implemental process has raised the old institutional problems of human sacrifice, slavery, colonialization and genocide when it is applied not for but to humanity itself; and it raises the modern, though not really new, institutional problems of "alienated class" and "mass society" when its application for the sake of humanity is "limited" or "incomplete".

In a critical consideration, we may simply draw a few important points. Various religious, political and philosophical views of "dogmatism", "absolutism" and "historicism" - sometimes extensively defended and conserved by institutions - are exercises in the abuse of the implemental nature of man's sociality; they attempt to endow men, our careers, societies and/or "universes", with eternal, ultimate, or fatal ends regardless of the lack of implements. And the predominant symbolic nature of implemental process is overlooked or de-emphasized by philosophical views of "materialistic or technological determinism"; these views take "means of production" or "media of communication", in their limited or narrow sense, to be the determinant of our sociality. On the other hand, in advocating various views of "free will" or "individualism" (or "anarchism") as implemental social attitudes or institutionalized policies, we cannot ignore the conditions of social implements which limit or preset the range of alternatives.

3.232 Implementation as Methodic Process

In a perspective of modern Western history, the method of science developed and refined in terms of the works of Galileo, Newton, Harvey, Boyle, etc. is obviously one of many implemental methods of man - prima facie distinct from, say, the method of early modern European guild systems, the Gutenberg method of printing, the Shakespearean method of writing historical drama, etc. And the works of scientists from these early modern "pioneers" to contemporary scientists has constituted an institution, one of a few social developments which has survived various historical upheavals and has come to "transcend" the political divisions of "provincialism" or "patriotism" (MT 168).

As for the import of modern science, its method and productions, Mead says:

From the point of view of a Darwinian evolution the various forms have arisen very largely through the changes that have taken place in the environment . . . . There we have the species more or less under the control of the environment. But when we reach the human form, we have one which determines what the environment shall be . . . . It can, to an amazing degree, determine what are the conditions under which life shall take place. There we reach a certain culmination in the evolutionary process . . . .

What has given it that control in the great degree in which it has been accomplished in these last three centuries has been the scientific method, which has found its greatest expression in the so-called "mechanical science". It is the scientific method by which the human form has turned around upon its environment and got control over it, and thus . . . presented a new set of ends which control human conduct, ends which are more universal than those which have previously guided the conduct of the individual and of mankind as a whole (MT 262).

Scientific method is dominant [today] not only in the study of nature, but in the study of all the social subject-matters, in religion, politics, in all social institutions. Scientific discoveries have made over the answer even to the fundamental question of who is my neighbor. Science is responsible for the view of the universe as a whole which must be the background of our theology as well as our philosophy and much that is finest in our literature. Science has changed sentiment to intelligence in divine charity, and has substituted the virtue of reformation of evil for that of resignation thereto in religion (SW 71-2).

Science is enabling us to restate our ends by freeing us from slavery to the means and to traditional formulations of our ends (PA 474).

There is nothing so social as science, nothing so universal. Nothing so rigorously oversteps the points that separate man from man and groups from groups as does science. There cannot be any narrow provincialism or patriotism in science. Scientific method makes that impossible. Science is inevitably a universal discipline which takes in all who think. It speaks with the voice of all rational beings. It must be true everywhere; otherwise it is not scientific (MT 168).

As Merritt Moore noted in his introduction to Mead's Movements of Thought in the Nineteenth Century, and as John Dewey commented in his review of the same work(52), Mead construes the "movements" of ideas and institutions from the Renaissance to the present in the West as a series of reconstructions to replace the "closed" order of the medieval world by the "open" perspective of modern science. In this work, he suggests a reinterpretation of Western history as an evolution from the society established on the authority and security of dogmas and traditions (rooted in "supernatural" revelations and mysteries) to the society based on the security of self-corrective scientific method (derived from the fallible powers of man).

In the large number of present societies where science, as a critical, elaborated method, has been developed or introduced, it has come into

---

(52) M. H. Moore, "Introduction" in MT, p. xi; J. Dewey, "The Works of George Mead", New Republic, July 22, 1936 (87), pp. 329-30.

conflict with attitudes or approaches based on dogmas and traditions.
On the strength of its remarkable efficacy in certain problematic contexts, especially in the study of physical nature and technological
application, the scientific method tends to undermine any traditional,
dogmatic, absolutistic approaches to problems; and it emerges as a
social institution which provides a basis for all the other institutions:
their common method of problem-solving. Today we are no longer
preoccupied with the age-old controversy between religious dogmas and
scientific theories. We have come to realize that their apparent conflict
lies not only simply in the difference between two views or theories, but
goes to the basic difference between their distinct approaches to problems.
Once the scientific method is accepted even for a limited area where its
efficacy is easily shown, it cannot be arbitrarily restricted to this area.
The "subversive" nature of the scientific method lies in its indifference
to the "off limits" signs which are not imposed by its own "logic" and
requirements.

In the mid-twentieth century, when the possible annihilation of mankind hangs nightmarishly before us, thanks to the latest production of
science, we are intensely aware of the extent to which science has
permeated large parts of human life. Mead says that the "importance of
scientific method in our period which has led to its elaboration is not
found in its novelty but in the successful invasion of this elaborated
method into fields where it was not previously employed" (PA 91). If the
permeation of scientific method presents certain problems in conflict
with other cherished values, the solution to these problems lies obviously
not in the simple rejection of science but in the attempt to realize all the
values involved in a given situation by the very application of scientific
method. And in view of the present problems of "overpopulation", it is
difficult to imagine the future of humanity without our reliance on the
method and production of science.

In 2.12, we have explained the nature of Mead's view that the teleological process of organisms in their evolution can be construed, by
analogy to the emerged method of science, to constitute a method of
successfully or appropriately selecting means for ends. As a corollary,
he suggests that "what science is doing is making this method of trial
and error a conscious method" (MT 367). (53) The scientific method is,
in one sense, a critical, refined, and systematic method of teleological
implementation, which has developed out of various implemental methods
in man's social evolution. Remembering that intelligence is construed in
terms of teleological process, we can understand Mead's following
statements:

> Science is a method that arises out of the criticism and
> direction of the intelligence that the most unscientific of us
> are constantly using (PA 517).

---

(53) It is also Prof. Quine's view that "science is self-conscious common
sense" (W. V. O. Quine, Word and Object [Cambridge: M. I. T. Press,
1960], p. 3).

Science is an expression of the highest type of intelligence, a
method of continually adjusting itself to that which is new
(MT 290).

Scientific method is not an agent foreign to the mind, that may
be called in and dismissed at will. It is an integral part of
human intelligence, and when it has once been set at work it
can only be dismissed by dismissing the intelligence itself
(SW 255).

It is Mead's attempt to formulate the common method of man's intelligence
or implemental process in terms of the method of science. He reinterprets
the scientific method in a broad sense, free from its narrow association
with the method of mechanical physics based on the language of mathematics. This historical association has been the common difficulty in generalizing the method of science for all contexts of implemental process.
Mead's task consists of isolating the common conditions of the scientific
method in consideration of, and yet without being confined to, its conditions which are found in its modern development in the fields of natural
sciences, especially mathematics and physics.

Mead speaks of the method or technique of implementation under various
names or descriptions in various contexts:

a) "the scientific method" (SW 13); (54)
b) "the research method" (SW 62);
c) "the experimental method" (PA 25);
d) the "technique . . . scientific" (PA 91);
e) the "rational procedure" (SW 404);
f) the method of "the calculation of means" for ends (PA 319);
g) the method of "the fashioning and selection of means" and of the
"restatement and reconstruction" of ends (SW 254-6);
h) "the method of the solution" of problems (SW 266);
i) "the method of meeting its [i.e., a society's] problems and the method
of reconstructing its environment and itself" (PA 508);
j) "the self-conscious method of the members of a human society"
(SW 266);
k) "the technique by which the individual perspective becomes the
perspective of the most universal community . . . ., that is, the technique
of the experimental method" (SW 311); etc.

In view of the diversity of concepts involved in these names or descriptions, we may ask if they refer to one and the same method. The answer
is that in accordance with Mead's contextualism explained in 2.2, they
are different (or contextually differentiated and useful) perspectives or
formulations of the method which is one and the same in a generalized
perspective. Here we may consider the relation of f) and g) based on

---

(54) As a common practice in this study, each of the quotations is
"footnoted" by only one reference to Mead's works. The reference given
may be regarded to be typical of many other available references.

"means and ends" to k) and i) based on "problems and solutions", leaving
the relation of the others for the occasions which will follow.(55)

In an examination of Dewey's concept of "the method of inquiry",
Prof. Buchler says: "The process of solving a problem does imply the
choice of a means to an end. But . . . the process of choosing a means
to an end does not necessarily imply problem-solving activity."(56) The
meaning of the second sentence is clearly indicated by the following case
he gives: "He [Hitler] could ingeniously select means to ends. On the
other hand, he typically solved no problems but only destroyed or
repressed the conditions under which they called for solution."(57) An
alternative interpretation is that "the methods of Hitler"(58) solved the
problems of seizing and holding the political power of a certain nation
insofar as he was "methodic" in selecting means to ends. Of course, he
did not, to say the least, solve many other problems in the situation of
the nation and of the world of which it was a related part.

In a common usage of the term "problem", Hitler's effort to organize
the Nazi party or to build the military power of Germany is a problem,
just as the attempt (of a man or group of men) to win a game, to find a
new material as a medium of sculpture, to cure a disease, to explain
the mystery of "flying saucers", to increase the net profit of a company,
to organize a labor union, or to look for a cause worthy of an inherited
fortune is a problem. Such an attempt is a problem in terms of its
(limited) context. Of course, it is another problem in a different (or
enlarged) context if the solution of, say, organizing a labor union is
contributory or antithetical - or, functional or dysfunctional - to the
solution of, say, the problem of economic improvement of a society or
to that of promotion of peace between nations. It follows that the solution
of, or the method of solving, a problem does not necessarily lead to that
of another problem. In this sense, if Hitler's activities were "methodic"
in the perspective of setting up the secret police or of organizing the
military power of a nation, they were not "methodic" in the perspective
of improving the economic conditions or of protecting the life of the
total population of the nation, etc.

In a perspective of social act, a problem, or a problematic situation,
was explained in 3.1.2 to be construed by Mead as a situation in which
impulses are inhibited and responses are delayed to "select", discover
and/or reconstruct, means for the consummatory ends involved (or to
revaluate and readjust the ends themselves in view of given conditions
of means). In short, a problem consists in the absence of (appropriate
or functional) means to an end which demands to be implemented in a
given situation. Here the implemental "selection" of means for ends
does necessarily imply problem-solving.

On the other hand, in the premediate field of a society, the social
act of using a contextually appropriate, readily available implement

---

(55) As for the relation of "perspective" and "self-consciousness", see
Appendix A.2 and A.3.
(56) J. Buchler, The Concept of Method, pp. 146-7.
(57) Ibid., pp. 147-8.
(58) Ibid., p. 147.

does not imply problem-solving in the above paradigmatic sense. Consider a simple case of the institutionalized method of eating with chopsticks in an Oriental country, or of sleeping with one's own husband in a monogamous society. In such a case, the implemental process is "immediate" in terms of symbolic and implemental premediation. That is, the problem has already been solved in an early anticipation of the act as an inhibitive or problematic situation. In this sense, we can understand Prof. Buchler's statement that "a task to be accomplished is not the same as a problem to be solved". (59) Thus, the same act of using an implement in the suggested cases does not also imply calculating various means and discovering and/or reconstructing, "selecting" - in an important sense of the term - one means out of many for the given end.

Of course, within the premediate field, the mediation of a social act commonly involves an elaborate process of evaluating many options and selecting one out of them. Since this process of selecting is mostly in terms of symbolic mediation of a variety of implements prepared, pre-arranged, etc., it may be distinguished from "selecting" in the above paradigmatic (or "stronger") sense. Even in this context, nevertheless, the process of calculating and selecting a means to an end does imply a problem to be solved insofar as the situation presents one alternative or more for discrimination. In such a situation our impulses are inhibited and our response is delayed for a decision to carry out our act in one way rather than in the other(s). In one sense, the development of the premediate field of society is in the direction of increasing our options for implementation. Hence we have, within a framework of institutions, the common "problem of choice" or the problem of deciding how to proceed: selecting one type of chopsticks for the evening's guests, one type of bed to sleep on with one's husband, one college among many for one's education, or one candidate among several for the mayor of one's city. The situations of these problems are no doubt variable in their logical and psychological complexity. But in each of the situations the functional or successful social act does necessarily imply the process of solving the given problem as well as the process of evaluating various means and selecting an appropriate one to the given end. And within the framework of an institution it can easily, though not necessarily, be a methodic process - provided that the institution itself is a method in (a perspective of) its present social context.

Thus, insofar as the implemental process of a social act constitutes a method in its situation (i.e., in a perspective of its situation), it is methodic in terms of the concept of the method of selecting means for ends (or reformulating ends for means), and in terms of that of the method of solving problems. Both of them refer to one and the same method of implementation. The methods noted earlier under the various names or descriptions, a) to k), are translatable into each other in a similar way. That is to say, they refer to the common method of methodic processes, although each of them characterizes it in different ways in various perspectives. By the common method we understand the

---

(59) Op. cit., p. 151.

common (functional) conditions of all methodic (implemental)(60) processes. In understanding Mead's concept of the scientific method, it is
not important whether his use of the term "scientific" is justified in
reference to this generalized view of implementation as methodic process
It is important to see whether implemental processes as methodic
processes present certain common conditions, which we will shortly
consider. Insofar as they do, Mead thinks we can conclude they have the
common method under whatever name it is given.

The fact that the common method of implementation has emerged and/
or "logically" been formulated in the premediate field of a society does
not imply that all members of the society practice it or are capable of
practicing it. Certainly, no more than the publication of, say, Beethoven'
Sonata No. 23 implies that all "piano-players" can and do perform it –
and well. (Here one may claim in some sense of "potentiality" that all
of them are potentially capable of doing it if one man is capable of doing
it.) Even in the field of modern sciences, "scientists" practice their
method to different degrees – assuming that it is commonly formulated
and known to them. The nature of methodic process, in general, can be
understood by analogy to familiar specific cases such as that of performing a published sonata (which is not a method, though one can be
methodic in composing or performing it), or that of theatrical acting in
accordance with Stanislavsky's method (which is a method presumably
in accordance with the common method of implementation).

In reference to the recent polemics of the "two cultures" which Snow's
lecture (61) started, on the other hand, we may draw a more definite
implication of Mead's view of the scientific method. The difference
between the sciences and the arts are no more great or radical (in
"kind") than the differences between two cultures or languages, say,
French gastronomy and Sicilian ethics, the Morse code and Chinese.
The consequences of the Industrial-Scientific Revolution, which Snow
sketches, (62) are striking, and they demand certain adjustments to
them in the societies in which they emerge, since members of each of
these societies desire or tend to live in an integrated culture. Similar
consequences were introduced in a transitional society such as the
Roman Empire in the early Christian era and India under British
colonialization, in which the two cultures have to be integrated and
lived by its members. In view of present societies such as England and
the U.S.A., Snow strongly presents a necessity and hope for the
integration of the "two cultures", but fails to point out some "intrinsic"

----

(60) These qualifications in parentheses are redundant since a method
is, at least, the functional process of an implementation.
(61) C. P. Snow, The Two Cultures: and a Second Look (New York: New
American Library, 1964). These "two cultures" as a social problem,
especially an educational problem, and an educational policy as a
solution to it, have been clearly anticipated in Mead's early articles
written in 1906, "The Teaching of Science in College" (SW 60-72) and
"Science in the High School" (School Review, 1906 [14:4], pp. 237-49)
as well as in his later articles. See Bibliography.
(62) Cf. MT, Ch. IX, XII & XIII.

grounds for the integration in terms of the functions of the sciences and the arts. Mead points out, as considered early in 2.1 and presently in this 3.23, that there are such grounds which can be, theoretically, effective for the integration of these "two cultures", in conjunction with the contingent condition that these cultures have to be lived by members of each of these societies.

3.233 Conditions of Functional Implementation

(i/c) (functional) implementation / condition of
(i/p) (functional) implementation / precondition of
(s/r) scientific method / rule of
(i/a) (functional) implementation / assumption of
(s/a) scientific method / assumption of

(i/c.1) An implemental process, as the solution of a particular problem, presents its situation in a unity (or unified relation) in a perspective in which all the pertinent factors of the situation are taken into consideration, and selected and/or reconstructed for appropriate adjustment or realization,
(i/p.1) so as to continue the on-going teleological process of social life.

(i/c.2) The implemental process is generalized to be repeatable in a perspective in which the given particular situation is construed to be an instance of a class of recurrent identical or similar situations (or a part of an enduring, "larger" situation),
(i/p.2) so as to facilitate the process of social life in anticipation of distant situations.

(s/r.1) A hypothesis, as the solution of a particular problem, presents its situation in a unity or unified relation.
(s/r.2) A theory (or law), as a confirmed hypothesis, is accepted as universal.

(i/a.1) Social acts can be implementally mediated.
(i/a.2) The factors involved in social acts are real.
(i/a.3) Implements are efficacious or functional.
(i/a.4) Implemental mediation can be undertaken insofar as it is free from any condition which is not functionl in the context of mediation.

(s/a.1) Nature is intelligible, or can be known.
(s/a.2) Nature as the subject matter of science is real.
(s/a.3) Knowledge (or statements of science) is "true".
(s/a.4) Science can be pursued insofar as it is free from any view (or belief) which is not "true" in the context of investigation or research.

In our attempt to explicate rationality, the common conditions of functional implementation can be formulated and justified insofar as implementation is construed as a methodic process. There are basically two conditions, related but distinguishable in a logical analysis: (c.1) the condition of unity (or unified relation) and (c.2) that of generality (or universality). In terms of the method of implementation, they are (c.1) the "methodic" requirement or rule of unification and (c.2) that of generalization (or universalization). We will see that any other contextually specific condition of functional implementation is derived from or subordinate to these two basic conditions. And they are the conditions of mediation which constitute the rationality of social act.

These two conditions of implementation may be stated in the following summary, generalized forms: (i/c.1) an implemental process, as the solution of a particular problem, presents its situation in a unity (or unified relation) in a perspective in which all the pertinent factors of the situation are taken into consideration, and selected and/or reconstructed for appropriate adjustment or realization, (i/p.1) so as to continue the on-going teleological process of social life. (i/c.2) The implemental process is generalized to be repeatable in a perspective in which the given particular situation is construed to be an instance of a class of recurrent identical or similar situations (or a part of an enduring, "larger" situation), (i/p.2) so as to facilitate the process of social life in anticipation of distant situations. (63)

These two statements are, for Mead, a translation, respectively of the two "methodological" requirements of science: (s/r.1) A hypothesis, as the solution of a particular problem, presents its situation in a unity or unified relation. (s/r.2) A theory (or law), as a confirmed hypothesis, is accepted as universal. (64)

It is suggested that these two conditions do, in a possible interpretation, correspond to Prof. Buchler's concepts, respectively, of 1) "order" and 2) "reproducible order" in his early quoted statement on method: "a

----

(63) Some of the basic concepts involved are explained in the earlier sections: "situation" in 2.22 and 2.4; "problem" in 3.12 and 3.232; "solution" in 3.13, etc. On the other hand, the concepts of "unity" (or "unification") and "generality" (or "generalization") are further explained in the following 3.3 in terms of symbolic process which, as a phase of implementation, determines the processes indicated by these concepts. "Perspective" as well as "identical" and "similar" is also considered in 3.3. (For an explanation of "perspective", see Appendix A.3.) The other terms have been used throughout this study, and their meaning could be understood in terms of their usage in context, which of course is largely based on the common philosophical and ordinary usage of them as much as on Mead's texts.

(64) Both of these statements are given in obviously simplified, "weaker" forms than the common formulations for the conditions of induction for synthetic universal statements. The above formulations presuppose no definite theory of "reality" and "truth" and no clear distinction between "analytic" and "synthetic" statements in general (or in a "metaphysical" sense). On the other hand, they do not deny the contextual usefulness or validity of the logical distinction between analytic and synthetic, or

method is a power of manipulating natural complexes, purposively and recognizably, within a reproducible order of utterance. "(65)

Mead states these two conditions of implementation in several different contexts:

1) the condition of unity:

Science cannot possibly tell what the facts are going to be, but can give a method of approach: recognize all the facts that belong to the problem, so that the hypothesis will be a consistent, rational one (MS 388).

We have to allow all the ends or values involved to get into our decision - that is about the only statement in terms of method, so far as the ends themselves are concerned, that can be set up (PA 465).

What scientific method does require, if it is to be consistently used, is that all the conflicting ends, the institutions and their hitherto inviolable values, be brought together and so restated and reconstructed that intelligent conduct may be possible, with reference to all of them . . . .

Its one insistent demand is that all the ends, all the valuable objects, institutions, and practices which are involved, must be taken into account. In other words, its attitude toward conflicting ends is the same as its attitude toward conflicting facts and theories in the field of research. It does not state what hypothesis must be adopted. It does insist that any acceptable hypothesis must take into account all the facts involved (SW 255-6).

In our reflective conduct we are always reconstructing the immediate society to which we belong. We are taking certain definite attitudes which involve relationship with others. In so far as those relationships are changed, the society itself is changed. We are continually reconstructing. When it comes to the problem of reconstruction there is one essential demand [if it is to be methodic] - that all of the interests that are involved should be taken into account. One should act with reference to all of the interests that are involved: that is what we could call a "categorical imperative" (MS 386).

---

deductive and inductive, types. Insofar as this logical distinction is made, these two methodological statements amount to one statement for the deductive and analytic types. These matters of science (or assertive statements), a special type of implementation, are not the problems in our present context.
(65) Buchler, The Concept of Method, p. 135; cf. pp. 137-9.

James's statement that unity is just something that is there seems to characterize our experience until we meet with problems. When a problem does arise, then the unity is gone so far as the content is concerned . . . . You set up a hypothesis. It is true, as Kant states, that the unity of the hypothesis is the unity of your object in that experience. But that is not your attitude with reference to other objects. You do not always assume that your hypothetical structure, your organization of the object, is responsible for the unity of the object. When that is the case, you undertake to form an object, but the other objects about you seem to be unified just as they are (PA 631-2).

2) the condition of generality:

He [a scientist] is simply occupied in finding [an hypothetical] order . . . . If he can fit his hypothesis into this world and if it anticipates that which occurs, it then becomes the account of what has happened. If it breaks down, another hypothesis replaces it and another past replaces that which the first hypothesis implied (PP 12).

Man is a rational being because he is a social being. The universality of our judgments, upon which Kant places so much stress, is a universality that arises from the fact that we take the attitude of the entire community . . . . We are what we are through our relationship to others. Inevitably, then, our end must be a social end, both from the standpoint of its content (that which would answer to primitive impulses) and also from the point of view of form. Sociality gives the universality of . . . judgments and lies back of the popular statement that the voice of all is the universal voice . . . The very form of our judgment is therefore social, so that the end, both content and form, is necessarily a social end. Kant approached that universality from the assumption of the rationality of the individual, and said that if his ends, or the form of his act, were universal, then society could arise. He conceived of the individual first of all as rational and as a condition of society. However, we recognize that not only the form of the judgment is universal but the content also - that the end itself can be universalized. Kant said we could only universalize the form. However, we do universalize the end itself. If we recognize that we can universalize the end itself, then a social order can arise from such social, universal ends . . . .

Only a rational being could give universal form to his act. The lower animals simply follow inclinations: they go after particular ends, but they could not give universal form to acts. Only a rational being would be able to generalize his act and the maxim of his act, and the human being has such rationality (MS 379-80).

A human being is a member of a community and is thereby an
an expression of its customs and the carrier of its values.
These customs appear in the individual as habits, and the
values appear as his goods, and these habits and goods come
into conflict with each other. Out of the conflict arise in human
social experience the meanings of things and the rational
solution of the conflicts. The rational solution of the conflicts,
however, calls for the reconstruction of both habits and values,
and this involves transcending the order of the community. A
hypothetically different order suggests itself and becomes the
end in conduct. It is a social end and must appeal to others in
the community. In logical terms there is established a universe
of discourse which transcends the specific order within which
the members of the community may, in a specific conflict, place
themselves outside of the community order as it exists, and
agree upon changed habits of action and a restatement of values.
Rational procedure, therefore, sets up an order within which
thought operates; that abstracts in varying degrees from the
actual structure of society. It is a social order, for its function
is a common action on the basis of commonly recognized
conditions of conduct and common ends. Its claims are the
claims of reason. It is a social order that includes any rational
being who is or may be in any way implicated in the situation
with which thought deals. It sets up an ideal world, not of
substantive things but of proper method. Its claim is that all
the conditions of conduct and all the values which are involved
in the conflict must be taken into account in abstraction from
the fixed forms of habits and goods which have clashed with
each other. It is evident that a man cannot act as a rational
member of society, except as he constitutes himself a member
of this wider commonwealth of rational beings (SW 404-5).

We observe particulars only in case of exceptions. We are
always seeing in things contents which we do not define as
particulars, since perception always has some sort of a
pattern which must be taken as universal. Yet the universality
which we perceive in the individual cannot be mere similarity.
Similarity has significance only as a basis for psychological
interpretation (PA 635).

As these quoted words of Mead suggest, the two conditions of implementation (given earlier in the "summary" formulation) can be easily
translated into "hypothetical imperatives" as the methodic or methodological rules of implemental process. But it does not follow from the
translation that in various contexts, individual members of social
situations must be able to state and assume these rules in order that
their implemental processes be methodic. For example, a frogman can
dive very well and methodically, exhibiting what may be construed in
the context of diving as the conditions of unity and generality; but he
may not be able to state a set of rules for diving. Nor must he be able
to state or explain that this set of rules fulfills the required conditions

of functional implementation in general. Nevertheless, the formulation
of the two conditions of implementation does imply that if an implementa
process exhibits these two conditions, it is a methodic process. After
all, an implemental process is not an "accident" nor an immediate act,
but a teleological attempt or "trial" to mediate the phases of an act. In
this context, the hypothetical rules of implemental process, if formulate
are methodological. On the other hand, if individual members of a socia
situation decide to implement their act methodically in terms of symboli
premediation, they can follow these rules, as in the case of research in
science. In this context, the rules are methodic (and methodological).

Not only in the cases of assuming and following (i/c.1 and 2) as
methodic rules, but also in the other cases, these conditions are
determined by symbolic processes which select the perspectives of
situations and mediate the factors involved. In other words, these two
conditions, as the functions of implemental process, are determined by
the functions of symbolic process, a phase of mediation. Thus, an
explication of these conditions requires, and can be more fully given in
terms of, a theory of symbolic process which we will consider in the
next section, 3.3.

These two conditions of implementation are distinguishable because
the experience of an individual man, as the basis of a solution, is
limited to a sample of particular situations, or the social act of an
individual man is carried out in a particular situation and can be repeated in a limited number of similar situations. Otherwise, that is, in
the context in which we can assume on some "prior" grounds that the
solution in one situation is universally or invariably repeatable in terms
of a selected perspective, the first condition, (i/c.1), is equivalent to
the second, (i/c.2). (66) In understanding these conditions, especially
the second, we may remind ourselves that we live by various recurrenc
which we refer to by the terms such as: 1) "per second", "per hour",
"daily", "quarterly", "annual", "centennial", etc.; 2) "generation",
"career", "dynasty", "era", etc.; 3) "rotation", "revolution", "cycle",
etc.

We may understand without difficulty that the condition of unity, (i/c.1
inclusive of (i/p.1), can be the common condition of all functional
implemental processes. Some kind of unity or unified relation of the
various factors involved in a given situation is necessary and exhibited
in a successful implemental process. A question may be raised as to
the condition of generality, (i/c.2) inclusive of (i/p.2): Is it another
common condition, say, in situations of gastronomy (or in those of
creation and appreciation of art objects)? It is, because the acts in such

---

(66) Here the use of the terms "a priori" and "a posteriori", or "analyti
and "synthetic" is avoided since they are in their usual sense limited to
assertive statements, especially those of the sciences. It is an open
question whether the context in which (i/c.1) is equivalent to (i/c.2) is
strictly limited to analytic - and "a priori synthetic" - statements. For
example, is it impossible in the field of sports and other games to
assume on some "prior" grounds that a certain process is invariably
repeatable (in some sense)?

situations are social(67) and the implemental mediation of them is determined by, and consists of, symbolic processes. (68) The fact that in these situations there are many diverse preferences or views is not an objection to our answer insofar as each of them can be generalized in terms of different contextual factors. (69)

The parts of (i/p.1) and (i/p.2) are what may be called the "precondition" of implementation as methodic process, or the "precondition" of functional implementation. It was considered in 3.12 in the name of the precondition of functional mediation in reference to impulses. While (i/p.2) is an extension of (i/p.1) in view of the fact that many situations of social acts are recurrent or cyclical, (i/p.1) means that a social act, which demands or requires implementation, is completed by an implemental process, not terminated by an attempt to eliminate or repress the contextually required process of implementation.

It is a "fact of life" that man strives not only to stay alive like other organisms, but also persistently and in complex ways "to live well" and "to live better". (i/p.1) and (i/p.2) are a recognition of this fact as a precondition of a type of human life, "life of reason". "The intelligence which makes society possible", Mead says, "carries within itself the demand for further development in order that the implications of life may be realized" (SW 404).

In the premediate field of society, certain implemental, even methodic and systematic, attempts against this very precondition of implementation have been made by some men, often as members of institutions. But this precondition is recognized even in various "destructive" cases of social process. We "understand" political assassinations, or even atrocious activities of the Mafia, while we find "senseless" and incredible the murder of a large number of passers-by from a "Tower of the University of Texas". The institutional, methodic production and use of deadly weapons are "officially" justified and accepted, in the name of defense of "our country" and "our allies" in murdering thousands or millions of soldiers, but not in murdering civilians. In view of the present reality of the enormous stockpiles of nuclear weapons in the U.S.A. and the U.S.S.R., which have provoked the science-fiction vision of the Doomsday Machine, the annihilation or suicide of mankind as a result of our activities is a possibility. But no one would suggest it is a problem in terms of the method of implementation, although the nuclear stockpiles

---

(67) See Appendix A.3 and A.4. Cf. Mead's article, "The Objective Reality of Perspectives" (PP. 161-175; SW 306-319).

(68) See the following 3.33.

(69) The gastronomical preferences or tastes of individual diners are said to be "subjective" (or difficult to generalize) in the sense that the judgments of individual scientists are not. In contrast to the fact that the judgments of scientists generally tend to be in agreement, it is the common case that these preferences or tastes appear to be diverse. But the diversity of preferences or tastes, which are largely reflections of different backgrounds and assimilations, implies their "subjectivity" no more than the diversity of nationalities in the UN General Assembly implies the "subjectivity" of these characters.

are a product of the method. If the possibility is ever realized, it would
be an accident or miscalculation, if not the madness of a few men.

In the face of the complexity of social conditions of human life, we
have the common difficulty of finding out what is the problem in a given
situation which emerges to inhibit our impulses. For that matter, we
have the problem of deciding what we want, what ends we will actually
pursue, even in a comparatively simple situation. And in the context of
a large society, we have the problem of isolating a problem among
related things in our attempt to solve it; or we have the problem of setting
up the "priority" of various problems of the society to be solved. Further
more, what is the problem of a given situation is, especially in a society
based on a "large" field of premediation, contingent upon the determinatio
of what implemental process is <u>possible</u>.

In a problematic situation, Mead says,

> We find ourselves tending to act or think or feel with reference
> to [the] situation in ways that are so opposed that they inhibit
> one another. The statement of just what is in the situation that
> calls out these inhibiting reactions is what we call gathering the
> data or facts. The effort to formulate these leads us to find like
> situations in the present or the past, but the goal of the process
> is such a definition of the facts that we are aware of exactly what
> the conditions which must be met to enable us to continue our
> action, or thought, or feeling, and such a statement is a state-
> ment or the problem in the form that invites solution (PA 82).

As an implication of the implemental precondition, the above requirement of isolating or stating a problem is in accordance with Mead's
"contextual functionalism" explained earlier in 2.22. In the situation
of a social act, all the factors are construed in terms of their functions
in it. In other words, in a situation where we methodically select an
end and a means to it, or formulate and solve a problem, we recognize
or accept no "extrinsic" or "superimposed" limit which is not a part of
the factors as functions in the situation.

In translating the traditional views of knowledge or sciences into
generalized statements on implementation, the implications of the
precondition in consideration may be construed to consist of the following
methodological or methodic assumptions:

(i/a.1) Social acts can be implementally mediated.
(i/a.2) The factors involved in social acts are real.
(i/a.3) Implements are efficacious or functional.
　　　　(Or: Implementation is the process of selecting or producing
　　　　efficacious or functional implements.)
(i/a.4) Implemental mediation can be undertaken insofar as it is free
　　　　from any condition which is not functional in the context of
　　　　mediation.

The above four statements are a translation, respectively, of the
following philosophically well known traditional assumptions in the
field of knowledge or sciences:

(s/a. 1) Nature is intelligible, or can be known.
(s/a. 2) Nature as the subject matter of science is real.
(s/a. 3) Knowledge (or statements of science) is "true".
  (Or: Science is the process of discovering "true" statements.)
(s/a. 4) Science can be pursued insofar as it is free from any view (or belief) which is not "true" in the context of investigation or research. (70)

(i/a. 1, 2 and 3) are what may be called, to borrow a term from Santanaya, man's "animal faith" in his "means of life", their availability, reality, and efficacy. If the traditional "epistemological skepticism" is translated as a skepticism in implementation - namely, a doubt or question of whether man's implements are efficacious, real, or possible, the absurdity of "universal skepticism" is clear. In a perspective of implementation, the general or "metaphysical" problem of reality does not arise. As for a specific implemental process, the problem of its possibility, efficacy and reality arises in a particular situation as an "isolated" part within the premediate framework of a society which is taken for granted to be implementally efficacious or functional and real.

On the other hand, as Mead says, "independent reality carries with it no implication of finality" (PP 106). The meaning of this statement is clear if it is considered in the general context of implemental process, not limited to its traditional, epistemological context (of knowledge). The objective, "independent" reality of functional implements - "independent" in the sense of not being dependent on one or several "exclusive" perspectives selected by individual men – does not imply the "finality", the "ultimate reality" of the implements in the sense that they may not become obsolete or be discarded in new situations. Consider the exemplary case of horses, their efficacy and reality, as vehicles of man's transportation (or the case of Euclidean geometry as the geometry of nature).

The above conclusion against the "implication of finality" is in accordance with (i/a. 4). As a corollary of the first three statements, it is what Mead calls the "postulate" of "freedom of action". It means, negatively, that no prior limit is set to a problematic situation, which is not functional or contributory to its solution; and positively, that solutions of problems further the development of man's social life. As an assumption or requirement of implemental process, (i/a. 4) is "methodic" in a more strict sense than the first three, since it can be justified, like (i/c. 1 and 2) exclusive of (i/p. 1 and 2), insofar as implementation is construed as a methodic process. The methodic nature of (i/a. 4) is analogous to the familiar specific case of (s/a. 4) which has been historically the grounds for the conflicts of sciences, as noted earlier in 3.232, with processes of traditional institutions based on religious dogmas.

Mead says:

---

(70) If the subjects of (s/a. 1) and s/a. 2), namely, "nature", are slightly modified, the original formulations of these assumptions can be traced back to the writings of Plato, e.g., Theaetetus.

We postulate freedom of action as the condition of formulating
the ends toward which our conduct shall be directed. Ancient
thought assured itself of its ends of conducts and allowed these
to determine the world which tested its hypothesis. We insist
such ends may not be formulated until we know the field of
possible action. The formulating of the ends is essentially a
social undertaking and seems to follow the statement of the
field of possible conduct, while in fact the statement of the
possible field of conduct is actually dependent on the push
toward action. A moving end which is continually reconstructing
itself follows upon the continually enlarging field of opportunities
of conduct (SW 209).

We should realize what is meant by the demand for scientific
freedom: that every problem that arises may be freely attacked
by the scientist; that he is justified in setting up any postulate
which will enable him to solve that problem; and that the only
test which shall be made is the success of his solution as
determined by actual experience itself (MT 259).

In the fields of science, politics, art, and others, the activities of
certain individual men to respond to new situations in a "free attitude"
or "creative spirit" tend to come in conflict with the attempts of other
individuals to conserve established institutions. In a perspective of
modern Western history, Mead says: "The so-called conflict of science
and religion finds its ground, insofar as such an opposition exists, in
the complete indifference of scientific method to the idea of a fixed
moral and social order, which has been an essential part of theological,
and in considerable degree of social, theory . . . . It never appears,
however, as a condition for the solution of a scientific problem" (PA 309).
The common problem of the political censorship of expressions of
critical journalists and avant garde artists does, in spite of complexities
involved in it, indicate a similar conflict between the "methodic" attitude
of openness to new situations and the "institutional" attitude of straining
the implements which once might have been methodic in earlier situations but are not longer so in changed situations.
    As the important implication of (i/p.1 and 2), the methodic assumption
of "freedom of action" implies that 1) all solutions of problems as
generalizations (or universals) are hypothetical, provisional implements
(or implemented values) for the mediation of social acts; and that 2) it
is possible and expected that changing situations present certain new
factors, namely "exceptions" to generalized implements, so as to make
it impossible to unify the situations and mediate the new social acts in
terms of these available implements. In short, insofar as we are
methodic, we assume no dogmas or veritas eternitas; we adopt the
open, free attitude of working on any possible novel factors of a future
situation in terms of their functions in it. (71)

---

(71) Here we may understand the nature of implements on analogy to
organisms. The implements as products of the human organism may

(i/a.1, 2, 3 and 4) as the implications of (i/p.1 and 2) could be construed, in another perspective, as the general "minimum" or common criteria of functional implementation, or for accepting and rejecting generalized solutions or implements. So, (i/c.1 and 2) - exclusive of (i/p.1 and 2) - are implicated and also explained in the explanation of (i/a.1, 2, 3 and 4).

The common method of implementation has developed in the social evolution of man, in which old implements have turned out to be dysfunctional and obsolete, and new implements are introduced, repeatedly in changing situations. (i/c.1 and 2) - exclusive of (i/p.1 and 2) - have been formulated and justified as the conditions of this common method, because the implemental process in terms of them provides the precondition of (i/p.1 and 2). (72) By analogy to a methodological argument for the principle of induction in sciences, we may argue that all implemental processes, methodic or otherwise, exhibit these two conditions insofar as they are functional or efficacious, and that any attempt at implementation in violation of these conditions would not produce functional or "working" implements. In other words, these conditions cannot be and are not discarded merely because some implements which have been produced under these conditions have turned out to be dysfunctional or obsolete in new situations. Rather, the method of implementation assumes and requires that new (functional) implements be found or produced under the conditions of (i/c.1 and 2) to provide the preconditions of (i/p.1 and 2) in the new situations.

In certain contexts of social act, the conditions of (i/c.1 and 2) are quite "trivial" in the sense that it is not very difficult to fulfill them. Consider the cases suggested by the following "antecedents": 1) "If I (or you or anyone else) want to cross this street (or such a street) with no traffic signs for cars . . ."; 2) "If I want to light a cigarette presently

---

have the limit of their "life". Of course, the "built-in" obsolesence of commercial products is the abuse of the process of implementation. On the other hand, not to speak of man's cravings or searchings for eternity in religion, the common practice of not dating or limiting the effective duration of legal and political rules appears to be one area of social life which we may revise. It is suggested that in the legislation of any statute, or regulation the definite date of its expiration is written in. Or, we may establish in terms of types of rules that all the statutes and regulations are invalid and have to be reaffirmed or revised after ten, twenty or thirty years.

(72) The apparent circularity of this statement in view of the previous paragraph is "dissolved" if it is understood by analogy to the relation of the principle of induction, or of (s/r.1 and 2), to the principles or criteria of truth and reality, or to (s/a.1, 2, 3 and 4), in empirical or "inductive" sciences. Namely, the principle of induction is justified as "the" (methodic or) methodological principle of scientific theories, because generalizations in terms of. or on the assumption of this principle are true theories of reality; on the other hand, an explanation of the criteria of truth and reality is also an explanation of the principle of induction.

with no match or lighter in my possession . . ."; 3) "If I want to buy a
new pair of shoes . . ." Supposing that these cases are construed to
present problems, their required solutions - as unitites of, and generalities in view of, the given situations - can be largely achieved in terms
of symbolic mediation to coordinate and organize premediated implements.

On the other hand, it is not very easy to fulfill the same conditions of
(i/c.1 and 2) in certain other contexts. And the fulfillment of these conditions is very important. Consider the cases suggested by the following:
1) "If I (or you or anyone else) want to travel to Mars . . ."; 2) "If I
want to eliminate war as an institutional instrument of nations . . .";
3) "If I want to write a contemporary version of Three Sisters . . ." In
the situations suggested, the required solutions are not entirely limited
to symbolic mediation on the basis of premediated implements, but lie
in the discovery or creation of new implements.

Furthermore, in various contexts of social act, there are certainly
many other specific conditions of implemental methods. Consider the
following exemplary conditions or requirements: 1) the "non-circularity
of confirmation or argument", or the "simplicity of theory", in sciences;
2) the "systematic connectedness" in communication networks; 3) the
"brevity" in communication of a telegram; 4) the "minimization of
production cost" in commercial manufacture; 5) the "maximization of
variation within the limit of unity" in a style of art; etc. They are all
important methodic conditions respectively in their contexts. It is not
very difficult to see that these and other specific conditions of functional
implementation are derived from or subordinate to the conditions of
(i/c.1 and 2) insofar as their implemental processes are methodic.
(What was presented earlier in Chapter 2 as the methodological requirements of philosophy is in a way derived from these two general conditions applied to the given context.)

In a broad (or abstract) perspective of a society, the extraordinary
import of certain implemental processes in comparison to others is not
fully accounted for in terms of the conditions of (i/c.1 and 2). In other
words, we have to understand the import of the introduction of, say,
penicillin or the mini-skirt on some contextual (i.e., socio-historical)
grounds as well as in terms of its fulfillment of the two conditions. Many
common-place processes - such as the use of water or chairs - fulfill
the two conditions as do the diffusion of penicillin and the mini-skirt.
Analogously, our extraordinary interest in a new abortion or tax law
lies as much in its fulfillment of the conditions of (i/c.1 and 2) as in
the other factors of its social effects. Many "trivial" rules - such as
"You shall learn to speak", or "You shall not bite your finger nails" -
also fulfill the two conditions as social rules.

As some of the previously quoted statements of Mead suggest, (i/c.1
and 2) inclusive of (i/p.1 and 2) are the conditions under which social
acts are construed to be rational. In another perspective, what we may
call rationality is the generic character of social acts, which is constituted by these conditions of implemental process. Thus, much of
what has been said about implementation as social mediation and as
methodic process is about man's rationality.

3.24 Implemental Mediation and Rationality

In the context in which a "Heracleitian" emphasis is called for against
an antithetical, "Parmenidian" view, Mead says: "With every breath
we are stepping into a world that has a novel element in it" (MT 116).
In view of this statement and also in view of the fact that such a situation
of novelty can become a problematic situation, we can understand the
full implication of the following statement: "The world is implicitly
rational up to the advent of the problem. It is again rational once the
problem is solved" (PP 98-9). In on-going, non-problematic situations,
man's social acts are rational insofar as they are anticipated and carried
out in terms of premediation (largely symbolic process) on the basis of
available implements (including symbols) which provide the conditions
of (i/c.1 and 2) in the acts. In problematic situations, social acts are
rational insofar as they are implementally mediated, or their problems
are solved, in terms of (i/c.1 and 2). Thus, these conditions of implemental mediation constitute man's rationality. And in the sense that
these conditions are observed and realized insofar as implementation
is construed as a methodic process, man's rationality is the common
trait or feature of methodic processes.
   "It [reason or rationality] is . . .", Mead says, "an ideal of method,
not of program. It indicates direction, not destination" (PA 519). As he
construed "method" in distinction from "institution" and in contrast to
"utopian" or "incorrigible" programs and to "eternal" destinations, his
concept of method does not have the implication suggested by Whitehead,
that "there is active interest restraining curiosity within the scope of
[a] method". (73) As Mead sees it, an implemental process is a method
in a perspective of a novel, problematic situation, or in a series of
such situations, insofar as it is functional in terms of the common
method of implementation (which, as we have seen, is nothing but the
method of solving problems in new situations). Such implemental processes as methods are man's developments and directions known by
the general name of rationality. Prof. Buchler says that "method informed by query is the essential expression of reason". (74) The qualification, "informed by query", is given, in Mead's view, by his way
of construing "methods" in terms of the common method of implementation.

---

(73) A. N. Whitehead, The Function of Reason, p. 17. This quotation
is preceded by the following statements which are basically in support
of Mead's concepts of "rationality" and "method": "The evolution of
Reason from below has been entirely pragmatic, with a short range of
forecast. The primitive deep-seated satisfaction derived from Reason,
a satisfaction arising out of an immediate heredity, is provided by the
emphatic clarification of some method regulating current practice. The
method works and Reason is satisfied." Here "reason" is what he calls
"practical reason" distinguished from "speculative reason". His concept of the latter and its relation to "method" is another matter. Cf.
J. Buchler, The Concept of Method, Ch. XII.
(74) Op. cit., p. 114.

Rationality is "an _ideal_ of method" in the sense that it is an attitude or effort (or task) to solve problems properly or pursue ends efficiently in given situations of social act, although this effort is not always realized. But rationality is not an "ideal" or end which is set up or pursued, exclusive of specific ends in given situations; it is an end or condition realized in the process of pursuing those given specific ends. It can be contrasted to irrationality, an attitude or attempt (or consequence) of refusing to solve problems properly or pursue ends efficiently (or of refusing to solve problems or pursue ends at all), in given situations. And it can be, in another sense, contrasted to bases of irrationality, certain ideals or ends which are set up or pursued, exclusive of or over specific ends in given situations. As an example, in a problematic situation where a society requires an adjustment of its population to its limited resources of life, the concept of "nature" which prohibits the use of the most effective available means of controlling the increase of its population as a "perversion" is an "ideal" - or an end, if the concept is actively pursued and instituted - which is set up over the contextually important end of providing the proper standard of living to its members. (Furthermore, this concept of "nature" is not generalized in a perspective of various situations to which it applies, i.e., if it is "natural" in terms of the same concept to take aspirin or travel by car.) Here rationality is the very condition which is realized when the required adjustment is made, or when the end of providing the proper standard of living is pursued, methodically without accepting such a concept of "nature" as an "imposed" limit to its required solution.

In changing situations of life, man's "animal faith" in the availability of means of life - and his "artisan craft" of finding or making them - does not require a system of eternal and perfect implements, ideas and tools. It requires only the "method of trial and error", or its refinement based on systematic, symbolic control, for repairing old and obsolete implements or replacing them with the new and functional, whenever necessary. The order and security of a society lies not in searching for the constitution of infallible or incorruptible institutions, nor in conserving the constitution of familiar or cherished institutions, but in working for the constitution of fallible institutions, of which their amendment or replacement - in the face of social changes - is an integral institutionalized provision. Man's rationality is the teleological or purposive task of finding and using functional or efficacious means of life in various situations. It lies in the steady discovery of methodic processes which contextually work. And it is not realized by any "schizophrenic" attempt to live up to eternal objects or structures which always turn out to be other than what they are supposed to be.

3.3 Symbolic Mediation

3.31 The "Genesis" of Symbolic Process

3.311 On the Genesis and Function of Symbolic Process

There is no question in the phylogenic perspective of man's evolution that the origins of his symbolic process go further in the past than his

earliest written form of which we have some remains. The study of
ancient history and primitive societies indicates that written languages
were preceded by spoken languages. Since oral and other symbolic
processes, which emerged earlier than those of writing, left no pre-
servable "record" or "fossil", various theories of the genesis of the
symbolic process have remained highly speculative.

Mead presents his theories of symbolic process, mind and self as
theories of their "genesis" as well as of their "function". Scholars of
his works have commonly understood his theories in the same way.
Mead speaks of "the history of the growth of language" (SW 312), "the
psychological theory of the origin of language" (SW 109), and "our social
theory of the origin and nature of minds and selves" (MS 227). "As
George H. Mead saw with incisive insight", Prof. Morris wrote, "the
crucial genetic problem in the origin of comsigns is to explain how an
animal that does something that another animal reacts to as a sign can
itself react to its own action as a sign with the same significance". (75)
And "it seems to me", Prof. Morris wrote in another context, "that he
[Mead] has shown that mind and self are, without reminder, generated
in a social process, and that he has for the first time isolated the
mechanism of its genesis". (76)

In his articles printed during his life and in other posthumously
published works, Mead seems to be concerned with the origin of symbolic
process after the "fashion" of Darwin. Mead repeatedly talks about the
problem of its genesis in the social evolution of mankind. But it is not
clear if he is inquiring into its phylogenesis, going back to the prehistory
of man as Darwin does in his Origin of Species in terms of remaining
fossils and other evidence. No attempt was made by Mead to date the
phylogenesis of symbolic process. Obviously this phylogenesis is such
a case that we have no remaining evidence which may be construed as
"fossils" of the pre-historical events of mankind in which spoken
languages emerged. In reference to this problematic context, Prof.
Randall says (in one of his characteristic moments of humor): "I wasn't
there, and know no one who was."(77) And it is commonly accepted that
the oldest records of written languages preserved belong to the period
long after the genesis of spoken languages.

On the other hand, Mead appears in some parts of the same articles
and works to be concerned with the ontogenesis and development of
symbolic process in the life of today's children. But he has not really

---

(75) C. W. Morris, Signs, Language, and Behavior (New York:
G. Braziller, 1955 [orig. 1946]), p. 39.
(76) C. W. Morris, "Introduction", in MS, p. xv. Cf. "It is necessary,
even at the risk of over-simplification, to summarize Mead's position.
. . . To attempt to account for phenomena like mind, consciousness,
and the self . . ., it is to no purpose . . . to start with mind or something like it, since this precisely is what is to be explained - not in
descriptive or phenomenological terms . . . but in terms of origin" -
G. R. Geiger, John Dewey in Perspective (New York: McGraw-Hill,
1964 [orig. 1953]), p. 144.
(77) J. H. Randall, Jr., Nature and Historical Experience, p. 255.

attempted to describe the step-by-step growth of the children's speech and reasoning, their learning process, after the fashion of Piaget. Mead' theory of symbolic process deals with the process of role-taking in general, not with the aspects of "role-acquiring", etc.; it is limited to what he calls the "mechanism" of symbolic process, not concerned with the problem of the development of its "content".

Furthermore, there are certain parts in Mead's articles which imply that he accepts the Hackelean hypothesis of the ontogenetic recapitulation of phylogenesis. Mead extends it to the aspect of symbolic process beyond the level of biological evolution. "It is an interesting study", he says, "that of the manner in which the self and its mind arise in every child, and the indications of the corresponding manner in which it arose in primitive man" (SW 288). In another context, he also says: "Antecedent to the reflective consciousness within which we exist, in the beginnings of the society of men and in the life of every child that arises to reflectiv consciousness, there must have been the condition of interrelation by acts springing from social instincts (SW 102).(78)

But it is not unreasonable to speculate that the ontogenesis of symbolic process is different from its phylogenesis at least for one aspect. Ancient men evolved their communication and symbolic systems without the benefit of the matured mind of today's parents and teachers, who have an important role in the genesis and development of children's symbolic processes. We have no clear evidence on the phylogenesis of symbolic process to decide if it is identical to the ontogenesis and the function of symbolic process in the present.

Prof. Bidney wrote:

> There is, in short, an irreducible gulf between the actual or potential human power of conceiving and symbolizing and the mental functions of man's nearest animal relatives. This explains why all attempts to reconstruct the origin of language have proved so futile and why linguists have reached the conclusion that "the data with which they are concerned yield little or no evidence about the origin of human speech".(79)

It has been recently suggested, as noted in 3.22, that "the ability to acquire language is a biological development [of man]" and that "language is due to as yet unknown species-specific biological capacities

---

(78) Among others, Freud and Piaget accept this Hackelean hypothesis in their psychological theories of man.
(79) D. Bidney, Theoretical Anthropology, p. 4. The inner quotation is from E. H. Sturtevant, An Introduction to Linguistic Science (New Haven: Yale Univ. Press, 1947), p. 40. Mead would agree with Profs. Bidney and Sturtevant in the sense that the philological or linguistic attempts to reconstruct the origin of spoken languages were not successful. See his article, "The Relations of Psychology and Philosophy", Psychological Bulletin, 1904 (1:11), pp. 375-91. Some of its pertinent parts are quoted in the following 3.12.

[of man]".(80) Even if this hypothesis is more fully confirmed and supplemented in details, the phylogenesis of symbolic process in the social evolution of mankind remains unexplained fully, unless the hypothesis implies that men simply speak or write like breathing or walking. Verbal or other symbolic processes are more like 1) shooting an arrow or driving a car than like 2) breathing or walking. (Note that man shares 2) with other organisms, while 1) is unique to man.) Symbolic processes have been socially evolved as devices, implemental processes. Thus, their phylogenesis and ontogenesis as well as their function cannot be fully explained in terms of biological factors.

The genesis of many processes (how they originated) determines, and is identical to, their present functions (what they do or how they work now). But for other processes, particularly human artifacts and institutions, their geneses are irrelevant to their present functions. Theoretically, "genesis" can and sometimes should be distinguished from "functions". It is a mistake to take an account of the present function of a process or object as the account of its genesis when that identity is not warranted by evidence; and this mistake may be called the functional fallacy, in contrast to the well-known genetic fallacy, the mistaken attempt to explain the present function of a process or object in terms of its genesis. For example, an explanation of the present function of the sun or the universal military draft may not be the same as that of their geneses in reference to their original contexts. It is a question of whether Mead is subject to a functional fallacy for his theory of symbolic process in which its genesis and function are not clearly delineated but identified for some of their common aspects.

3.312 On the "Functional Genesis" of Symbolic Process

It is possible to understand Mead's genetic theory of symbolic process to be a theory of its arche in the ancient Greek sense: "not a commencement in time but a 'first principle' . . . (which is) logical rather than chronological". (81) Not unlike such early modern social philosophers as Hobbes, Locke, and Rousseau in their conceptions of the "state of nature", (82) Mead is basically interested in locating the logically primitive condition in which symbolic process "originates", that is, functions in its "minimum" characteristic way.

As he derives his theory of the origin of symbolic process from the observation of its function, it is the arche, the principle of what may be regarded as the "functional genesis", not the chronological or historical genesis, which may not be "accidentally" related to the function. The assumption behind Mead's theory is that an object (or form or process) originates properly out of its function. In the sense that the genesis of

---

(80) Lenneberg, "A Biological Perspective of Language", pp. 40 and 45. See 3.225, fn. 37.
(81) E. Cassirer, The Myth of the State (New Haven: Yale Univ. Press, 1946), p. 54. Cf. J. H. Randall, Jr., Aristotle, pp. 35 ff.
(82) Of course, their concept of the "state of nature" has been commonly understood by a large number of their interpreters in the phylogenic sense.

an object is a past of the present in which the object functions, the genesis is reconstructed in the present. In the case of the genesis of symbolic process, it is largely reconstructed in terms of its present function insofar as no other, contrary evidence can be found in the present. (83)

Through his works, Mead employs various terms, as noted below, in the place of the "genesis" of symbolic process as well as of mind and self. His use of these "sibling-terms" is, as explained in 2.22, justified by his contextual criteria of the act. It may be noted that some of these terms, (e-j), could imply the concept of "function".

a) genesis (PP 196)(84)   a') generate
b) origin (SW 104)   b') originate
c) beginning (SW 136)   c') begin
d) evolution (SW 273)   d') evolve
e) emergence (PA 640)   e') emerge
f) appearance (SW 267)   f') appear
g) development (SW 243)   g') develop
h) growth (SW 104)   h') grow
i) rise (SW 306)   i') arise
j) basis (SW 82)   j') be based on

It is clear that Mead takes his social psychological theory of symbolic process as a theory of "the process of language or speech - its origins and development" (MS 6) in one context and as a theory of "the origin, development, nature, and structure of the self" (MS 379) in another context. In one of his important articles printed during his life, "The Genesis of the Self and Social Control", Mead says: "It is my desire to present an account of the appearance of the self in social behavior" (SW 267). Here the "genesis" in the sense of "appearance . . . in social behavior" implies the "function" of the self in general more than the phylogenesis or ontogenesis in the chronological sense.

---

(83) Susanne K. Langer came to a conclusion quite similar to Mead's theory of the "functional genesis", though not entirely in behavioristic terms, in her 1960 article, "Speculations on the Origins of Speech and Its Communicative Function", which has references to Dewey's Experience and Nature but no reference to any of Mead's works (Quarterly Journal of Speech, 1960 [46], pp. 121-34; reprinted in Philosophical Sketches, New York: New American Library, 1964 [orig. 1962], pp. 30-52). "The great step from anthropoid to anthropos, animal to man", Langer wrote, "was taken when the vocal organs were moved to register the occurrence of an image, and stirred an equivalent occurrence in another brain, and the two creatures referred to the same thing. At that point, the vocal habit that had long served for communion assumed the function of communication" (p. 50). Note that this process of two similar organisms "referring to the same thing" is not simply admitted but explained by Mead in terms of their reflexive act of role-taking; see 3.3.3.
(84) Only one paradigmatic reference is given after each term.

Mead's theory of symbolic process is a reconstruction of its arche, which may be regarded as a theory of its function in reference to the on-going present and as that of its genesis in reference to the past of its genetic context which the present implies. In a genetic perspective, it is his contention, as explained earlier in 2.34, (85) that if one attempts to explain, in view of the present theory of evolution, how society, mind, and self are evolved, one cannot go by the earlier theories which assume that men have mind first of all in the ontological and/or psychological order. They "cannot explain the existence of minds and selves" in terms of which social processes are explained. As an alternative, the bio-social theory of the symbolic process, mind and self, is in accordance with the implication of evolution: it can explain the origin of symbolic process in terms of on-going bio-social processes as well as the existence of social process in terms of physiological and environmental factors involved.

In one of his early articles, "The Relations of Psychology and Philosophy", Mead discusses the problem of the phylogenesis of symbolic process in reference to the 18th and 19th century philological theories based on the traditional concept of substantial, pre-existing mind:

> The difference between the Herbartian treatment of a language and Wundt's is . . . not confined to the nature of the subject-matter itself. The distinction is that with which we are familiar under the terms intellectualistic [associational psychology] and voluntaristic [functional psychology]. It is the advantage of this latter type of psychology that it is able to start with the act in the form of an impulse. The striking illustration of this advantage is to be found in the theories of the origin of language.

> From the standpoint of an associational psychology – one that recognizes only ideas and their connections, at least depends upon these for the psychological analysis of the contents of consciousness – language is almost unavoidably conceived of as an invention. While the more modern psychologist would not be guilty of the absurd theories of the origin of language, of religion, of government which belong to the rationalism of the eighteenth century, a thorough-going associational psychology, whether Herbartian or English, can give no account of language processes which in principle differs from these. For typical associations lie between contents of consciousness which have been analyzed out of objects and have become symbolic. The sensuous content and its meaning have been separated from each other and in so far the content is arbitrary . . .

> Wundt, on the other hand, is able to refer the beginning of language to the primitive impulse to expression. The sound is at first but a gesture . . . Articulation, as a muscular process,

---

(85) Also see Appendix A.

is explained in the same way that movements of the fact, of the hands, of the whole body are accounted for under the influence of emotional tension. Instead, therefore, of having to assume unknown or exceptional conditions as the antecedents of the origin of speech, we can find the conditions present in our own movements, in first activities of children, in the gesture languages of primitive peoples or the deaf-mutes . . . .

Such a conception of the beginning of gesture language passes over easily to that of the beginning of spoken language, through the recognition that articulate sounds are in their beginning but sound-gestures and take the same place in the act of emotional expression that is taken by the gesture. Perhaps there is no better illustration of the importance of psychology to the comprehension of language than such a natural and simple presentation of the beginning of the interchange of ideas through the simple sympathetic interaction of gesture expression within a common emotional situation. There could be no better illustration of the advantage of beginning one's psychological analysis with the act in its primitive form of the impulse, instead of being forced to build it up out of intellectual elements . . . .

The question of the beginning of language is not attacked [by Wundt] from the standpoint of the comparative philologist. There is no generalization from the earliest forms of speech with which we are familiar, nor are there any inferences drawn from the Ursprachen which can be constructed out of the identities between kindred tongues. The problem is attached as a psychological problem. Speech is an act and like any other act has its natural history which psychology can undertake to give to us from a study of its nature and its analogy to other acts. It is, in its primitive form, emotional expression, not because primitive languages are more emotional, but because gestures and cries are the external parts of emotional acts. Sympathetic reproduction of seen gestures, and the change in them which answers to the difference of conscious content they arouse are facts with which psychology deals, and out of these facts arises a theory of the origin of language which whether it is correct or not is psychological, and not philological in the ordinary sense of the word . . . .

The philologist has not been successful enough in his efforts to reconstruct a primitive language, to care to contest with the psychologist his right to form theories within his own field . . . .

I think there can be no question that he [Wundt] has succeeded in locating the problem of the origin of language within the field of psychology . . . .

In the question of the origin of language the psychological

treatment enables the philologist to dispense with a reconstruction based on historical remains and inferences drawn
from these . . . . (86)

In developing the Wundtian theory of symbolic process, Mead goes
further than Wundt to its logical end to eliminate the residue of the
traditional concept of substantial, pre-existing mind as its precondition:

In order that Wundt's theory of the origin of language may be
carried out, the gesture which the first individual makes use
of must in some sense be reproduced in the experience of the
individual in order that it may arouse the same idea in his
mind. We must not confuse the beginning of language with its
later states . . . . We are supposed to be at the beginning of
these developments of language . . . . In the very beginning
the other person's gesture means what you are going to do
about it. It does not mean what he is thinking about or even
his emotion . . . .

How, in terms of Wundt's psychological analysis of communication, does a responding organism get or experience
the same idea or psychical correlate of any given gesture
that the organism making this gesture has? The difficulty is
that Wundt presupposes selves as antecedent to the social
process in order to explain communication within that process,
whereas, on the contrary, selves must be accounted for in

---

(86) Op. cit., pp. 379-388. The same view is given in a summary form
in MS: "The study of the process of language or speech - its origins
and development - is a branch of social psychology, because it can be
understood only in terms of the social processes of behavior within a
group of interacting organisms; because it is one of the activities of
such a group. The philologist, however, has often taken the view of the
prisoner in a cell. The prisoner knows that others are in a like position
and he wants to get in communication with them. So he sets about some
method of communication, some arbitrary affair, perhaps, such as
tapping on the wall. Now, each of us, on this view, is shut up in his own
cell of consciousness and, knowing that there are other people so shut
up, develops ways to set up communication with them" (MS 6 fn).
This philologist's theory of symbolic process, as Mead shows,
describes the case of the communication of prisoners between their
cells in Arthur Koestler's Darkness at Noon (1941). The event of the
novel presupposes a common symbolic system, mind, as well as "a
like position" among them; it is certainly not analogous to the phylogenetic (or ontogenetic) situation of symbolic process. Although the
event is a highly interesting, powerful device for a novel, it is doubtful
that such a communication process of tapping can be constructed so
easily as it appears in the novel without some pre-arranged code system.
This negative consideration implies the difficulty of the philologist's
theory of the origin of symbolic process.

terms of the social process, and in terms of communication.
. . . If, as Wundt does, you presuppose the existence of mind
at the start, as explaining or making possible the social process
of experience, then the origin of minds and the interaction among
minds become mysteries. But if, on the other hand, you regard
the social process of experience as prior (in a rudimentary form)
to the existence of mind and explain the origin of minds in terms
of the interaction among individuals within that process, then not
only the origin of minds, but also the interaction among minds
. . . cease to seem mysterious or miraculous (MS 48-50).

As suggested so far and as will be more fully considered in the following
3.32 and 3.33, Mead's theory of symbolic process as that of its arche
does explain the relation of factors involved in the possible genesis and
function of symbolic process. In reference to the genesis in particular,
the theory is not an attempt to give a full chronological account after the
fashion of a Darwin or a Piaget. It explains only the basic "mechanism"
of symbolic process in its proper genetic - both phylogenetic and ontogenetic - and later purely functional context, on the basis of the social
conditions and highly developed physiological functions of men.
    In taking Mead's theory of symbolic process as a psychological
explanation of its "functional genesis" as well as of its function, we can
understand why Mead talks of the genesis of symbolic process often
indiscriminately in reference both to its phylogenesis and ontogenesis,
while he emphasizes the bio-physiological "primitive" context of communication in terms of vocal gesture. (87) It is also apparent why he is
concerned with the symbolic process as the present functional act of
role-taking, not as the learning act of "role-acquiring", etc. Thus, we
can see why, limited to his concern with the discovery of the basic
mechanism of symbolic process in its "functional genesis", Mead
construes "signs . . . [as] biological mechanism which function socially"
and "has biologized it [reflexive communication]", as Prof. Buchler
presents. (88) But Mead does not limit the symbolic process in its present
functional context to the original or primitive communication of vocal
gestures, "an inscrutable succession of animal postures". (89) The most
complex forms of symbolic process, the theories of modern science as
well as the productions of modern communication media, can be explicated in terms of Mead's theory of symbolic process.

3.32 Symbolic Process: Connotation and Denotation

3.321 Symbolic Process in a Functional Perspective (1)
    In the perspective of man's sociality and teleology, which we have
explained in 3.1 and 3.2, symbolic process is a special type of the
implemental mediation of his social acts. Implements of the acts are

---

(87) Cf. SP 306.
(88) J. Buchler, Nature and Judgment, pp. 66 & 155.
(89) Op. cit., p. 66.

dysfunctional or obsolete unless they are symbolically mediated. In
this sense, symbolic process is the "mechanism" of the social acts.(90)
In contrast, their "contents" range, in various contexts, from impulses
to sensitivities, from implements to consummatory ends, and from
institutions to common values. And they are "vivified" and "digested"
by men as members of a society in terms of the mediate functions of
symbolic process.

We are aware of what it is like to be a pioneer exploring on a frontier,
an étranger lost in a foreign land, or a "victim" caught in a bureaucratic
maze. In such a problematic situation, shapes, colours, and sounds are
unrelated and indifferent to us; they are purposeless and useless. That
is, they are "meaningless". As Mead says, "men live in the world of
Meaning" (SW 294). The socialized environment of implements we live
by is doubly premediated by a complex matrix of symbols, their meanings.
These symbols are the "roles of others", social objects, which we can
assume in anticipation of their responses or reactions to ourselves. In
this sense, the objects of our environment as our symbol-mediated
implements, "speak" and cater to us, warning and challenging, or
inviting and encouraging.

Of course, the functions of symbolic process are heavily implemented
by other implements - from brushes and megaphones to typewriters and
televisions. And symbols as produced works of men are values or ends
themselves in a permanent implemental field of society, to which other
implements - from libraries and museums to scholarly researches and
educational digests - are also applied for their assimilation and conservation. In our attempt to explicate the functional conditions of social
act, we are concerned with symbolic process mainly for its mediational
function.(91)

By "symbol"(92) we refer to those units which are (or are supposed
to be) functional in the mediation of social acts. That is, we refer by
symbols not to "atomic" units of sign-vehicles such as abstracted
alphabets or words but to exclamations made, orders given, questions
asked (and answered or not answered), propositions asserted, coins
exchanged, checks signed, clocks observed, traffic lights watched,
race records printed, applications filled out, labels attached, instructions
read, hands waved, letters written, stories narrated, sonatas played,

---

(90) MS 120, PA 547, SW 314, etc.
(91) As a study of symbolic process, 3.3 is limited in its scope in view
of the contemporary literature on "meaning" and "referring", "sign"
and "symbol", "natural languages" and "artificial" (or formal) languages,
etc. In terms of the common divisions of semiotic, it is a study of basic,
general problems of "pragmatics" and "semantics"; it has no concern
with "syntactics". And it is not within its scope to delineate types of
man's implemental processes and to explain divergent functions of
symbols which are prominent in the field of each specific type of them.
(92) In view of common practice and convenience, the term "symbol"
is consistently used in reference to what Mead variously terms as
"significant gesture", "significant symbol", "language symbol",
"universal", etc. Cf. MS 79, SW 247, etc.

films screened, etc.(93)
  Mead says:

> Signification has . . . two references, one to the thing indicated,
> and the other to the responses . . . . It denotes and connotes.
> . . . But it neither denotes nor connotes except, when in form
> at least, denotation and connotation are addressed both to a self
> and to others, when it is in a universe of discourse that is
> originated with reference to a self. (SW 246).

We may take this short quotation of Mead for a functional interpretation
of symbolic process without concern with his suggested reference to its
genetic problems. In a functional perspective, symbolic process refers
to the social act(94) in which a symbol - or a set of symbols - has its
denotative and connotative references related as it is addressed by an
individual to others and to himself. And it involves three logically
distinguishable factors: 1) the relation of connotative and denotative
references, 2) that of others to oneself, and 3) that of the above two
relations.

  First, the connotative and denotative references of symbolic process
are related in a functional unity; that is, they must presuppose or posit
each other within a context of social act. Second, the individual and
others as its members are related in terms of a common or invariant
perspective of the social act; that is, the individual takes the role(s) of
others and realizes himself in adjustment to them. Third, in the
"genetic" perspective Mead commonly takes, the first relation is derived
from the second; but in a functional perspective, the second is based on
the first. In the functional perspective, symbolic process may be said to
be a process in which an individual is able to address to himself what
he addresses to others in terms of (the functional unity of) a symbol in
its connotative and denotative references.

  Symbolic process is considered in reference to a whole social act,
not in reference to single words or other logically separable parts. A
series of words uttered as part of a social act may not be subject to the
three functional relations or conditions mentioned in the previous paragraph. It is the whole series, such as a complete sentence or paragraph,

---

(93) This Meadean approach to symbolic process is suggested, in
principle, by Prof. Randall's statement on "languaging" or "communicating": "The unit of language is not the term, not even the sentence,
but rather the paragraph, the related context of 'use' - as any functional
and contextual view must maintain" (J. H. Randall, Jr., "The Art of
Language and the Linguistic Situation: A Naturalistic Analysis", Journal
of Philosophy, 1963 (60:2), p. 56 fn).
  Cf. "It therefore remained appropriate . . . to treat sentences and
not words as the wholes whose use is learned - though never denying
that the learning of the wholes proceeds largely by an abstracting and
assembling of parts" (W. V. O. Quine, Word and Object, p. 13).
(94) Mead's concept of social act has been explained earlier in 2.2 and
2.4.

or an entire lecture or cinema, which is, in the context of its use, subject to these conditions. It is not uncommon, on the other hand, that on certain occasions long "sentences" are uttered by men without fulfilling these required conditions. They are cases of what is commonly known as "nonsense" or "breakdown in communication". They involve inadequate significations, derived from or resulting in the disunity or separation of one or more of the three required relations. In the exigency of man's social processes, all these conditions of symbolic process may not be fully satisfied, but in the history of mankind, there has been a good record of pervasive occurrences of those social acts in which these conditions are fulfilled.

In a perspective of symbolic process, these three relations involved in symbolic process constitute the required conditions of the functional mediation of social act. As we will see, they "formulate" or "determine" the implemental conditions of "unity" and "generality" (i/c. 1 and 2), in social act, which we have explained earlier in 3.233. And so they determine the rationality of social act.

3.322 The Relation of Connotation and Denotation

As suggested by Mead's statements (SW 246) quoted in the previous section, 3.321, a symbol in its denotative(95) reference is the signification or designation of a range or type of objects (or processes) in social, implemental relations: objects as implements, objects implemented, or their relations. These things "indicated", as Mead says, range from distant events and contact objects to contextually private phases of individual men and relations of symbols themselves. They exist or prevail by no means in one and the same way but in various ways. And a symbol in its connotative (96) reference is the signification of a common or identical (or similar) response – or range of responses – for an end in terms of a generalized perspective of a social act to which any difference between individual members is irrelevant. In this sense of common or identical response, symbols are socially invariant or universal, at least logically or "in form". These invariant responses "formulate" or "determine" the general natures or universal characters of those denoted objects or relations as they endure or recur as common objects of the responses. (97)

---

(95) Cf. SW 246, PA 223, etc. Here Mead's use of the term "denotation" is taken, as we will see, in the sense of what Prof. Morris calls "designation" in contrast to the traditional notions of "denotation". Cf. C. W. Morris, Foundations of the Theory of Signs (Chicago: Univ. of Chicago Press, 1938), pp. 5, 25, 32, etc.

(96) Cf. MS 73 ff, SW 246 etc. In reference to the same aspect of a symbol, Mead also uses various terms other than "connotation" in different contexts: "meaning", "significance", "interpretation", "concept", "ideation", etc.

(97) Cf. "Meaning is not indeed a psychic existence; it is primarily a property of behavior, and secondarily a property of objects" (John Dewey, Experience and Nature, p. 179). Dewey's emphasis on the order of the relation of connotation and denotation is entirely in support of

Accordingly, a symbol in its functional unity of connotation and denotation is a symbol, or a "universal", (98) if it is used by an individual man in relation or in view of members of a social act, "others and himself", (C) to stimulate or guide some common or identical (or similar) response or disposition to respond, (D.1) in reference to some particular objects or relations in view of a large number or a repeatable series of similar ones, (D.2) in spite of certain variations among them, and (D.3) even in absence of any one of them or their substitutes (i.e., "signals")(99) as immediate or direct stimuli.

The connotation and denotation of a symbol are logically distinguished. But in the context of a social act, a symbol is used in terms of its functional unity or relation. That is, a symbol used denotes (D) something if it presupposes (discloses or indicates) some common or identical response as its connotation in reference to (D); a symbol used connotes (functions as a direction, expression, information, etc.) for (C) some further response, or disposition to respond further, if it presupposes certain common objects or relations as its denotation in reference to (C). What is required in denoting a symbolic process is that members of a social act are able, in a common perspective of their situation, to divide their "universe of discourse" into two or more parts (individuals, classes, or relations) and to select or indicate one or more pertinent parts in contrast to the others in the same way in reference to what is connoted. And what is required in connoting is that the members are able, in a common perspective of the situation, to respond in their related roles in the same way in reference to what is denoted. This requirement of the functional relation of connotative and denotative references could not be properly considered if single words or other logically separate parts were taken as symbols and if symbols were considered apart from the contexts of their uses.

Prof. Strawson argues, in considering what he calls "uniquely referring expressions", that "referring", i.e., denoting, is the function

---

Mead's theories of man's perspectives and symbols. (See Appendix A.3.)

A similar emphasis is suggested by Prof. Randall's theory of the "two different modes of signification", the "primary" and "secondary" (J. H. Randall, Jr., Nature and Historical Experience, pp. 239 ff). His theory is explained in terms of four different "levels or responding to": 1) "ways" (or "universals"); 2) "signs", a "special kind" of 1); 3) "linguistic signs", a "special kind" of 2); 4) "symbols", a "special kind" of 3) and so of 2) and 1) - in one context of analysis (ibid., p. 248) - or, a "special kind" of 1) which is construed not to be any "kind" of 2) and 3) - in another context (ibid., p. 263). Prof. Randall's theory is complicated enough to suggest a simple comparison to Mead's theory of symbols under study without going into details.

(98) Cf. "A sentence is not an event of utterance, but a universal: a repeatable sound pattern, or repeatedly approximable norm" (W. V. O. Quine, Word and Object, p. 191).

(99) As for the distinction between "symbol" and "signal" - or, in Mead's terms, between "significant symbol" and "non-significant gesture", see the following 3.331.

of the use of these expressions in contexts.(100) His argument was presented as a criticism of Russell's view that "definite descriptions", i.e.,
one type of "uniquely referring expressions", are quantifiable or existential propositions (which are true or false), and that they "do not
(logically or necessarily) denote anything".(101) " 'Mentioning', or
'referring' ", Prof. Strawson concludes, "is not something an expression
does; it is something that someone can use an expression to do. "(102)
The implication is that if a symbol denotes anything, it denotes something in the contexts of its use. As for meaning or connotation, he says
that "meaning (in at least one important sense) is a function of the
sentence or expression".(103) But in another important sense, the
"meaning" of a "sentence" is the function of its use in contexts in relation to its denotation, as suggested by common examples: "Would you
offer him a chair?" or "How did you find your angel?" "Look at the
sentence as an instrument", Wittgenstein stated, "and its sense as its
employment. "(104)

3.323 Denotation

In a genetic perspective, Mead commonly explains that symbolic
process emerges in man's "primitive" situations of "conversations of
gestures" which are "non-significant" or without connotation and which
are directly stimulated by objects (to be denoted). He takes these social
acts to be "co-operative" - even for cases where members of a social
act are in conflict over their identical or similar ends. In these situations which we assume to be recurrent, non-significant but "reflexive"
gestures - such as vocal gestures which one says and hears at the same
time, that is, gestures which stimulate others and oneself in the same
way - logically fulfill the necessary functional condition of symbols to
signify common or identical responses and to designate common objects
or relations which are direct stimuli. These reflexive gestures are
ultimately transformed into symbols to arouse responses, or dispositions
to respond, in situations where the denoted objects, or their substitutes
(signals), are not present as direct stimuli. In present contexts in which
new symbols are originated, certain non-significant signs are used in
conjunction with other symbols to guide or control certain responses in
the same way in reference to certain common objects, regardless of
whether these objects are present as direct stimuli; and these new signs
are transformed into symbols themselves to connote and denote.
   Mead says:

(100) P. F. Strawson, "On Referring", Mind, 1950 (59), pp. 320-44;
reprinted in Essays in Conceptual Analysis, ed. by A. Flew (London:
Macmillan, 1956), pp. 21-52.
(101) B. Russell, "On Denoting", Mind, 1905 (14), pp. 478-93; reprinted in Readings in Philosophical Analysis, ed. by H. Feigl &
W. Sellars (New York: Appleton-Century-Crofts, 1949), pp. 103-15.
(102) Essays in Conceptual Analysis, p. 29.
(103) Op. cit., p. 30.
(104) L. Wittgenstein, Philosophical Investigations, trans. by
G. E. M. Anscombe (New York: Macmillan, 1953), 1.421.

124

Whatever endures in the midst of passing events (. . . some
sensuous content . . . or a structure of the thing . . . or an
aesthetic, logical, or ethical content . . .) is in so far universal,
for it is a character of which there are a number of instances
and of which there might be an indefinite number . . . . It is
these persistent characters which can be indicated to others or
to one's self, for only that which persists can be indicated . . . .
Such an indication of a character by a specific social gesture,
generally vocal, with the tendency to respond to the character
pointed out, is what is called an idea that answers to the universal
content.

It is the attitude of response to these universal characters which
answers to them in the individual. The responses are universal
because they may be called out by any number of different
stimuli and so answer to that universal character in the object
which calls them out. In the experience of individuals they are
the criteria by which we identify the universal characters in
things. Whatever one tends to sit down [on] is a chair. Whatever
one places in a scale of colours is a certain blue. We identify
the universal contents in things by presenting ourselves as
responding to them, and we call these responses aroused by the
significant symbols of social gestures, or language, the meanings
of things. It is because we can summon ourselves, as organizations of responses, into the field of experience by means of
these symbols, that we are able to isolate these meanings [and
denote objects as objects of these meanings] and so further the
reorganization of our responses in a plan of action. (PA 371)(105)

In one sense, objects and their relations denoted by symbols are "there
in the world" to be selected and/or to stimulate. "Nature", Mead says,
"has meaning and implication but not indication by symbols" (MS 78 fn).

---

(105) In view of these statements and others, it is difficult to understand
a certain criticism of "his [Mead's] . . . failure to grasp the denotative
function of the language symbol" (W. Percy, "Symbol, Consciousness,
and Intersubjectivity", Journal of Philosophy, 1958 (55:15), p. 633.
"I would . . . suggest", Percy says, "that a recognition of the denotative
function of the symbol, as a real property, yields the intersubjectivity
which is not forthcoming from Mead's sign-response psychology"
(op. cit., p. 640). First of all, it is mistaken to suggest that Mead's
theory of symbolic process is merely a "sign-response" theory in the
sense of "conditioned reflex" and that it is without an explanation of the
denotative function of symbolic process. Secondly, the problem of
"intersubjectivity" would have more to do with connotation than with
denotation if the two were separated in a logical analysis. Such a mis-
interpretation of Mead is possible if one is limited to a superficial
reading of Ch. 2 of MS in which Mead is mainly concerned with the
"genetic" problem of the "connotation" of symbols. One has to turn to
PA to find Mead's full discussion of the problem of denotation.

But in another sense, common responses as connotations of symbols
"constitute" these objects, because common or universal natures of the
former answer to unities or identities of the latter, and classify them
as members of classes. "Symbolization", Mead says, "constitutes
objects not constituted before, objects which would not exist except for
the context of social relationships wherein symbolization occurs.
Language does not simply symbolize a situation or object which is
already there in advance; it makes possible the existence or appearance
of that situation or object, for it is a part of the mechanism whereby the
situation or object is created" (MS 78).(106)

Objects of nature are noticed or selected insofar as common responses
to them are possible (that is, insofar as a response of one individual to
a gesture or symbol of another is, in a logical analysis, taken as the
meaning of the latter). In this sense, symbols as connotations are social,
and objects denoted by symbols are "constituted" by social process.
Various, distinct objects of nature, including those of culture, are
determined by the variety and distinction of man's responses in implemental process which mediate social acts initiated or based on his
impulses or needs.(107)

The well known philosophical problem of objects raised by Stebbing
against Jeans and Eddington - which goes back to the ancient controversies of Zeno's paradoxes and others - can be answered by Mead's
social, contextual view of symbols and their objects, as Prof. Hook
pointed out in his review of Mind, Self, and Society.(108) Whether an
object in a situation is appropriately designated by a symbol (e.g., a

---

(106) Mead's terms, "create", "constitute", etc. could be understood
in the sense of Prof. Randall's "formulate" when he says that "sentences
. . . can be said to 'formulate' features, traits and structures" (J. H.
Randall, Jr., "The Art of Language and the Linguistic Situation: A
Naturalistic Analysis", p. 39). In another context, Mead speaks of
"ideas" or connotations of symbols "as attitudes or organized responses
selecting characters of things" (PP 75-6; italics added). Or, in a
"genetic" perspective, Mead says that "it is the gesture arising in
human conduct as means of controlling cooperative conduct which has
become a symbol and thus endowed objects with the meanings by means
of which we can think them" (G. H. Mead, "The Philosophy of John
Dewey", International Journal of Ethics, 1935 [46:4], p. 78; italics
added).
(107) Cf. "Every classification [of 'symbolic forms'] is directed and
dictated by special needs, and it is clear that these needs vary according
to the different conditions of man's social and cultural life" (E. Cassirer,
An Essay on Man, p. 136).
(108) Prof. Hook wrote: "The contrasts between the 'illusionary' solid
substance of things and their 'real' non-experimental scientific character,
dramatically exploited for different ends from Democritus to Eddington,
vanishes in the light of careful inquiry into the role of signs and symbols
in thinking" (S. Hook, "A Philosophic Pathfinder: Mind, Self, and Society
By George H. Mead", The Nation, 1935 [140:3632], p. 196).
As for Stebbing's views against Eddington and others, see: L. S.

symbol in the language of nuclear physics) rather than by another symbol (e. g. , a symbol in ordinary language on furniture) is the problem of appropriate response in reference to the object. The response has to be indicated by the symbol used, and the appropriateness of the response is determined by the end or purpose of the whole act in a perspective of the situation. In denoting an object, a symbol or a type of symbol is not appropriate (or "true") or functional by the "nature" of the symbol in an abstract sense. Only in a perspective of the situation, i. e. , in a consideration of the end involved, can we decide whether one symbol rather than another is appropriate.

And whether an object designated by a symbol is "illusory" or "real" is determined in a perspective of the situation of which the object is a part and in which a certain response, indicated by the symbol used, is carried out as a phase of the whole act. Any object denoted by a symbol is real (in a perspective of the given situation) insofar as the symbol is appropriately used to indicate the response involved in the situation. Certain "illusions" (or "delusions"), as suggested by paranoiac behaviors or as dramatized by some of Don Quixote's misadventures, are the dysfunctional or mistaken efforts in the use of symbols to indicate and carry out certain responses in the situations of which the objects designated by the symbols are not parts. But no object designated by symbolic process is in general or intrinsically "illusory" or "unreal" in terms of some fundamental or unique perspective of situations. (109) Furthermore, there is no justification for the attempt of some philosophers to imagine or presuppose a perspective or a universe in which all the objects designated by symbolic process are illusory or unreal and in which only "things in themselves" or "transcendent forms", or "the unspeakable", are real.

Stebbing, Philosophy and the Physicists (London: Methuen & Co. , 1937). A chapter of its basic argument is reprinted in Philosophy of Science, ed. by A. Danto & S. Morgenbesser (New York: World Publishing Co. , 1960), pp. 69-81.

Cf. G. Ryle, Dilemmas (Cambridge: Cambridge Univ. Press, 1954), Ch. V & VI; N. Goodman, "The Way the World Is", Review of Metaphysics, 1960 (14:1), pp. 48-56.

(109) Cf. PA 7, etc. And J. H. Randall, Jr. Nature and Historical Experience, pp. 131 ff; J. Buchler, Metaphysics of Natural Complexes, Ch. I. In view of Prof. Buchler's briefly suggested criticism of Mead's view of "reality" (p. 4), it is a question whether the above interpretation of denotation is in accordance with Mead's views. We may note that Mead has no generalized hierarchical typology of objects or things as a theory of Reality, and that his views do not imply any "principle of ontological priority" (pp. 30 ff). Mead's statement, "reality exists in a present" (PP 1), is a suggestive, abbreviated version of his view that the question of whether any specific object or process is real in a problematic situation is solved in a present context of human act or experience. This view is a methodological statement. See 2.2.

Cf. "For Mead, an object is anything that can be designated or referred to. It may be physical as a chair or imaginary as a ghost, natural as a

The Meadean contextual approach to symbolic process does not presuppose a metaphysical thesis that a real, substantially distinct world of denotation provides the basis of symbolic process, namely, its connotative function. Nor is it in accord with another thesis that the structures of symbols as connotations "copy" or "picture" (or "isomorphically represent") the relations of what they denote. The iconic aspect of symbols is a function of symbolic process, predominant in certain contexts such as those of making and using maps. But they are a contextually limited or "secondary" function of symbolic process. Fundamentally, symbols are the "instruments of human conduct", implements of man's social mediation. As implements, they are more the extensions of his physiological functions than the "imitation" of nature. In common contexts, the "best" map is not a large, bulky map which "represents" all the details of a given region in miniature and which is too large to be seen in a glance. It is a small, easy-to-see map which "presents" pertinent aspects of the region and which guides our activities of travel, etc. without misleading us. The map is an extension of our visual and other sensitivities as well as of our gestures of isolating and indicating.

For Mead's view of denotation, we do not have to deny that some symbols may be predominantly "expressive" or "exhibitive" in certain contexts in the sense that such a function is not denotative. The contrast of "denotation" with "expression" or "exhibition" is a problem if denoting, especially in the sense of "isomorphic representation" on the basis of some "realism", is construed "exclusively" to be the function of symbols in terms of their connotation. Of course, a four-letter word-sentence, when uttered, does not denote in the same way a biological model does, though it denotes in its own way by selecting and indicating a relation of phases in a type of social situation. Nor does an "abstract" painting, as created or appreciated, denote in the way a unit item in a calendar or directory does. But in spite of a certain thesis of aesthetic "purism", such a work of art as a medium of symbolic process denotes in its way by selecting and formulating a complex of shapes and colours (and motions) as a reproducible, unified form possible in the milieu of human life. Such an aesthetic form is or prevails "in the world" no less than the longitudes and latitudes of the earth, though it may not be very "useful" and so not widely shared. A symbol of one implemental type or genre is likely to denote in a different way from the way a symbol of another type or genre does. In various situations, symbols are used for purposes of social mediation other than that of communicating in terms of clear connotations and distinct denotations.

---

cloud in the sky or man-made as an automobile, material as the Empire State Building or abstract as the concept of liberty, animate as an elephant or inanimate as a vein of coal . . ., definite as a multiplication table or vague as a philosophical doctrine. In short, objects consist of whatever people indicate or refer to" (H. Blumer, "Sociological Implications of the Thought of George Herbert Mead", American Journal of Sociology, 1966 [71:5], p. 539).

3.324 Connotation

Insofar as symbols function to formulate or relate particular objects as examples of universal natures or members of classes, they presuppose at least a logically primitive condition that an individual man's use of them enables him to stimulate certain identical or common responses (or dispositions to respond) in others and himself - in himself as an "other" - in reference to these objects. In this sense, symbols basically designate common responses as their connotations. "The symbols as such are", Mead says, "simply ways of calling out responses. They are not bare words, but words that do answer to certain responses; and when we combine a certain set of symbols, we inevitably combine a certain set of responses" (MS 269).

The development of symbols as implemental sets or systems of organizing and controlling responses is contingent upon their evolved syntactic structures as well as upon common objects in a society, in reference to which they are used. In certain developments of symbols, such as mathematics and metaphysics, their connotations may be very abstract or "vague", and be logically regarded to transcend all particular situations. But, as these symbols logically imply some definite, distinct responses, they still have reference to situations of (actual or possible) social acts.(110)

"I depart", Brewster wrote, "from Mead on two basic points. He held that the relation of meaning exists only in an overt social act, whereas I find meaning present even in non-social behavior. Secondly, he attempts to explain language on the basis of individual gestures, whereas I am forced to conclude that linguistic symbols are by nature the common property of a group, and that it is for this reason that they can function as universals."(111) These two criticisms of Mead's view of "meaning" or connotation amount to a failure to read his statements in their contexts of problems with which he is concerned, and/or to see their proper implications.

First, in the contexts - e.g., MS 10-1 which Brewster quotes from and refers to in stating the above points - where Mead suggests that "the relation of meaning exists only in overt social act", he is concerned with the "genetic" problem of symbolic process. He points out that an explanation of the process of mind or meaning does not presuppose "ideas in mind" in a traditional, subjectivistic sense. He does not imply 1) that "meaning" in the sense of sensitively selected, teleological response to stimuli is not present in situations which are "non-social" in the sense that man's symbolic process is "social". (On the other hand, he uses "social" in a broad sense in certain contexts of his works to refer to both these two different situations.)(112) Nor does he imply 2) that the meaning or connotation of symbols cannot be "internalized" by individual men; and 3) that the "internalized", provisionally private symbolic processes of individual men are not commonly a basis for introducing

---

(110) Cf. PA 117-8.
(111) J. M. Brewster, "A Behavioristic Account of the Logical Function of Universals", Journal of Philosophy, 1936 (33:19 and 20), p. 507.
(112) See 3.11.

new meanings and symbols to social situations.

As for Brewster's second criticism, we may note Mead's view that an attempt to explain symbolic process in a genetic perspective would result in an analysis of the "primitive" situation where individual gestures, as common, reflexive signs, are transformed into mutually significant symbols in role-taking processes. Brewster says that "Mead's logic [of the analysis of such a situation] is flawless."(113) The implication of Mead's view is that a complex or system of symbols develops as the shared property of a given society by means of diffusion and conservation (i.e., in the process of an "infinite" series of role-taking, especially taking roles of generalized others). (114) On the other hand, Brewster makes no attempt to give or suggest an account of how "linguistic symbols [have become] by nature the common property of a group", which an account of the logical function of their universality presupposes.

It is Mead's view that "universals" in traditional philosophy - from Plato's "eternal forms" to Descartes' "innate ideas" and Kant's "transcendental concepts" - can be reinterpreted in terms of symbols as signs of common responses. It would be unnecessary to construe them as more than "common symbols" (PA 52), what Prof. Morris calls "com-symbols". (115) Symbols do not imply any "intrinsically mental ideas", "transcendental essences", or "eternal objects", nor do they require any logically "subsistent" entities to be universally meaningful. The universality of symbols requires only the social unity and identity of responses as long as that sociality is logically open to any possible member who may be able to find himself in the same or similar situations. On the other hand, the universality of symbols does not lie in signs or "names" themselves, as symbolic process always presupposes situations which are involved with more than particulars and signs - that is, it presupposes social situations in which responses to particulars are common or identical. (116)

Symbols are not "surrogates" of objects, but as Mead says, "they bring into the experience of the individual the surrogates of the objects which would complete the acts which the individual initiates" (PA 223).

---

(113) Op. cit., p. 547.
(114) Mead's theory of "role-taking" is explained in the following 3.33.
(115) C. W. Morris, Signs, Language and Behavior, pp. 253 ff.
(116) On this problem of "universality", Prof. Morris notes "five types of universality" or "generality" in terms of his analysis of semiosis: 1) "generality of sign vehicle", its variability; 2) "generality of [legisign] form"; 3) "generality of denotation"; 4) "generality of the interpretant" or connotation; and 5) "social generality" of common, similar response (C. W. Morris, Foundations of the Theory of Signs, pp. 48-52). It is the implication of Mead's views that these five types of "generality" are based on the social process of role-taking. Namely, the first three types are in one important sense derived from or determined by the social conditions of the last two types which are construed to constitute one type, what is considered as the universality of connotations of symbols in the present study of Mead.

Symbols as "universals" function to mediate social acts, providing the control of one's future consequences or distant objects in terms of present, contact factors. Thus, symbolic process brings about or determines the coordinated adjustment of responses and the appropriate use of implements, which constitute the functional condition of social acts, their rationality.

3.33 Symbolic Process: Reflexiveness and Regulativeness

3.331 Symbolic Process in a Functional Perspective (2)

In referring back to Mead's statements (SW 246) quoted in 3.321, we state once more that symbolic process has its function in the social act in which an individual man is related - "in form at least" - to one or more others. In this relation of the individual to the others, symbolic process has two distinguishable functions or processes which may be called 1) "reflexive" (or "role-taking") and 2) "regulative" (or "rule-assuming").

First, a symbolic process is reflexive if in using a symbol the individual stimulates himself as he stimulates others in the given situation. Here the individual takes himself to be an object (or experiences himself as an object) in the way the (specific) others respond to him as an object (or experience him as an object). In this sense, the individual takes a role of the others.

Second, a symbolic process is regulative if in using a symbol the individual stimulates the others and himself as he would stimulate any individual (in the same way) in the situation. Here the individual takes himself to be an object in the way any other individual would respond to him as an object.

In the language of Mead's theory of perspective, (117) we may say that in using a symbol the individual acts in a common perspective which selects an invariant aspect of the others' and his perspectives, so as to open this common perspective to any other individual's perspective which has the invariant aspect. This common or generalized perspective requires only that any variant aspect of the individuals' specific perspectives, which is not selected or "organized" by the generalized perspective, is irrelevant or insignificant in the situation in which the symbol is used. In other words, if some variant aspect of the specific perspectives, which is not or cannot be selected by the given generalized perspective, is found to be relevant in (the individual's specific perspective of) the situation in which the symbol is used, then the generalized perspective is irrelevant or inappropriate for the use of the symbol. Or, such a variant aspect presents to the use of the symbol what is known as an "exception", and the symbolic process is not regulative. In this sense of acting in a generalized perspective or taking the role of a generalized other, the individual assumes a rule.

Symbolic process may be said to be like 1) looking at oneself in a mirror made of others and 2) improvising one's acts in the world (or

---

(117) See Appendix A.3. Cf. MS 89, PA 545 ff. etc.

theater) of this mirror in search of repeatable working roles.

The distinction of reflexiveness and regulativeness is based on Mead's views of "role of others" and "role of generalized other". It is commonly given by him in reference to genetic contexts of symbolic process, but it is construed here in reference to present functional contexts. In a genetic perspective, Mead explains that regulative process is derived from reflexive process. For proper uses of symbols in their contexts, these two functions are inseparable, though they are logically distinguishable. The functional unity or connection of reflexiveness and regulativeness can be understood in the sense 1) that in taking roles of others, one would generalize them, or take them as particulars of a generalized other; or 2) that in taking the role of a generalized other, or assuming a (generalized) rule, in reference to a number of others, one would still interact with each of them as a concrete, particular individual.

In a genetic, especially phylogenic, perspective, we may assume that the genesis of symbolic process requires a series of recurrent, "concrete" relations with others in similar contexts since their responses constitute the significance or connotation of one's reflexive vehicles as symbols. Thus, symbols as unities of denotation and connotation emerge in or are derived from the relations of others to oneself; these relations provide certain "primitive" preconditions of the reflexive and regulative functions such as reflexive vehicles (e.g., vocal gestures) and recurrent common situations. But in functional contexts of the use of symbols, these reflexive and regulative functions are based or dependent on the unities of connotations and denotations. This basis or dependency is evident if it is noted that a symbol signifies a common or identical response in reference to a type or class of particular situations - that is, a response in a role of generalized other or under a universalized rule of act.

The concept of "reflexiveness" is distinct from that of "unity" as an implemental condition, (i/c.1) - namely, the unified relation of the phases of a situation of social act. In a situation, such a unity is "formulated" or "determined" by a reflexive process (or a series of reflexive processes). A symbolic process, or a symbol, presents as its own order or structure a unity insofar as it formulates or determines an implemental unity. And the implemental condition of generality or universality, (i/c.2), is formulated or determined by a regulative, reflexive process. Thus, a symbol is a "universal". In a social, symbolic process, the phases or objects of a situation are related in a unity which is generalized; and in such an order or structure of the unity, each of the objects, including individual men, is respectively "identified", or "unified" in a generalized perspective.

"The self is a social object", Mead says, "like other social objects and is reconstructed like other objects in . . . experience [of social mediation]" (PA 155). In a reflexive, regulative process of using symbols, an individual man organizes and coordinates his functions in a unified, generalized perspective; that is, he forms ("formulates" or "determines") or reforms himself to function as a self, a unitary, consistent individual or a self-conscious person. In a genetic perspective, Mead commonly explains that in a social, symbolic process an individual man emerges and develops as a self: (118)

> In our statement of the development of intelligence we have
> already suggested that the language process is essential for
> the development of the self. The self has a character which is
> different from that of the physiological organism proper. The
> self is something which has a development; it is not initially
> there, at birth, but arises in the process of social experience
> and activity . . . . The intelligence of the lower forms of animal
> life, like a great deal of human intelligence, does not involve a
> self. In our . . . moving about in a world that is simply there
> and to which we are so adjusted that no thinking is involved,
> there is a certain amount of sensuous experience . . ., a bare
> thereness of the world. Such characters about us may exist in
> experience without their place in relationship to the self.
> (MS 135)

> A self . . . is as much a result of the process of evolution as
> other biological forms. A form that can co-operate with others
> through the use of significant symbols, set up attitudes of
> others and respond to them, is possible through the development
> of great tracts in the central nervous system that are connected
> with our processes of articulation, with the ear, and so with the
> various movements that can go on in the human form. But they
> are not circumscribed within the conduct of a single form. They
> belong to the group. And the process is just as much an evolution
> as is the queen bee or the fighter among the ants. In those
> instances we get a certain particular evolution that is taking place,
> belonging to a particular society, one which could exist only in
> such a society. The same is true of the self. That is, an indi-
> vidual who affects himself as he affects another; who takes the
> attitude of the other in so far he affects the other, in so far as
> he is using what we term "intelligible speech"; who knows what
> he himself is saying, in so far as he is directing his indications
> by these significant symbols to others with the recognition that
> they have the same meaning for them as for him; such an indi-
> vidual is, of course, a phase of the development of the social
> form. This is a branch of what we term "behavioristic psy-

---

(118) See Appendix A, especially A.2 and A.3. In various contexts
Mead refers to a "self" by other terms such as "social self" (SW 142),
"social individual" (MT 382), "organized self" (MS 162), "empirical
self" (SW 142), "reflective self" (SW 145), "me" (SW 245), and "socially
self-conscious individual" (MS 347). In the perspective of the present
study, the polar concept of these terms is not what Mead calls "I" (see
the following fn. 3), but "generalized other", "other", "other individual"
or "other social object", on one hand, and "individual organism", "body"
or "biologic individual", on the other. The organism or body is an
abstraction of social objects in the sense that "physical objects" are
explained to be abstractions of social objects.

chology", one in which we can see how the self as such has developed (MT 382-3).

In the organization of the baby's physical experience the appearance of his body as a unitary thing, as an object, will be relatively late, and must follow upon the structure of the objects of his environment. This is as true of the object that appears in social conduct, the self. The form of the social object must be found first of all in the experience of other selves. The earliest achievement of social consciousness will be the merging of the imagery of the baby's first responses and their results with the stimulations of the gestures of others. The child will not succeed in forming an object of himself - of putting the so-called subjective material of consciousness with- in such a self - until he has recognized about him social objects who have arisen in his experience through this process of filling out stimulations with past experiences of response . . . . The mere presence of affective experience, of imagery, of organic sensations, does not carry with it consciousness of a self to which these experiences belong. Nor does the unitary character of the response which tends to synthesize our objects or per- ception convey that same unitary character to the inner ex- perience until the child is able to experience himself as he experiences other selves (SW 139).

The self that is central to all so-called mental activities has appeared only in the social conduct of human vertebrates. It is just because the individual finds himself taking the attitudes of the others who are involved in his conduct that he becomes an object for himself. It is only by taking the roles of others that we have been able to come back to ourselves . . . . The social object can exist for the individual only if the various parts of the whole social act carried out by the other members of the society are in some fashion present in the conduct of the individual . . . . The self can exist for the individual only if he assumes the roles of the others. The presence in the conduct of the individual of the tendencies to act as others act may be, then, responsible for the appearance in the experience of the individual of a social object, i.e., an object answering to complex reactions of a number of individuals, and also for the appearance of the self. Indeed, these two appearances are correlative (SW 283-4).

In a functional perspective, the condition that symbolic process is reflexive and regulative is equivalent to the condition that in the process the individual is a self and the others are social objects. In the symbolic mediation of a social situation, its members function "correlatively" to take the role of each other in terms of the role of a generalized other, or to assume a rule (in a generalized perspective). This condition may be called the "correlative unity" of social members. In another, or a new, perspective of the given situation, the reformation of the individuals

134

as new selves is a consequence of the symbolic mediation. And their society in the situation is reconstructed to the extent that their symbolic process has been based on a certain sustained "correlative unity" between them as social members.

"A universe of discourse that is originated with reference to a self" (SW 246) is a condition of symbolic process. But the unity of a self is no more a presupposition or precondition of a symbolic process than the unity of social objects which are phases of the symbolic process. The condition that symbolic process is reflexive and regulative is equivalent to the condition that a symbolic process is unitary and universal in its function, or that insofar as objects of a social situation are mediated by a symbolic process, they are unified and generalized (in a perspective). In spite of the traditional mode of discoursing on the problem of the unity of judgment or perception in terms of "self" or "ego", (119) we consider the problem in terms of reflexive and regulative processes within the frame of Mead's social behaviorism.

The usefulness of the concepts, "reflexiveness" and "regulativeness", may be suggested in an approach to the problem of distinguishing symbols from other signs, what Mead calls "non-significant gestures" or "signals" (120) The problem can be approached without introducing the substantial notion of "self" and "ego" as a precondition or presupposition for symbolic process, or without relying on the unsatisfactory notion of the "fixed particularity" of denotation for other sign processes. Mead accepts the common observation that certain organisms other than man, such as bees and chimpanzees, communicate for their "limited" ends by means of their "gestures" in conjunction with their sensitivities. Not without a reservation, (121) however, he explains that in distinction from man's symbolic process, such a communication is a "conversation of gestures" which function as "signals" to other organisms but not to the organisms who make them. That is, the "conversation" is not reflexive (and so not regulative).

First, in a social situation - "social" not necessarily in the anthropo-

_____

(119) Mead's concept of "I" or "ego" (MS 199) - in an analysis, his concepts of "I" - is a residue of the substantial concept of "ego" or "subjectivity" in traditional philosophy. For a number of reasons, it is not construed to be a basic, required concept of social act and rationality in the present anthropological study of Mead's works. In certain contexts Mead explains quite diverse phases of social act in terms of "I", but in other contexts he explains the same diverse phases in terms of organic functions and environmental conditions, on one hand, and in terms of other phases of social act and self (or self-consciousness), on the other, without invoking 'the invisible 'I' " (MS 373 which is supposedly "never experienced" in the context of its function. Cf. W. L. Kolb, "A Critical Evaluation of Mead's 'I' and 'Me' Concepts", Social Forces, 1944 (22:3), pp. 291-6.
(120) Cf. MS 63, 81, 190, etc. Also see: C. W. Morris, Signs, Language, and Behavior, pp. 25 ff.
(121) See 3.13, fn. 9.

logical sense(122) - any phase of the activities of an individual organism is a "signal" if it is not reflexive, that is, if the individual is not stimulated by it in the way another organism (or self-conscious person) is stimulated by it, as a sign of something else. Here the individual does not take the role of the other, and the sign is not significant to the individual as it is to the other. The individual is unable to control, assert or modify, his own further activities by adjusting himself to the other's subsequent activities as the consequence or effect of the signal-stimuli unless the other's activities are introduced to the individual as a signal (or a symbol). In an anthropological perspective, such a signal is a "symptom" in a broad sense; it is what Prof. Morris calls a "diagnostic sign".(123) On the other hand, we extend the use of the terms "sign" or "signal" in this sense to contexts of "physical" objects so as to designate relations of various processes. For example, we take "smoke" as the sign of "fire", or "falling of leaves" as the signal for the "coming of winter", in a certain context.

Second, any phase of a given social situation is merely a "signal" if the individual is stimulated by it as a sign of something else for his further activities without taking the role of the other, to whom this phase is a signal in the first sense or a symbol.(124) Here a signal is a sign which substitutes a contextually confined particular object or specific type of objects for a stimulus to the individual, and which determines his response in the way the object(s) itself does. The explanation of "signal" in this second sense is the common approach of explicating signs or signals distinguished from symbols. "A sign or signal is related", Cassirer wrote, "to the thing to which it refers in a fixed and unique way."(125)

---

(122) See 3.11, especially its fn. 2.
(123) C. W. Morris, Foundations of the Theory of Signs, p. 39.
(124) Here "social" is not, once more, necessarily in the anthropological sense. And "other" does not necessarily refer to organisms; it can be an inanimate object.

If we understand "social" in the anthropological sense, a sign or "signal" is "not . . . in itself inherently social" (J. H. Randall, Jr., Nature and Historical Experience, p. 255). Thus, we may understand Prof. Randall's following statement in which the above quoted words are found: "Linguistic or group signs are social and shared. 'Signifying' in general does not seem to be in itself inherently social - I think Mead was mistaken on this point. Signifying occurs whenever conditioning of responses has taken place. But linguistic signs and conditioning are obviously a group or social matter" (ibid.). "Signifying" in the sense of "signal" is, of course, not social in the sense symbols are social.
(125) E. Cassirer, An Essay on Man, p. 16. His term "fixed" has a double connotation in the ordinary sense: first, "narrowly confined" or "inflexibly limited"; second, "permanently set" or "durably established". In the context of the statement, Cassirer's emphasis is, properly, on the first connotation - properly because there is some question whether communication in terms of "signals" is necessarily "fixed" in the sense of the second connotation.

What is called the "conditioned reflex" or "Pavlovian conditioning" (126) is a habit formation of an individual organism by means of signals in the second sense. In contrast, what Mead calls a "self-conditioning" (127) is a habit formation of an individual organism by means of his use of symbols, i.e., his self-conscious process. (When a group of individua. men go through an identical or similar habit formation, they constitute an institution as explained in 3.231.) In a self-conditioning, the effect or consequence of denoted objects is indirect or mediate on the individual In one important sense, that is, the objects are not necessarily required to be present in "localized" or "spatio-temporally limited" situations in which the symbols function. Here the response of the individual to the objects is "intrinsically" inhibited and delayed, as explained in 3.12 and 3.13, though it may not be blocked and delayed by external conditions in certain contexts. In a Pavlovian conditioning, the effect or consequence of denoted objects is direct, if not immediate, on the individual. That is, the objects are necessarily required to be present in "localized" situations in which the signals function. Here the responses are "intrinsically" uninhibited and undelayed, though they may be blocked or destroyed by external conditions in certain contexts.

The above explanation of "signals" in both the first and second sense suggests that the concepts of connotation and denotation which we have construed for symbols are respectfully modified in applying them to "signals". In present contexts of man's social acts, however, what may be, in an analysis, construed as "signals" - such as certain mannerisms (in the first sense) or certain fetishistic stimuli (in the second sense) - functions commonly as parts of symbolic process, that is, they are mediated by symbols like all other implements - except in extreme cases of pathological disorders. Consider the case of criminals who skillfully remove their fingerprints and other traces from the scene of the crime, or the case of obese persons who try to stay away from certain types of food and from the conditions related to them. It is difficult to point out some contexts in which an individual man's social acts are completely determined by a "signal" or a set of "signals" which is not, for better or worse, intertwined with and manipulated by some contextually involved symbols.

In a society in which a large body or system of symbols emerges, its individual members who have assimilated the mechanism of symbolic process can transform and extend "the relation with others", i.e., the reflexive process, to carry on symbolic process with individuals, including objects other than men, who are not "reflexive" in their response. Such a transformed extension appears, "uncritically" in anthropomorphic mythical attitudes and rituals, and "critically", in our attitudes and activities in aesthetic creations and in living with sick or helpless men and domesticated animals. (128) In a similar way, a man can respond to his own "body" as an "other" to interpret its non-reflexive symptomatic

---

(126) MS 9 and 102 ff; MT 190-1. Cf. I. P. Pavlov, Conditioned Reflexes.
(127) MS 108 and 121 ff.
(128) Cf. SW 313, MS 154 fn., etc.

manifestations reflexively and regulatively in terms of other symbols, or to transform them into symbols as in contexts of medical analysis, theater, and other implemental processes.

In the beginning of 3.321, we have explained in what sense Mead construes symbolic process as the "mechanism" of man's social acts. Prof. Buchler also speaks of "communication, the guiding <u>mechanism</u> of proception", (129) man's "directed activity". (130)

"If we understand 'sign' ", Prof. Buchler wrote, "in the narrower sense (as a proxy for something else) rather than in the possible broader sense (as a means of further judgment), we must surely conclude that communication is not carried on in terms of signs alone."(131) Here the distinction of "sign" in the two different senses breaks down if a "sign" as "a means of further judgment" is construed to be a repeatable medium of communication in the recurrence of similar situations of communication.(132) Prof. Buchler goes further: "But even in the broader sense of 'sign', there can be essential phases in a communication situation besides the uses of signs."(133) On the other hand, precisely because a communication or symbolic process is a process of using "signs" as "proxies" to select and relate important, pertinent - i.e., "essential" - phases of various situations, the symbolic process is effective in its functions of selectively manipulating and assimilating certain phases of the given situation in anticipation of future situations as well as in relation to past situations, and in its functions of informing, directing, inviting, and persuading others.

In the life of men as members of a society, no situation is so isolated or unique that it is encountered or experienced in itself without some "signs" recalled from past situations and assimilated in view of future situations. The common problems or tasks in situations of human communication, as those of the purposive, directed mediation of social acts, are not so much whether we can interact and adjust somehow, possibly by our physiological sensitivities, or whether we can manipulate or use all phases of a situation as signs or symbols; as whether we can selectively manipulate and reformulate, and communicate and assimilate, contextually pertinent phases of a given situation in terms of a limited set of repeatable symbols. In the "arts" or "crafts" of politics, economics, sciences, and other enterprises of man, our crucial and pervasive tasks are to invent (or learn) and use certain means by which we can anticipate and control our further activities and by which we can intensify and preserve what have been valuable activities. These means are provided by a type of communicative articulation, namely, symbols

---

(129) J. Buchler, <u>Toward a General Theory of Human Judgment</u>, p. 54; italics added.

(130) <u>Op. cit.</u>, p. 4.

(131) J. Buchler, <u>Nature and Judgment</u>, p. 156.

(132) This assumption is supported by Prof. Buchler's following statement: "In fact it is doubtful that any product of query can be considered the outcome of a 'single' project" (<u>Toward a General Theory of Human Judgment</u>, p. 54).

(133) <u>Nature and Judgment</u>, p. 156.

in the sense we have used, which mediates the use of implements in social situations. (134)

3.332 Reflexive Process: Role-taking

In 3.224, we have explained that human intelligence is basically the individual man's capacity to be reflexive, his sensitivity to his own stimuli in the way they stimulate other persons and things, and that social implements are, in one sense, the extension and elaboration of this reflexive function in the development of human life.

In a genetic perspective of symbolic process, Mead says:

Communication is a social process whose natural history shows that it arises out of cooperative activities, such as those involved in sex, parenthood, fighting, herding, and the like, in which some phase of the act of one form, which may be called a gesture, acts as a stimulus to others to carry on their parts of the social act. It does not become communication in the full sense, i.e., the stimulus does not become a significant symbol, until the gesture tends to arouse the same response in the individual who makes it that it arouses in the others. The history of the growth of language shows that in its earlier stages the vocal gesture(135) addressed to another awakens in the individual who makes the gesture not simply the tendency to the response which it calls forth in the other, such as the seizing of a weapon or the avoiding of a danger, but primarily the social role which the other plays in the cooperative act. This is indicated in the early play period in the development of the child, and in the richness in social implication of language structures in the speech of primitive peoples (SW 312).

In a functional perspective, Mead says:

In the human group . . ., the person who uses [a symbol or significant] gesture and so communicates assumes the attitude of the other individual as well as calling it out in the other. He himself is in the role of the other person whom he is so exciting and influencing. It is through taking this role of the other that he is able to come back on himself and so direct his own

---

(134) Cf. "When we learn to do something, what we learn is always a principle . . . . To learn to do anything is never to learn to do an individual act; it is always to learn to do acts of a certain kind in a certain kind of situation; and this is to learn a principle . . . . Thus without principles we could not learn anything whatever from our elders . . . . But even if each generation were able to teach itself, it could not do so without principles; for self-teaching, like all other teaching, is the teaching of principles" (R. M. Hare, The Language of Morals, New York: Oxford Univ. Press, 1964 [orig. 1952], pp. 60-1).
(135) Mead's emphasis on the import of vocal gestures as reflexive vehicles has been explained in 3.224.

process of communication. This taking the role of the other, an
expression I have so often used, is not simply of passing
importance . . . . The immediate effect of such role-taking
lies in the control which the individual is able to exercise
over his own response . . . . It is this control of the response
of the individual himself through taking the role of the other
that leads to the value of this type of communication from the
point of view of the organization of the conduct in the group.
It carries the process of co-operative activity farther than
it can be carried in the herd as such, or in the insect society
(MS 254-5).

In functional contexts of symbolic process, responses of others are
anticipated by oneself in terms of the common denotation and connotation of symbols; and one's responses to others' are pre-disposed or
prepared in advance. In a functional perspective, Mead says: "symbol
is nothing but the stimulus whose response is given in advance" (MS 181).
Insofar as symbols are used reflexively, i.e., to stimulate oneself as
they stimulate others, we arouse in ourselves the attitudes or dispositions of others and place ourselves in their roles; and we can respond
to others to further the adjustment of our responses. And insofar as the
others respond through the same reflexive process, we are able to
transact in our "correlative" roles in terms of a common, "mirrored"
perspective of symbols.
On Mead's concept of role-taking, Prof. Morris wrote:

Mead seems to vacillate somewhat on this point: at times he
talkes as if role-taking were a precondition of the significant
symbol and at times as if it were made possible by such symbols. The ambiguity is at least partially resolved if we recognize
two senses of role-taking: 1) the sense in which a person simply
as a fact responds to a sound he makes as others respond, and
2) the sense in which a person identifies the response he makes
to this sound as the kind of response another person makes.
. . . The distinction is important since there is no evidence
that taking the roles of the other in 2) the latter sense is
required to explain the genesis of the language sign. Mead
seems at times to avoid the difficulties in the analysis of
language by invoking the notion of role-taking. (136)

The "ambiguity" of the concept of "role-taking" Prof. Morris finds in
Mead's theory of symbols arises if we do not observe that although his
theory is predominantly presented in a perspective of their "genesis",
or, as explained in 3.31, of their "functional genesis", many of his
statements in his works are misleading unless they are entirely taken

---

(136) C. W. Morris, Signs, Language, and Behavior, pp. 45-6. The
numbers "1" and "2" are added. Just before what is quoted here, Prof.
Morris specifically refers to SW 244-5 by quoting a part from it, which
is written entirely in a functional perspective of symbolic process.

in a perspective of their functions. In his genetic perspective, further-more, Mead presents a logical reconstruction of the transformation of "non-significant gestures" into symbols. Here Mead's reconstruction presupposes the recurrence of similar common situations, the diffusion of selected common gestures and other signs of communication, etc. Mead speaks of "what a long road speech or communication has to travel from the situation where there is nothing but vocal cries to the situation in which significant symbols are utilized" (MS 67). In a functional per-spective, role-taking in the first sense is an abstraction in the sense that man's signs of communication without common connotative and denotative references are abstractions.

In both a genetic and a functional perspective, gestures and other vehicles of physiologically (or implementally produced) reflexive nature - namely, the mechanism of role-taking in the first sense - is a precon-dition of symbols. But in the contexts of their use, they function as symbols of common connotative and denotative references. Thus, role-taking in the second sense of identifying or anticipating the responses of others and the objects in distant experience is the very function of the use of reflexive vehicles as symbols, not a consequence made possible or followed by the use of symbols. Of course, the reflexive function is a matter of degree contingent on various contextual factors, as Mead says: "The more we do call out in ourselves the response which our gestures call out in the other, the more we understand him" (MS 271).

In certain contexts, a non-reflexive or reflexive (in the first sense) vehicle is transformed into a symbol by the reflexive function (in the second sense) based on the use of other symbols. Consider a comedian's discovery of an unusual body posture as a suggestive satire, or a foreigner's discovery of a new use and meaning of an old implement on his visit to a new land (e. g., one of his country's old folk songs as an-other country's national anthem). In reference to the new vehicle, the reflexive function of taking a new role of the other (or the role of a new other) emerges in the very use of the vehicle as a reflexive symbol.

We may consider the reflexive function of symbolic process in reference to three different social situations. 1) In the situations which are commonly occasions of impulsive or emotional reactions, men can utter words or make gestures in undelayed immediacy or urgency, stimulating others without fully indicating to themselves the significance of their words or gestures and anticipating the others' responses even when they hear their own words or see their own gestures. 2) In the situations of persuading or commanding others, formulating theories, creating works of art, etc., the significance of symbols - at least as a gestaltic unit - is re-introduced or emerges reflexively in the second sense. 3) In the situations of "absent-minded" or routine acts, men immediately interact with each other in adjustment of their responses without requiring any effort of role-taking in terms of the use of specific symbols. The third type of situation is based on the second type, as the acts of the third type are (implementally and) symbolically pre-mediated. And the first type can occur as provisional parts of a person or a society without a destructive or disintegrating effect only if the person or the society as a whole is largely based on the second type. In the sense that symbolic process refers primarily to the second type, role-taking in the second sense (Prof. Morris explained) is the function of symbolic process.

Mead says:

> It is by means of reflexiveness – the turning-back of the experience of the individual upon himself – that the whole social process is thus brought into the experience of the individuals involved in it; it is by such means, which enable the individual to take the attitude of the other toward himself, that the individual is able consciously to adjust himself to that process in any given social act in terms of his adjustment to it. Reflexiveness, then, is the essential condition, within the social process, for the development of mind (MS 134). (137)

Reflexiveness is the basic social process of man's organized and creative life. Because we are reflexive in relation to other persons and things, we live together as members of a society (or a society of societies), and we reconstruct our environment as our implements. We may translate Descartes' cogito, ergo sum in the following way: We speak to other persons and ourselves and we think of other things and ourselves; therefore, we are. The translation is not the fundamental "intuition" of "mind" or "ego" (or "soul"), from which a whole "metaphysical" system of the universe can be deduced. Instead, it is a conclusion from social experience, which is supported by, and which supports, other generalizations about man and his universe. A doubt – not a Cartesian "universal doubt", (138) but a doubt in a contextually limited situation – is a difficulty in reflexive process. A failure in or an inability for reflexiveness is commonly a problem or an indication of a problematic situation. Any prolonged and/or extensive indifference to the reflexive process needed in a society is commonly an indication of a forthcoming crisis.

---

(137) In another context, Mead suggests: "Spearman's 'X factor' in intelligence – the unknown factor which, according to him, intelligence contains – is simply . . . this ability of the intelligent individual to take . . . the attitudes of others, thus realizing the significations . . . of the symbols . . . in terms of which thinking proceeds; and thus being able to carry on with himself the internal conversation with these symbols . . . which thinking involves" (MS 141). Cf. C. E. Spearman, The Abilities of Man, their Nature and Measurement (New York: Macmillan, 1927); C. E. Spearman & L. W. Jones, Human Ability (London: Macmillan, 1950).

(138) Descartes' "universal doubt" may be, in Mead's language, translated as a question whether the totality of others (persons and things) is real or not, as it appears in himself or appears to constitute his self. Descartes' "immediate" restoration of his doubting being, a symbol-using "ego", implies prima facie the affirmation of the reality of the others.

A doubt, or an experience of doubting, appears in a perspective of a given or selected context in which an individual man is not certain if some phase of an act appears in the experience of others, or any other,

3.333 Reflexive Process and Other Social Processes

We may consider how or in what sense the reflexive function of symbolic process is the basic "mechanism" of man's social mediation by distinguishing it from and yet relating it to other types of his social process.

Mead makes a distinction between "role-taking" and "role-playing". The distinction is not clearly indicated by these terms as understood in ordinary English. Possibly for the same reason, the distinction is not clearly made in the contemporary literature of sociology and psychology in which the concepts are used. (139) But an elementary distinction must be clearly kept between 1) "role-taking" or "reflexive process", on one hand, and 2) "role-playing" (or "role-performing", or "role-presenting"), "playing-at-a-role" (as in games of children and in theatrical acting), "role-originating" (or "role-creating"), and "role-acquiring" (or "role-learning"), on the other. The pertinent distinction involved is that between 1') taking or (anticipating) a role of others in relation to oneself and 2') playing (or carrying out, or presenting) one of one's own roles in relation to others.

For example, a woman takes or assumes her son's role as a baby in relation to herself in calling him for dinner and feeding him. And she plays or carries out her role of a mother or parent in relation to him. At the same time, she may be taking a role of her "former self" as a child in relation to her mother, and she plays her own role of a parent, which may not be, in an important aspect, like the role her mother played to the child. She may be also taking a role of another child in relation to his mother, as portrayed in a novel, and she plays her own role of a parent, which may be, in an important aspect, like the role this mother plays in the novel. In turn, the son who cries and is fed plays or carries out his role of a baby in relation to his mother, probably without taking her role of a parent. Furthermore, in relation to a neighbor who happens to watch the whole scene of the dinner at a distance, the woman may have merely "presented" her role of an indulgent parent or something else without taking the role of a "watcher"

---

in the way it appears to himself. The context, or the perspective itself as a whole cannot be doubted within the given context or perspective. As soon as it is subject to a doubt, it is placed in another, a more "inclusive", perspective, or in a perspective of another, a "larger", context.

It is impossible in experience or "in principle" to doubt everything "at once", or to try to formulate a question whether the universe as a whole, including the question itself and the questioner himself, is real or not. If the given universe as the total complex of actual and possible experience is subject to doubt as a perfect deception of the Devil or a coherent dream, it still exists as, and is, what it is, because that is all we have.

(139) Cf. W. Coutu, "Role-playing vs. Role-taking: An Appeal for Clarification", American Sociological Review, 1951 (16:2), pp. 180-7; L. J. Neiman & J. W. Hughes, "The Problem of the Concept of Role - A Re-survey of the Literature", Social Forces, 1951 (30:2), pp. 141-9.

in relation to herself as a "person watched". On the other hand, she may have, self-consciously, taken the role of a yet-to-be-born grandchild, to whom her own son will play his role of a parent.

It is possible that an individual man plays a role, his role, without taking the role of others which is related to his own role. It is possible only to the extent that his role-playing, as an isolated social process, is based on signals in both the first and second senses of "signal" as explained earlier in 3.331. Otherwise, that is, insofar as the individual plays his roles in terms of symbolic mediation, his role-playing is based on his role-taking, even in the context where he refuses to relate or accommodate himself to the others' role-playing.

In another perspective, we can distinguish "role-taking" from common types of man's activities such as 1) cooperation and sympathy, 2) strife and war, 3) projection and "interpersonal analogy", and 4) imitation and conformity. (140) But all of them are, not in one and the same way but in various ways, based on role-taking as a function of symbolic process. One of these types such as "imitation" has been selected by philosophers and psychologists as the basic, pervasive process of man to explain all the other activities, including symbolic process. It is Mead's view that in terms of the reflexive function of symbolic process all of them can be explicated, while in terms of such a process as "cooperation" or "imitation", symbolic process as well as the other activities could not be fully explicated.

Symbolic process is, in a broad sense, a "cooperative", "sympathetic" act with or toward others. Not only in a genetic, but also in a functional perspective, symbolic process, including its reflexive function, is largely based on and supported by the social attitudes or dispositions of cooperation and sympathy. The common responses connoted and the common objects denoted by symbols presuppose the experiences and histories of cooperative activities in various degrees in a given society. As Mead says, "the probable beginning of human communication was in cooperation, not in imitation" (SW 101). On the other hand, cooperation as elaborate, prolonged and/or organized activities, and sympathy as actively cooperative and/or implemental dispositions (especially in reference to distant or future persons and objects) are mediated by symbolic process, its reflexive (and regulative) function.

Mead says:

To take a distinctively human, that is, self-conscious, social attitude toward another individual, or to become aware of him as such, is to identify yourself sympathetically with him, by taking his attitude toward, and his role in, the given social situation, and by thus responding to that situation implicitly as he does or is about to do explicitly . . . . Human social activities depend very largely upon social co-operation among the human

---

(140) Commonly related to the present problem are other types such as "empathy", "identification", and "learning". Cf. R. E. O'Toole, "Experiments in George Herbert Mead's Taking the Role of the Other ", Ph. D. Dissert., Eugene: Univ. of Oregon, 1963.

individuals who carry them on, and such co-operation results
from the taking by these individuals of social attitudes toward
one another (MS 300).

Furthermore, symbolic role-taking appears to be distinct from, and
fundamental in comparison to, the activities of cooperation and sympathy.
Human conflicts and strifes, which occur mostly in institutional matrixes,
can be explained in terms of the former, but not in terms of the latter.
In certain situations, men are involved in conflict precisely because they
have failed to "cooperate" or take the role of the opponent; "peace" lies
in further cooperation and communication toward taking the roles of
each other. On the other hand, in the situations where certain identical
or common ends of men or communities emerge to be in conflict in the
face of the scarcity of implements, etc., men go to "duel" or battle
precisely because they are symbolically able to take the roles of the
opponent.
"Role-taking", as Mead understands it, is an entirely different concept in contrast to "projecting" or "analogical reasoning" from one's
self to other persons, or from one's mind to other minds, as understood
in the traditional philosophy and psychology of empiricism. As a
methodic approach of introducing and justifying the use of certain symbols in reference to the "subjective" (or "physiologically inaccessible-
to-others" and "provisionally private")(141) phases of man, the traditional concepts of "projection" and "interpersonal analogy" present a
skepticism and a "solipsistic" psychology, which are not justified by
common experience and by the practice of contemporary psychologists.
"In human social conduct", Mead says, "certain gestures . . . arouse
in the individual who makes them a response that is of the same nature
as that which they call out in those with whom [he is] engaged . . . .
One finds oneself already in the attitude of the other.. . . It is a mistake
to assume that the self has projected itself into the other, for the self
arises as an object in the same process. Solipsism is a psychologically
impossible doctrine" (PA 150).
"Role-taking" is distinguished from "projecting" in the sense understood in contemporary psychoanalysis and ordinary language. A "projecting" of a phase of oneself to another person is not the process by
which a symbol (or a set of symbols) which suggests or states what is
projected is produced and used to function as a symbol of common
connotation and denotation. In social, symbolic process, we can project
many things into others on the basis or as a consequence of role-taking.
When an individual projects a specific attitude, for example, in uttering
or entertaining the statement that "we all hate our parents", the significance of the statement is not based on the process of projecting in a
"solipsist" fashion that "I hate my parents and so everyone else hates
his or her parents." The significance is probably a result of a previous
series of symbolic processes. When he utters such a statement to a
friend in a new situation, its significance (or non-significance) is re-
introduced by (or emerges to) himself as the friend responds to it. After

---

(141) See Appendix A.4.

a new conversation with the friend, he may change his "mind" or reform his "self" to project the same attitude more "strongly", or to project a modified attitude to the effect of concluding that "everyone, except the sissy boys like his friend, hates his or her parents". In a genetic perspective, Mead says: "The content of [an] act . . . is projected into the other only in the sense in which it is projected into the self" (SW 314).

If we resort, in a certain problematic situation, to an interpersonal analogical argument for the justification of the use of a symbol, it is nothing but a new attempt of role-taking as a consequence of other role-takings. It is not radically different from other analogical arguments used in contexts such as our relations with physical objects, in which some factor is technically or otherwise difficult to experience and explain directly. As an example, a psychologist or an ordinary man may have a problem of knowing, in view of certain physiological differences, what process or state of process a person of the other sex exactly refers to by the idea of "orgasm". In certain contexts, we resort to an analogical reasoning, but in the long run we may attempt to achieve certain symbols of common connotations and denotations after a series of experiments or experiences.

In a logical analysis, "projections" may have the proper "logical form" of analogical argument. But these social processes are characterized, as a psychological concept, by the fact that they are commonly directed or determined by some "strong" or "preoccupied" motives or ends of the individuals who project. On the other hand, "interpersonal analogies" are a type of projection which is directed by the general end of introducing and justifying some symbols in certain problematic contexts. It is prima facie evident that the complex of man's symbols has not developed primarily on the basis of "analogical reasoning" and "projection", because in a good part of symbolic process they are simply not necessary. On the other hand, they are symbolic processes. In this sense, "analogical reasoning" and "projection" are based on the reflexive function of symbolic process.

As a criticism of Mead's view of the reflexive function of symbolic process, it is suggested that "we do not think of ourselves as others think of us, but as we think others think of us". (142) If the quoted statement implies that the difference between "ourselves as others think of us" and "ourselves as we think others think of us" is invariably constant, though in different degrees, in all contexts of social life, it is very difficult in terms of such a view of man's social process to explain the common basis for the development and function of symbols. On the other hand, the very process of discovering such a difference presupposes a common basis of social processes in spite of differences. Furthermore, certain differences between "ourselves as others think of us" and "ourselves as we think others think of us" in certain limited contexts can be explained in terms of social conditions of symbolic process and in terms of the physiological capacities and acquired capacities and dis-

---

(142) K. D. Naegele, "Editorial Foreword" to a section, "Interaction: Roles and Collectivities", in Theories of Society, ed. by T. Parsons et al. (New York: Free Press, 1961), p. 155.

positions of social members for role-taking in the contexts.

Mead's view of symbolic, reflexive process does not imply that all men always use symbols in carrying out their acts in social situations, or that all men are always reflexive in their social situations. Men are reflexive in the situations in which we mediate our acts in terms of symbols. That is, we can think of ourselves as others think of us in these situations. On the other hand, Mead's view does not imply that we always accept what others think of us, or we always imitate or conform to others in the symbolic process of social acts. Such an act of communication is a process of "correlative" role-takings, in which not only an individual takes the roles the others play, but also the others are expected by the individual to take the roles he plays.

In one of the recent experimental studies on Mead, his theory of "taking the role of the other" was "operationalized" and tested in terms of the three experiments of "baby feeding", "body sway" after the motion of others, and identification of the left and right "sideness" of others; it was concluded that "in each of the experiments the TRO [i.e., taking the role of the other] model could account for more of the observed behavior than alternative models", mainly that of imitation, and that "the TRO concept . . . has validity as a concept which signifies a process of interaction". (143)

Mead says:

> Under the influence of social instincts, animals and young children or primitive peoples may be stimulated to many reactions which are like those which directly or indirectly are responsible for them without there being any justification for the assumption that the process is one of imitation . . . . But by what possible mechanism, short of a miracle, the conduct of one form [i.e., organism] should act as a stimulus to another to do, not what the situation calls for, but something like that which the first form is doing, is beyond ordinary comprehension . . . . An organization of social instincts gives rise to many situations which have the outward appearance of imitation, but these situations - those in which, under the influence of social stimulation, one form does what others are doing - are no more responsible for the appearance in consciousness of other selves that answer to our own than are the situations which call out different and even opposed reactions . . . . The sight of a man pushing a stone registers itself as a meaning through a tendency in ourselves to push the stone, but it is a far call from this to the statement that it is first through imitation of him or some one else pushing stones that we have gained the motor-idea of stone-pushing.

> The important character of social organization of conduct or behavior through instincts is not that one form in a social group does what the others do, but that the conduct of one

---

(143) O'Toole, op. cit., p. 68.

form is a stimulus to another to a certain act, and that this
act again becomes a stimulus at first to a certain reaction,
and so on in ceaseless interaction. The likeness of the actions
is of minimal importance compared with the fact that the actions
of one form have the implicit meaning of a certain response to
another form. The probable beginning of human communication
was in cooperation, not in imitation, where conduct differed and
yet where the act of the one answered to and called out the act
of the other.

The conception of imitation as it has functioned in social
psychology needs to be developed into a theory of social
stimulation and response and of the social situations which
these stimulations and responses create. Here we have the
matter and the form of the social object, and here we have
also the medium of communication and reflection (SW 100-1).

It is clear that imitation in the sense of an attempt to repeat and model
after the processes of others presupposes or is based on a symbolic
process of taking roles of others – persons or things. In spite of the
common fact that certain birds can be conditioned to "imitate" the sounds
of others, it is Mead's view that "imitation seems to belong to the
human form, where it has reached some sort of independent conscious
[or self-conscious] existence" (MS 59). It is not denied, on the other
hand, that the conditioning process which is evident in the "imitative"
process of birds and other animals is also a part of man's processes,
particularly in our physiological conditioning involved in habit forma-
tions which symbolic process utilizes and controls.

For some reason, Mead's concept of "role-taking" has been sometimes understood as a strange mixture of "passive receptivity" and
"active imitation" in the sense of "conformism" or "other-directed
determinism". It appears that Mead's common statement, "one takes
the roles of others", is read as "one plays the roles of others". One
does not, according to Mead, play the roles of others in taking them;
he plays his own roles. (On the stage, an actress "plays" or "plays at"
the role of Cleopatra; but she plays the role of an actress in taking the
role of an audience.)

Consider the following three statements:

1) One is determined by the process in which one takes or
assumes the roles of others. (E.g., in a situation where an old
woman and a little boy are involved, she takes or assumes the
role of a grandchild.)

2) One is determined by the process in which one plays or acts
out one's own roles, the roles one plays. (E.g., the old woman
plays the role of a grandmother.)

3) One is determined by the process in which one plays or acts
out the roles of others, the roles others play. (E.g., the old
woman plays or acts out the role of a grandchild.)

The first and second constitute Mead's concepts of "role-taking" and "role-playing", but the third is not necessarily implied by Mead's concepts. In taking the roles of others, one is not necessarily determined, in a sense of "imitating" or "conforming", by these roles any more than one is not necessarily undetermined by them.

3.334 Regulative Process: Role of Generalized Other

If one speaks of a society of men as a structure, it is, in one important sense, a structure of institutionalized roles (144) ranging from those of family and school to those of economic and political organizations. Individual men participate in a variety of these roles in their daily living, and organize them as a large part of their career and personality. In terms of these institutional or "habitual" roles in which members of a society engage, they "correlatively" anticipate carrying out certain pre-assigned functions and responding in certain pre-set ranges of act.

Besides these institutional roles, individual men find themselves in certain prevalent roles - from those of "visitor-host" and "questioner-answerer" to those of fighters and lovers - in terms of casual or exigent events they encounter or choose to encounter. These roles are recurrent in a society, but they are not clearly pre-defined or pre-arranged for the range and variety of response within them. In the sense that the individuals respond within certain socially developed "limits", and, in some contexts, against certain dominant institutions, these roles are only "negatively" pre-defined. In their recurrent prevalency, they also constitute institutions in a society, though they are usually not any "habit" of individual men in the ordinary sense of English.

Over these institutional roles - not necessarily against them - individual men can engage in "extraordinary" roles of pioneer, discoverer, prophet, revolutionary, and so forth. In certain contexts, these roles are against or apart from on-going conditions of social life, and appear to transcend any relation with members of the given present society. Nevertheless, they do presuppose the present society as well as distant or future societies; they are social roles in relation to other members of the present society, ultimately confronting these members with crisis or "drama".

We may note certain aspects of these roles in view of relating them to the reflexive and regulative functions of symbolic process. First, these roles are transactional or interactional between members of a society. Second, they are implemental in social processes in which man's common impulses, biologically undetermined as principles of social organization, are expressed and determined. Third, in the "core" of all these roles are symbols which organize and mediate the relations of social members in, before and/or after their direct transactions. If we understand symbolic process, as Mead construes it, in terms of common responses in reference to common objects in social situations, roles as structures of responses are symbolic structures. These roles are what Mead calls "roles of generalized others", roles prescribed or

---

(144) "Institution" as an implemental process, and its relation to "habit", have been explained earlier in 3.13 and 3.231.

defined by symbols of common generalities: unwritten or written statutes institutional policies, religious myths, political ideologies, conventions of commerce, theories of science, forms of arts and crafts, rules of games, labels and names, and so forth.

In other words, the role of a generalized other in a social act is the invariant implemental function of the others - including oneself as an "other" to others - as a whole in reference to their common or identical end. It emerges in or is based on an organized common perspective of their situation, to which any individual difference other than those subservient aspects involved in their invariant function is irrelevant. And the common perspective is selected and indicated by a symbol.

The roles of others an individual man takes in a social act are specific or unique as the others are particular individuals. But in the predominant contexts of social act in which the roles are taken in terms of symbols which designate common responses in reference to common objects, they are regarded as the specialized or particularized roles of "generalized others". "The individual does not . . .", Mead says, "assume the attitudes [or roles] of the numberless others who are in one way or another implicated in his social conduct, except insofar as the attitudes of others are uniform under like circumstances. One assumes . . . the attitudes of generalized others" (SW 291). Insofar as a social act is mediated in terms of symbolic process, the role of a generalized other is re-introduced to, or emerges in, the situation of specific or particular others with reference to the particular objects involved. And the individual functions as a self, a "generalized" unity in which phases of the act are related and organized and in terms of which identical or similar acts have been and/or will be repeated. As suggested in 3.331, the function of symbolic process which mediates social acts in terms of the roles of generalized others is regarded as its "regulative" function.(145)

---

(145) In this context, we may note one of the criticisms against Mead in G. A. de Laguna's article, "Communication, the Act, and the Object with Reference to Mead" (Journal of Philosophy, 1946 [43:9], pp. 225-38). "The fundamental fallacy of Mead's treatment of communication is . . .", de Laguna wrote, "akin to that of the English empiricists. It lies in his reduction of the shared universality of symbolic significance to a mere identity of particulars" (p. 234). It is her conclusion that "both speaker and hearer must, in short, play the role of the universal other in order to play the role of the particular other" (ibid.; italics added). Contrary to her intention, her conclusion is entirely in accordance with Mead's view that in a functional situation of symbolic process members of the social situation are implicated in a role of generalized other. In her attempt to criticize Mead, she quotes a part of p. 67 of MS, and then overlooks the fact that in this part Mead is mainly concerned with the "genetic" problem of symbolic process. In a proper study of his works, one can easily find that the significance or meaning of symbolic process is not merely limited to "a mere identity" of particular responses in given contexts, but that it is fully introduced in terms of the (reflexive and regulative) process of taking roles of specific others in view of the role of a generalized other.

In a genetic perspective, roles of generalized others are the basis
for the development of symbolic process. In a functional perspective,
its regulative function, which presupposes or is based on its reflexive
function, is the condition of the functional mediation of social act: the
"communicability" (or "intelligibility") and "objectivity" (or "universality"), in terms of which one can appropriately or successfully take
the role of others, not as the particular members of a given social
situation, but as the particularized members of a "universal" type of
recurrent situation. (146) In functional contexts, the roles of generalized
others appear as attitudes or dispositions of the individual, as a self,
in the early mediate phase of his social acts.

Mead says:

The individual experiences himself as such, not directly, but
only indirectly, from the particular standpoints of other . . .
members of the same social group, or from the generalized
standpoint of the social group as a whole to which he belongs.
For he enters his own experience as a self . . ., not directly
or immediately, not by becoming a subject to himself, but
only in so far as he first becomes an object to himself just as
other individuals are objects to him or in his experience . . . .
The importance of what we term "communication" lies in the
fact that it provides a form of behavior in which the organism
or the individual may become an object to himself. It is . . .
not communication in the sense of the cluck of the hen to the
chickens, or the bark of a wolf to the pack . . ., but communication in the sense of significant symbols, communication which
is directed not only to others but also the the individual himself.
So far as that type of communication is a part of behavior it at
least introduces a self (MS 138-9).

The organized community or social group which gives the
individual his unity of self may be called "the generalized
other". The attitude of the generalized other is the attitude of
the whole community. Thus, for example, in the case of such
a social group as a ball team, the team is the generalized other
in so far as it enters - as an organized process . . . - into the
experience of any one of the individual members of it. If the
given human individual is to develop a self in the fullest sense,
it is not sufficient for him merely to take the attitudes of other
human individuals toward himself and toward one another within
that . . . social process, and to bring that . . . process as a
whole into his . . . experience merely in these terms: he must
also, in the same way that he takes the attitudes of other individuals toward himself and toward one another, take their attitudes toward the various phases or aspects of the common . . .
activity . . . in which, as members of an organized . . . group,
they are all engaged; and he must then, by generalizing these

---

(146) Cf. SW 310 ff.

. . . attitudes of that . . . group itself, as a whole, act toward
different social projects . . . [and] toward the various larger
phases of the general social process . . . of which these projects
are specific manifestations. This getting of the broad activities
of any given social whole . . . as such within the experiential
field of any one of the individuals involved or included in that
whole is . . . the essential basis and prerequisite of the fullest
development of that individual's self . . . . And on the other
hand, the complex co-operative processes . . . and institutional
functionings of . . . human society are also possible only in so
far as every individual involved in them or belonging to that
society can take the general attitudes of all other such individuals
with reference to these processes . . . and . . . functionings,
and to the organized social whole of experiential relations . . . -
and can direct his behavior accordingly (MS 154-5).

As explained earlier, the roles of generalized others range from 1)
clearly delineated roles of established institutions to 2) prevalent,
flexible (or "negatively pre-defined") roles in casual or exigent encoun-
ters, and 3) "extraordinary" roles which transcend local societies and
yet are played in them in view of a past and/or future society. In another perspective, they range from a) relatively concrete roles of
family, school, employment, parties, and sports to b) relatively abstract
roles of "Renaissance man", "the Romantic", "petit bourgeoisie",
"proletariat of the world", and "the liberal" and to c) the most abstract
role of "the logical universe of discourse" which is especially the foundation as well as the production of the community of "thinking men" and
their "technique of the experimental method", the refined method of
translating one particular role to another or of transforming various
roles into one generalized role. (147)
    In certain parts of his works, Mead speaks of "the total generalized
other" in the singular, inclusive sense, not merely in reference to "the
whole community", but ultimately in reference to "the logical universe
of discourse (or system of universally significant symbols)". (148) In a
way, he renders his view open to a Hegelian concept of the Absolute as
a historical process, or to a Whiteheadean concept of God as a "super-
jective" process. "How far", Prof. Morris asks, "does the generalized
other provide the psychological equivalent of the historical concept of
God, and of the Absolute of the idealists?"(149) If one undertakes a re-
interpretation of these traditional concepts in terms of Mead's concept
of "generalized other" (in spite of his well-known personal refusal to
do so), it would still remain a sociological or psychological "equivalent".
Insofar as the generalized other is construed in Mead's sense as a contextual concept, its reality lies within contexts of social acts without
any metaphysical ultimacy in the traditional sense.
    On the other hand, Mead has been subject to certain criticisms when

---

(147) Cf., MS 157, SW 311, PA 375, etc.
(148) MS 90 and 154 ff.
(149) C. W. Morris, "Introduction" in MS, p. xxx.

his "inclusive" concept of "generalized other" is considered in view of psychological or sociological observations of individual experiences. "I do not believe (as Mead does . . .)", Prof. Mills comments, "that the generalized other incorporates 'the whole society'; but rather that it stands for selected social segments. Mead's statements regarding this point are, I believe, functions of an inadequate theory of society and of certain democratic persuasions. These are not, however, logically necessary to the general outline of his social theory of mind." (150)

This kind of criticism is possible if one overlooks the basic nature of Mead's "social psychology" in general, and his theory of symbolic process in particular. In contexts where "generalized other" is considered in his "genetic" perspective, Mead is concerned with the "arche" of symbolic process, its functional conditions in a logical reconstruction. (151) Generalized others, in an inclusive sense as well as in the other senses, are realized and possible in symbol-mediated social acts; and in proper contexts of the acts they are the function of symbolic processes. But it is not implied that all acts or experiences of man exemplify these functions.

On the other hand, as the criticism emphasizes that a social act has its generalized other in a selective or contextual sense, Mead's "generalized other" is thoroughly contextual in accordance with his general contextual criteria of act. (152) In explaining the problem of "generalized other", he commonly refers to "the given social group or community" (MS 154), and says that "whether this group is of restricted or indefinite number depends upon the character of the co-operative activity that is going on" (PA 390). For Mead, the functional character of a given social act, namely, the implemental relation of ends and means in a given situation, contextually determines the "scope" of its generalized other.

"Generalized other" as a contextual concept is evident as it is frequentl explained by Mead in terms of "games" as its "paradigm" context. A game such as chess, bridge, hunting, or football has "a definite end to be obtained", with reference to which all the members of the game are related to each other in an organization of attitudes and responses. This organization Mead construes as the generalized other in the game. (153) As for his favorite example of "a person playing baseball", Mead says: "Each one of his own acts is determined by his assumption of the action of the others who are playing the game. What he does is controlled by his being everyone else [in the game], at least in so far as those attitudes affect his own particular response. We get then an "other" which is an organization of the attitudes of those involved in the same process" (MS 154). (154)

---

(150) C. W. Mills, "Language, Logic, and Culture", American Sociological Review, 1939 (4:5), p. 672 fn.
(151) See 3.312.
(152) See 2.22.
(153) Cf. MS 159, PA 374, etc.
(154) In using "game" to explain the generalized other, Mead always contrasts it to "play", particularly those of children, in an ontogenic

Consider the following situations which can be suggested by the ordinary language of English: 1) "Check-mate!"; 2) "Mom, Sue is crying"; 3) "One third of the population of this continent suffers from poverty"; 4) "'I'm starving' is a stronger expression in English than 'I'm hungry'"; and 5) "It is a mistake to think that one times one is two." In these five different situations one would, insofar as one could, respond to the others involved in terms of the roles of respectively different generalized others (in reference to the objects involved). On the other hand, all of these situations presuppose, respectively for their limited purposes, the generalized role of the members of the community of English as well as of the community of symbolic process itself, the "logical" universe of discourse - insofar as the roles involved in the situations are taken regulatively in terms of the symbols involved.

The role of a generalized other may be that of a definite chess game with two members or a definite family of five members in a contextually limited sense; or it may be that of the indefinite community of all the chess players or those who are involved in the institutions of family in various societies; or that of the community of "all beings speaking the same language" or "a group that . . . takes in all rational individuals . . ., all individuals who could indicate to one another universal characters and objects in co-operative activity".(155) In a situation of life an individual man may take the roles of a multitude of generalized others, some in a more important way than the others, and ultimately in the generalized role of the symbolic process of regulative role-taking.

---

perspective. In comparison to the definite organization of role-takings in a game, a play is an activity of "taking different roles", each on different occasions, in a loose manner (cf. MS 150). Mead says that "the game represents the passage in the life of the child from taking the roles of others in play to the organized part that is essential to self-consciousness in the full sense of the term" (MS 152). For Mead, "game" is the polar concept in contrast to "play", not to the other concepts such as "labor", "serious work", or "commitment".

In ordinary English, the term "game" has a double meaning. Thus, it is quite misleading to suggest vaguely, as in certain contemporary writings of psychology, that all social acts of generalized others are "games" to which no polar concept is clearly given. (Cf., e.g., E. Berne, Games People Play [New York: Grove Press, 1964]. Mead is mentioned as one of the original sources for the author's theory of "games".)

In philosophy, economics, and other sciences, the term "game" is used respectively in different, technically defined senses, but it is just as misleading as the above case of psychology for the same reason if the term has no definite polar concept to contrast.

Mead's distinction of "game" and "play", though useful as a logical distinction in certain genetic contexts, breaks down in general contexts of social acts, namely, those of adults, precisely because it is difficult to isolate acts as pure forms of play except in certain pathological cases.

(155) MS 335 and PA 375.

3.335 Regulative Process: Rule-assuming

Insofar as individual men are able, in a symbol-mediated social act, to take the roles of each other in terms of the role of a generalized other, they assume, or act in view of, a rule or a set of rules. The role of a generalized other refers, as explained earlier, to a common or invariant way of responding to a situation in the perspective which any individual must accept for the given end of the situation; it constitutes a rule. In the situation of a "game" as the paradigm of social act, the role of its generalized other is "the rules of the game".(156)
Mead says:

[An individual] comes to address himself in the generalized attitude of the group of persons occupied with a common under-taking. The generalization lies in such an organization of all the different co-operative acts as they appear in the attitudes of the individual that he finds himself directing his act by the corresponding acts of the others involved - by what may be called the rules of the game (PA 192).

In the game [or other social act of taking the role of generalized other] . . ., there is a set of responses of [the] others so organized that the attitude of one calls out the appropriate atti-tudes of the other[s]. This organization is put in the form of the rules of the game . . . . The rules are the set of responses which a particular attitude calls out. You can demand a certain response in others if you take a certain attitude. These responses are all in yourself as well (MS 151-2).

Symbolic process is regulative, i.e., rule-assuming or rule-setting, not merely because symbols are constructed 1) in terms of their "grammatical" or "syntactical" rules, but especially because symbols are themselves the rules of act or response 2) in reference to the objects they designate to denote and 3) in reference to the relation of others to oneself. A rule, or a symbol as a rule, is a social or socially derived way or order of implementation which determines and indicates the relation of an end and a means in a social act. In another perspective, it is a direction or guideline for the repeatable (implemental) solution(157) of a problematic situation and its kind, which has been and/or is anticipated to be inhibitive, primarily in the consummation demanded by an impulse. A symbol in its regulative function is a teleological and conditional (or, hypothetical and contextual) rule. Here we may say that implemental process, which we have considered in 3.2, is basically the

---

(156) "Game" is used here in contrast to "play", not to "work" or "labor". (See 3.334, fn. 154.) "Play" is understood by Mead to refer in one sense to man's activities in which definite, consistent rules are comparatively absent (MS 150 ff).
(157) Symbols are solutions themselves in certain contexts, as we have explained in 3.231 that symbols are implements themselves as well as the implements for other implements.

process of discovering and using symbols as rules.

Thus, the implemental conditions, (i/c.1 and 2), are determined by the regulative function of symbolic process. A symbol as a rule unifies, or relates various factors into a unity, in each of the situations in which it is discovered or to which it is applied; and it generalizes one of the given situations to relate to the other situations, or determines a classification of them against the rest of the "universe of discourse". The import of symbols can be seen here in the fact that distant or future situations are anticipated and mediated (i.e., "classified", "familiarized", etc.) in terms of some contextually pertinent symbols. A problem arises in a situation of social act in which the anticipated application of a symbolic rule fails to unify its phases, as much as in a situation to which no symbolic rule is available to apply in anticipation. On the other hand, rationality, as the condition of a social act in which a problem is solved or which is functionally mediated by an implemental process, is brought about or determined by the regulative function of a symbolic process.

In symbol-mediated social situations, men act in view of rules, and in accordance with them, basically not because they are "universal" in some absolute sense, but because they are conditionally required or necessary for implemental mediation in the situations. In Kant's terms, given in his Critique of Practical Reason, all rules are "hypothetical". What he regards as the "categorical imperative"(158) is not so much to be taken in contrast to "hypothetical imperatives" to delineate the condition of "morality", but as a general precondition under which the hypothetical rules are used. We may recall the precondition of (functional) implemental process, (i/p.1 and 2), as explained in 3.233, which is in a way a translation of Kant's formulation of the categorical imperative based on the concept of man as "an end in itself". A Kantian or deontological attempt to delineate morality in terms of the concept of the categorical imperative fails because "morality" or valuation is something more than the observation of the categorical imperative, though it is, at least, the prerequisite or precondition of "morality". In other words, many of man's important problems cannot be solved solely in terms of the criterion of this precondition, because the solutions of them require a choice between alternative "hypothetical" rules, all of which are anticipated to fulfill the precondition.

Generally, Mead explains his concept of "role of generalized other" and "role of self", as explained earlier, in terms of "games" and "institutions", and construes "symbolic process" in a broad, inclusive sense for which "assertive statements" are only a type of symbol. His concept of "reflexive, regulative process", or "rule-assuming process of role-taking" is analogous, among traditional concepts, to "knowing", if it is not construed in the intellectual sense of "knowing that". Of course, "role-taking" carries an emphasis on the social origin or

(158) Cf. "So act that the maxim of your will could always hold at the same time as a principle establishing universal law" (Critique of Practical Reason, trans. by L. W. Beck [New York: Liberal Arts, 1956], p. 30; Fundamental Principles of the Metaphysics of Morals, trans. by T. K. Abbott [New York: Liberal Arts, 1949], p. 38).

basis of symbolic process, namely, that a symbol is "primarily [a] social role" (SW 312). In certain contexts, Mead explains the process of taking the role of a generalized other as a "cognitive" process in contrast to an "emotional" or "affective" process (MS 173). But it is clear that he uses the term "cognitive" not in a traditional sense of "assertive statement", but in a sense for which "knowing that" and "knowing how" are included. Mead's use of "rule-assuming" in an inclusive sense does not necessarily deny the contextually useful distinction between "rules of convention" and "laws of nature", as his view of the "universality" of all symbols does not deny the distinction of "form of universal statement" and "form of particular statement" in formal logic. The concept of social, symbolic rule is construed to be used not only in reference to conventional, legal, and moral contexts, but also in reference to those of theories of science on one hand, and to those of "forms" of art on the other.

Of course, rules are variable in their "prevalence" and "endurance" in terms of the nature of social acts, and the relation of means to ends in them, in which these rules function. On one extreme, we have various rules in the areas of imagination, fashion, taste, and subgroup relations. These rules are limited in their prevalence and endurance, though hypothetically universal in their implications, to the extent that the acts in these areas are "localized" and constantly change, and that the ends of these acts are remotely related to the physical, organic, and social basis of human life and are open to various alternative means. On the other extreme, we have various rules of the social, organic, and physical conditions of human life. In a narrow sense, these rules prevail and endure, and so are universal and necessary, since they indicate the invariant "preconditions" which any social act of man is based on or presupposes in his "present" environment. Suppose that, thanks to the mysterious power of Allah, every man could, and were forced continuously to, play chess as a precondition of human life - then, the rules of chess would be as invariant, as universal and necessary, as the laws of physics or biology.

The above contrast of the two extreme cases of rules may have suggested the traditional distinction of "rules of convention" and "laws (and theories) of nature". In certain contexts, this distinction is useful as a criterion of differentiating one type of "roles of generalized others" from the other, e.g., a traffic regulation from a chemical principle of combustion. But the traditional distinction breaks down for a number of reasons. Insofar as a rule, or the role of a generalized other, is functional in a social act, it has both a dimension of "convention" and a dimension of "nature". In certain important cases such as the methodological assumptions of science (or, the conditions of [functional] implemental process we have considered), the principles of logic, and some elementary theories of psychology as well as of physics, we have a difficulty in explaining them in terms of the traditional distinction. Furthermore, the traditional concept of "rules" and "theories" does not explain a common basis of or relation between them, which Mead's theory of man's social act suggests.

The "laws" and "theories" of science as assertive, descriptive universal statements of "deterministic" relations are a special way of formulating certain rules of social acts in view of the nature of these relations, which endure over various changes in the contexts of the acts. They are "derivatives" of the social rules in general at least in the sense 1) that they are formulated in terms of the "generalized rules (or roles)" of the community of "scientists", i.e., the methodological rules of science; and 2) that their "physical" and other scientific objects can be construed as abstractions from social objects.(159) The traditional problem of deriving prescriptive rules ("ought-statements") from descriptive theories ("is-statements") is based in part on a misconception of the relation between them. The problem is not how we derive certain rules from theories, but how we decide if certain rules (or "values") are theories (or "facts").

Laws and theories of social sciences, including psychology, as those of man's social acts are the "statistical uniformities" or "logical limits" of the acts, to which symbolic processes of rule-assuming provide a pivotal determining part. In this context, it is Mead's conclusion that 1) "it is only insofar as the individual acts not only in his own perspective but also in the perspective of others, especially in the common perspective of a group (i.e., in the role of generalized other) that a society arises and its affairs become the object of scientific inquiry (within the society)"; and that 2) "in the field of any social science the objective data are those experiences of the individuals in which they take the attitude of the community, i.e., in which they enter into the perspectives of the other members of the community" (SW 310). Thus, the laws and theories of social sciences - as works of a society on its "affairs" - are derived from and presuppose social acts of rule-assuming in the given society.

There is an "intrinsic" relation between (a.1) "rationality" as a social process of rule-assuming or rule-setting and (a.2) "rationality" as a theoretical, determinate structure of social processes - or between (b.1) the fact that men act in view of generalized roles or rules and (b.2) the fact that their acts are investigated and abstracted in terms of their uniformities or limits as their determinate structures. In view of this relation between the two phases of man, we may dissolve the traditional problem of the metaphysical duality of man: (c.1) his free being and (c.2) his causally determined being - in the language of Kant, (d.1) the rational being of free will and (d.2) the "natural" being subject to the principle of causality. A society of men is "free" to the extent that its members determine (or "self-condition") themselves in terms of their use of symbols in their social acts. An individual man as a member of a society (or a complex of societies) is "free" to the extent that he determines (or "self-conditions") himself in terms of his use of symbols in his social acts.(160) The discovery of the determinate structure of man's social acts, namely, that of the theories of sciences of

---

(159) Cf. PA 190, 328, 377, etc.
(160) C. W. Morris, "The Mechanism of Freedom", in Freedom, Its Meaning, edited by R. N. Anshen (New York: Harcourt, Brace & Co.), 1940, pp. 579-89; Foundations of the Theory of Signs, p. 42; Signs, Language, and Behavior, p. 275.

man, is the very process of symbolic, social premediation in which we
are trying to prepare for our self-determining or self-conditioning. In
other words, it is the process of producing symbols (and other implements), in terms of which we can determine ourselves in our acts
so as to be "free" from unanticipated consequences of the acts.

In certain social acts or "games" of man's life, it may be noted, it
is one thing to take, assume, and/or carry out, the role of a generalized
other; it is another thing to present this role as a set of rules in verbal
statements in a logical or systematic manner. That is, it is one thing
to play chess, write poems, or lead a nation; it is another matter to
explain in lectures or books how to do them. It is the common contingent
fact of human life that the first type does not necessarily require the
second type, and vice versa, although they are obviously related and
their union in some individuals is sometimes realized. In this sense,
what is commonly construed as "theoretical reason" is not the prerequisite or presupposition of man's rationality.(161) On the other hand,
in certain contexts of social acts, the two types may be functionally
required to be united, or are the same "thing", as in the case of "un-
perished" professors.

3.34 Symbolic Mediation and Rationality

We have explained earlier in 3.2 that in a social act, the condition of
its functional or successful completion, namely, its rationality, is constituted by an implemental mediation. As the conditions of functional
implementation are determined by a symbolic process as a part of the
mediation, the rationality of the act is determined by the symbolic process. In a social act, rationality is determined by the role of a generalized other which an individual man takes as a function of his symbolic
process. In the early phase or through the mediate phase of the act, the
symbolic process functions as a disposition or attitude of the individual
which determines the functional mediation, i.e., the rationality, of the
act. "When the activity [i.e., a social act] is an organized one", Mead
says, "in which the different roles because of the organization all call
for an identical response, as in an economic or political process, the
individual assumes what may be called the role of the generalized other,
and the attitude is a universal or rational attitude" (PA 445).

We have explained in 3.32 and 3.33 that the mediational function of
symbolic process is provided by its unity of regulative and reflexive
functions, which is based on its unity of connotative and denotative functions. In terms of this function of symbolic process, we select and
manipulate phases of a social act and relate them in unity in a selected
perspective, and we generalize the unified situation of the act in view
of past and future situations. In the mediation of the act, accordingly,
symbolic process determines the implemental conditions of "unity" and
"generality" (i/c.1 and 2), which constitute the rationality of the act.
Thus, much of what has been said about symbolic process is about man's
rationality.

---

(161) See 4.2.

Mead says:

Language is a process of indicating certain stimuli and changing the response to them in the system of behavior. Language as a social process has made it possible for us to pick out responses and hold them in the organism of the individual, so that they are there in relation to that which we indicate . . . .

Whether one points with his finger, or points with the glance of the eye . . . or the motion of the head . . ., or by means of a vocal gesture in one language or another, is indifferent, provided it does call out the response that belongs to that which is indicated . . . . However slight, there must be some sort of gesture. To have the response isolated without an indication of a stimulus is almost a contradiction in terms . . . .

This process of communication . . . furnish[es] those [reflexive] gestures [or symbols] which in affecting us as they affect others call out the attitude which the other takes, and that we take in so far as we assume his role. We get the attitude, the meaning, within the field of our own control, and that control [i.e., regulative function] consists in combining all these various responses to furnish the newly constructed act [i.e., role of generalized other] demanded by the problem [or situation]. In such a way we can state rational conduct in terms of a behavioristic psychology (MS 97–8).

If symbolization can be stated in terms of the behavior of primitive communication, then every distinctly human being belongs to a possibly larger society than that which he actually finds himself. It is this, indeed, which is implied in the rational character of the human animal. And . . . patterns [of such a larger society] afford a basis for the criticism of existing conditions (SP 306).

We may consider what Mead construes as the relation of symbolic process and rationality in terms of two different types of man's social situation: 1) situations of mediation based on premediated implements, and 2) situations of mediation based on new implements.
1) In the preserved field of premediated implements in a society, men as its members live, basically depending on the use of premediated symbols as a part of the field. All other implements and their relations are premediated in terms of these symbols. Under the prevalent condition that the premediated implementation presents a series of alternatives for a given situation, an individual man can solve his problem of selecting one of them basically in terms of his symbolic process. In view of the complexity of such a condition, members of the society establish various institutions of education and other ways of assimilation as a part of premediation. In this field, a social act is rational as long as its required implemental mediation is functionally (or appropriately) determined in terms of a symbolic premediation. Consider a modern

man who chooses and uses a multitude of complicated gadgets needed in his home by reading simple directions without going through a complex or theoretical and technical problems involved in the production of these gadgets. In contexts of this field, irrationality is the failure or refusal of individual men to act in terms of symbolic premediation; it implies that their acts are not functionally implemented. Otherwise, that is, if a symbolic premediation does not, especially repeatedly, determine the condition of (functional) implemental mediation required for a social act, the symbolic premediation is dysfunctional (or inappropriate), and the implemental premediation determined by it is dysfunctional (or obsolete).

2) In situations where an implemental mediation desired or required is not found in the premediated implemental field of a society or where a part of the field breaks down or is obsolete, members of the society turn, as explained in 3.2, to a delayed process of implementation in terms of a method, of which the method of modern science is a refined paradigm. A method itself, as a preserved implement – highly institutionalized in certain societies – is premediated in terms of symbolic process. In such a problematic situation, an implemental process is mediated in terms of those symbols in the premediated field which remain untouched by the given problem, while its solution lies in a selective reconstruction of phases or factors of the situation, which are significant or meaningful. The solution encloses new implements, including new symbols, which are integrated into the premediated field, or in terms of which the whole field is radically reconstructed. The reconstructed situation is mediated in terms of these new symbols, as they provide a reflexive and regulative function for members of the situation in reference to the emerged implemental objects. Here the rationality of the social act is determined by these new symbols in the perspective of the reconstruction, while this rationality is constituted by the implemental mediation, inclusive of the symbolic process, as a whole. In such a problematic situation, irrationality is the refusal or failure of individual men involved to attempt a functional (or appropriate) implementation.

Thus, rationality is determined by symbolic process not only in 1) social acts of premediate implementation but also in 2) those of methodic and other new implementation. In this sense, symbolic process is the "necessary" condition of rationality, while methodic or other implemental process is its "sufficient" condition. In view of the import of the second type of social act, we can understand Prof. Buchler's statement that "reason is a form of love . . . , love of inventive communication".(162) Mead says:

The identification of language with reason in one sense is an absurdity, but in another it is valid. It is valid, namely, in the sense that the process of language brings the total social act into the experience of the given individual as himself involved in the act, and thus makes process of reason possible (MS 74 fn.).

---

(162) J. Buchler, Toward a General Theory of Judgment, p. 168.

In the same footnote, Mead goes on to say: "But though the process of reason is and must be carried on in terms of the process of language - in terms, that is, of words - it is not simply constituted by the latter" (MS 74 fn.). As for what there is other than "language" or symbolic process, constituting the "process of reason", Mead could have meant the physiological functions of individual human organisms, particularly those of the nervous system, insofar as they are regarded as "mental" or self-conscious process. On the other hand, this "process of reason" - even in the traditional sense of "reasoning" - is not limited to the self-conscious, private, "mental" process, which is largely a physiological function "programmed" in terms of symbolic process. It is carried out by various social implemental processes such as talking, writing, experimentation, computer programming, group improvisation, etc. In a final analysis, what there is other than symbolic process, constituting the rationality of social act, is implemental process as a whole, including the physiological functions as a phase of the social act.

Insofar as a social act is meditated and is rational, it implicates the role of a generalized other as a social rule which is assumed, or introduced to be assumed, by its members. In a logical sense, this role may be construed to be "a priori". But the symbolic process involved is thoroughly contextual, and the role assumed can be, in traditional terms, an a posteriori rule of how to start a fire, or an a priori rule of "excluded middle". The rationality of a social act may contextually presuppose a host of social roles or rules as its preconditions. In Mead's view of social act, however, rationality is not constituted by a set or system of a priori forms (structures or orders) which are metaphysically ultimate or eternal in contradistinction to a posteriori matters (or contents) as another type of reality. In this sense, as we will further consider in 4.3, rationality is a contextual, social concept, distinguished from the traditional concepts of rationality as an innate faculty or transcendental structure of mind, or as a transcendent realm of eternal forms.

An articulate "defense" of certain irrational conditions and phases of man is only a witness to the common task of man's rationality - whether it is a Schopenhauerian metaphysical discourse in German, a Dostoevskian fictional prose in Russian, a Beckettian tragi-comedy in French, or a Barrettian "existential" study in English. "Irrationalism" is self-contradictory and self-defeating because he who claims it knows and generalizes enough. The only "irrationalism" which has been a delusive, sanguinary part of human history is the silence of the gods. On the other hand, what is deprecatingly called "rationalization" is the homage man pays to his "stronger" phase for the "sin" of his self and others in their "weaker" moments. Man's irrational phase lies largely in his refusal or failure to listen to . . . and in "the rest [which] is silence".

As Mead construes man's rationality in terms of social act and as its functional or appropriate implemental relation, symbolic process determines this rationality under the condition that it mediates the implemental process of the act functionally. In terms of the emphasis on the contextual functions of symbolic process in the mediate phase of social act, rather than in terms of the "innate" structure of mind as the a priori condition of experience, we can re-interpret Kant's statements on reason: "Percepts without concepts are blind" and "concepts without percepts are empty". (163) Translating liberally, we may say that implements without symbolic mediations are blind and symbols without implemental functions are empty.

Thus, the problem of rationality in Mead's perspective of social act can be stated in the following variation of Kant's well known question: How is symbolic process possible for its mediate function in social act? We have tried to answer this question in 3.2 and 3.3.

3.4 On Experimental Studies of Mead's Theories
- a justification of his concept of rationality

We have gone through some 150 pages to explain a "common sense" statement in the basis of Mead's theories, that men live together in a complex of social relations, and have developed and used symbols and other implements in their processes of social life. This elementary anthropological statement is analogous to a biological statement that organisms have appeared, at least on the earth, and will likely continue to live for some time in the universe; or to a cosmological statement that all things go through change and yet their relations endure relatively in various ways and periods. The analogous relation lies in the fact that there will be no great dispute in present days against these elementary, "trivial" statements, though they can be re-stated "better" in different sentences. But disputes and problems arise as soon as we try to fill in these statements with explanations to make them "non-trivial" statements.

In a recent study of Mead's works, Prof. Swanson wrote:

Mead is peculiarly unfortunate in having proposed as a major social psychological premise a dictum that seems untestable, whatever its heuristic value. I have in mind his judgment that self-awareness and reflective thought are products of social interaction mediated by language signs and products of it alone.

The only relevant test of this notion would require a population of biologically normal human adults who had managed, without undue trauma, to become knowledgable about a differentiated environment, who had learned to employ certain common vocal gestures instrumentally but not reflexively, and who lacked all human contacts [i.e., contacts with men of other, reflexively symbolic communities] from birth to maturity. (164)

(163) Critique of Pure Reason, A 51 (B 75). The translations given are from: J. H. Randall, Jr. The Career of Philosophy, II, (New York: Columbia Univ. Press, 1965), pp. 199 & 198. Cf. Critique of Pure Reason, trans. by N. K. Smith (London: Macmillan, 1929), p. 93.
(164) G. E. Swanson, "Mead and Freud: Their Relevance for Social Psychology", Sociometry, 1961 (24:4), p. 336.

Prof. Swanson's proposed test may be relevant in testing the aspect of
Mead's "judgement" suggested by the phrase, "mediated by language
signs", but may not be relevant in testing the other aspect suggested
by "social interaction" since "a population of biologically normal human
adults" implies a life of "social interaction". A better alternative test
of, and perfect counter-evidence against, Mead's theory of man's social
act and implemental, symbolic mediation would be the discovery of a
singular "feral" man who survived alone on an island where his parents
and everyone else had died at his age of, say, one in the conflagration
of their households and who has matured to dress and speak like a
Descartes or a Chomsky, though respectively in an insular fashion and
in a language he has devised.
Prof. Swanson went on to comment:

> I believe it is time to label as irrelevant for Mead's premise
> all of the materials on feral men, infra-human primates,
> aphasics, schizophrenics, and children. None of these provides
> a reasonable test of Mead's idea. The accounts of ferals are of
> doubtful validity. The chimpanzees and gorillas lack human
> biology as well as symbols. It is as plausible to explain the
> aphasic's difficulty from the damage to his brain as from his
> conceptual disorders. Schizophrenia seems more a result of
> traumatic rearing than of miseducation in symbol usage. The
> very young child is biologically and experientially immature
> as well as unskilled in language.

> Although I am disposed to believe that Mead's premise is sound,
> I am also disposed to believe that it cannot be demonstrated to
> be so. I would propose that whatever use we may make of Mead
> should not depend on the truth of this particular premise, and
> that we stop fruitless debate about its validity. (165)

In the background of Prof. Swanson's above conclusion is the fact that
Mead's methodological approach of "social behaviorism" and his theory
of symbolic process have provided a foundation of "symbolic inter-
actionalism" in the contemporary fields of sociology and psychology. (166)
On the other hand, his theory (or theories) of "social act" (or "rationality") as a whole, at least as presented in the present study, is
prima facie not limited to what Prof. Swanson meant by "Mead's
premise" or to his theory of symbolic process. And the problem of
"justifying" such a broad or "philosophical" anthropological theory is
not easily solved by one or two "crucial" experiments or arguments.
We may consider Prof. Buchler's following statements on the problem
of "acceptibility" of a theory in general and "a philosophic theory in
particular". In the preface to his work on "a general theory of human
judgment", Prof. Buchler stated:

---

(165) Ibid.
(166) Cf. A. M. Rose (ed.), Human Behavior and Social Processes: An
Interactionist Approach (Boston: Houghton Mifflin Co., 1962).

Every theory aims, in the last analysis, to exhibit a structure among data ordinarily regarded as disparate: by the use of a relatively small number of categories a scheme is devised which requires to be self-consistent and consistent with other schemes that have come to be thought part of the fabric of knowledge. The burden that a philosophic theory in particular bears is likely to be great; for beyond these primal requirements it dedicates itself to the difficult union of a high level of generality with interpretative justice. In the case of such a theory the circumstances of verification are usually very complex, and the acceptability of the results depends ultimately, perhaps, upon the presence of a sense of philosophic satisfaction in the reader, who is both spectator and participant.(167)

We may accept (or reject, or revise) a theory as an implement,(168) at least, in terms of considering its fulfillment of the implemental conditions, (i/c.1 and 2), in a contextually appropriate, refined version. Consider Mead's theory of "role-taking" in a "limited" scope without implicating it, especially, with his theory of implemental process, as prevalently done in the contemporary studies of Mead in psychology and sociology. It can be selectively reformulated as a theory of (the process and development of) self-consciousness, as a theory of self or personality formation, as a theory of institutions, or as a theory of symbols. In view of the common practice of science, we would consider a) whether such a theory is "internally" consistent, and b) whether it explains and predicts the process of various situations to which the theory is applicable. Furthermore, we would consider the theory c) in comparison to alternative theories available, d) in view of whether it is related to and in accordance with pertinent theories of "broader scope" (or, whether it is an implication of them in some way), and e) in view of whether pertinent theories of "narrower scope" are implied by it and are accepted or acceptable in the present field of sciences.

In a similar way, we may approach Mead's theory (or theories) of man's social act (or rationality) as a whole, namely, as presented in this study. But since the generalization of the implemental conditions, (i/c.1 and 2), are a part of this whole theory, we have an apparent "circularity" which is analogous to the attempt to "justify" the principle (or "general rules") of induction itself inductively. As Prof. Goodman suggested for the "problem of induction",(169) we have to approach the

---

(167) J. Buchler, Toward a General Theory of Human Judgment, p. vii.
(168) Cf. S. Morgenbesser, "The Realist-Instrumentalist Controversy", in Philosophy, Science, and Method: Essays in Honor of Ernest Nagel, edited by S. Morgenbesser, P. Suppes, and M. White (New York: St. Martin's Press, 1969), pp. 200-18.
(169) Cf. "An inductive inference . . . is justified by conformity to general rules, and a general rule by conformity to accepted inductive inferences. Predictions are justified if they conform to valid canons of induction; and the canons are valid if they accurately codify accepted inductive practice . . . . The traditional smug insistence upon a hard-

problem of "justifying" Mead's theory, inclusive of the generalizations of (i/c.1 and 2)(170) and regulative process, in terms of a "reciprocal" relation between his theory and various theories of "narrower scope". Namely, we have to consider if the former is justified by the latter, and if the latter are derived from or justified by the former. This consideration would, in a way, cover b) and e) of the above paragraph. The present study of Mead's works has begun with the understanding, and has shown on various occasions, that his theory of social act, at least as presented in this study, is justified in the considerations of b) and e) as well as in those of a), c), and d) of the above paragraph.

In view of a recent experimentally controlled "study of the social-psychological theory of G. H. Mead", (171) we may justify the present interpretation of Mead's theory of man's social act as his theory of man's rationality. In an attempt to test the applicability and validity of Mead's theory of role-taking in terms of a number of verifiable hypotheses derived from it, Prof. Stryker came to the following conclusion: "To the degree that these characteristics [of rationality in general in the sense of the present study - or, as he distinguishes, of 'rationality,

---

and-fast line between justifying induction and describing ordinary inductive practice distorts the problem . . . . The problem of induction is not a problem of demonstration but a problem of defining the difference between valid and invalid predictions" - N. Goodman, Fact, Fiction, and Forecast (Indianapolis: Bobbs-Merrill Co., 1965 [orig. 1955]), pp. 64-5.

(170) The "justification" of (i/c.1 and 2) was, according to Mead, given in 3.2.3.3 as the methodological assumptions or rules of methodic implementation.

(171) S. Stryker, "Attitude Ascription in Adult Married Offspring-Parent Relationships: A Study of the Social Psychological Theory of G. H. Mead", Ph. D. Dissert., Minneapolis: Univ. of Minnesota. 1955. Its conclusive parts are printed in the following articles: 1) "The Adjustment of Married Offspring to their Parents", American Sociological Review, 1955 (20:2), pp. 149-54; 2) "Relationships of Married Offspring and Parent: A Test of Mead's Theory", American Journal of Sociology, 1956 (62:3), pp. 308-19; revised and reprinted under a new title, "Conditions of Accurate Role-taking: A Test of Mead's Theory", in Human Behavior and Social Processes, pp. 41-62; and 3) "Role-Taking Accuracy and Adjustment", Sociometry, 1957 (20:4), pp. 286-96.

It is a conclusion from this study as well as from the following experimental studies that Mead's basic theory of "role-taking", interpreted as various theories of "limited scope", fulfills a methodological requirement of theory in science: it is "operationally" definable and falsifiable.

Cf. S. F. Miyamoto & S. M. Dornbusch "A Test of Interactionist Hypotheses of Self-Conception", American Journal of Sociology, 1956 (61:5), pp. 399-403; L. G. Reeder, G. A. Donohue & A. Biblarz, "Conceptions of Self and Others", American Journal of Sociology, 1960 (66:2), pp. 153-9; R. E. O'Toole, Experiments in George Herbert Mead's "Taking the Role of the Other".

utilitarianism, and organization'] (172) are present in social relationships, observation of role-taking will more completely support hypotheses based on Mead's theory."(173) On the other hand, in other cases
where the characteristics of rationality are not dominant, the hypotheses
based on Mead's theory fail to predict the roles taken.

As a plausible account for the difficulty in predicting in certain cases
of social relationships in terms of the hypotheses derived from Mead's
theory, Prof. Stryker suggested:

> Mead's social psychology is highly rationalistic. Weber analyzed
> social action in terms of four ideal-typical modes of orientation
> . . ., traditional, affective, evaluative and rational . . . . From
> the standpoint of a schema of this, it is clear that Meadean social
> psychology focuses upon the last of these categories of action, the
> rational, to the virtual exclusion of the remaining three. Mead's
> concern is with and his emphasis upon rational behavior, or at
> least with conditions which permit rationality, while behaviors
> involving absolute ends, affect or tradition remain by and large
> outside his view. (174)

> It is suggested that a qualification be incorporated into the body
> of theory derived from Mead to take into account differentials
> in the degree of rationality, utilitarianism, and organization in
> various sets of social relationships. For Mead these are im-
> plicitly assumed constants of social situations; we are proposing
> that they be treated as explicit variables in the theory, vari-
> ations among which would be pertinent to predictions. (175)

Prof. Stryker's conclusion supports the interpretation of the present
study that Mead's theory of social act is not an inclusive, systematic,
typological theory of man's diverse conditions and social psychic processes, but a theory of a certain type of human act, the rational, which
is very fundamental in the general explanation of man's social, psychic
processes. (176) We can understand Mead's case by analogy to a chemical
theory of water as H_2O which is applicable only to "pure" or distilled
water, not to any "water" in rivers and bathtubs. A pertinent implication
of the analogy is that in ordinary contexts of life all acts of man are not
rational in a "pure" form but are "mixed" in various degrees. Rationality

---

(172) These characteristics are interpreted in terms of criteria such
as level of education, degree of interest in personal relationships, etc.,
independent of the data from observation of role-taking in question.
(173) Human Behavior and Social Processes, p. 59.
(174) Attitude Ascription, p. 200. Cf. Human Behavior and Social
Processes, p. 58.
(175) Human Behavior and Social Processes, p. 59; italics in the
original.
(176) Cf. "Mead's social behaviorism finds its major problem in
accounting for rationality" (G. E. Swanson, "Mead and Freud: Their
Relevance for Social Psychology", p. 322).

may be regarded as a variable in the diverse conditions, but Mead explicitly explains, not just implicitly assumes, that it is the "constant" of a social act insofar as its situation is "controlled" in a certain way as a whole and it is carried out properly to its end. Rationality is the "conditional constant or necessity" of social act as a functionally implemented social process – or as a "successful social conduct" (SW 131). In both a genetic and functional perspective, Mead is interested in and emphasizes the crucial, working conditions of the social acts of men as members of society, which real-izes culture or civilization – symbols and tools: arts, sciences, technologies, institutions, ideals, games, and so forth.

Mead does not isolate and focus upon the rational phase of social process "to the virtual exclusion of" what is regarded in a typological schema as other types of social situations or actions. Such an "exclusion" would be contrary to his interest in providing a theoretical basis for explaining and controlling the complex of social processes. As Prof. Stryker implies, Mead's theory of social act does provide a basis in terms of which the other types – if the typology is necessary and useful in certain contexts – or, as Mead would consider, various factors of a given social situation, can be investigated and controlled. Furthermore, in terms of his view of methodic implementation, a solution of problems – say, from insanity to cults and dogmas – lies in his contextual, methodic approach of relating all the factors of a social situation involved as parts of a rational process under a plausible, enlarged perspective.

Unless it is clearly understood that Mead is basically concerned with the rational phase of man as social being, it would be easy to be taken in by various misreadings or impertinent criticisms of his works. In classes of ethics and social philosophy where his works have been read, a common critical question has been raised by students: How can a "descriptive" theory of anthropology provide any "prescriptive" principle of valuation, moral conduct, and social reform?

In an article on Mead's "social philosophy", Prof. Smith commented:

> How can a mind formed by assuming conflicting roles have differential value for making harmonious the divisions that produce and constitute it? To put it more intimately, how can a mind so constituted ever become a unity anyway? . . . The simple truth seems to be that in his ameliorative impetus, Mead assumes a unified self because only from a self could there issue differential hope of a unified society. But on a sober second thought, to get such a self would require a unified society in advance. Each here must rely upon a perfection in the other which the other cannot achieve because of the imperfection in it itself.(177)

In another article on Mead, Prof. Smith went on to comment:

---

(177) T. V. Smith, "The Social Philosophy of George Herbert Mead", American Journal of Sociology, 1931 (37:3), p. 381.

168

> An empirically social derivation of personality is not enough to
> guarantee a humane social order . . . . We have seemed to
> detect in Mead some remnant of the general philosophic pre-
> dilection to count "isness" for "oughtness" in operative efficacy.
> (178)

In terms of the problem of the descriptive vs. the prescriptive, or the
"is" vs. the "ought" statement, Mead's theory of social act and its
rationality is descriptive. But it is a description of a highly selected
type of social process or human conduct and so appears to be prescriptive in relation to other types of human conditions and conducts. This
"dual" nature of Mead's theory explains the practice and possibility of
the comparison and criticism of certain conducts and institutions within
the frame of his descriptive theory of man. Nowhere does he, however,
"guarantee a humane social order", or require every man to harmonize
social divisions; nor does he assume the possibility of a "unified society"
or its rationality less (or more) than that of a "unified self" or its rationality. Mead observes that the symbolic, implemental process of rationality has been "operative" - that is, individuals have been formed in
social, symbolic processes, and problems have been solved through a
method or other process of implementation. And he concludes that its
continuation is highly probable for some time.

---

(178) T. V. Smith, "George Herbert Mead and the Philosophy of
Philanthropy", Social Service Review, 1932 (6:1), p. 39.

RATIONALITY AS MAN'S VOCATION

> The rationality of man and the universe makes it possible
> for us to accept defeat without despair.
>
> G. H. Mead, The Philosophy of the Act (c. 1916-31)

4.0 The Preliminary Remarks and Questions

In this concluding chapter, we will attempt to re-interpret the traditional concept of reason as the "essence" of man and to consider some of its basic problems in view of Mead's concept of rationality, "social reason" (PA 508) - or, what one may, in a historical perspective, call "impure reason".

In Mead's perspective of man's social act, rationality is a concept of human sociality. It is distinguished, on one hand, from teleology and intelligence in the biological sense. As an inclusive anthropological concept, on the other hand, it is distinguished from reason as the "faculty" of assertive discourse or the truth function of assertive statement in the traditional or present exclusive sense of epistemology, and from reason as the "innate faculty" or "a priori structure" of individual mind in the traditional sense of metaphysics and epistemology.

The following questions are considered:

4.1) In what sense is the question of the "essence" of man understood? How or in what sense is man's rationality distinguished from teleological intelligence in the biological sense? How is rationality construed to be the basic, common "vocation" of man?

4.2) How is rationality not exclusively the "truth" function of assertive discourse?

4.3) How are certain social rules (or roles) construed, in a social perspective, to be the a priori structure of reason, or the "pure reason" of mind, but not the "innate" structure of individual man's mind and not the veritas eternitas?

In 4.4, a suggestion is made as to how the ancient myth of Prometheus may be re-interpreted in Mead's perspective.

4.1 On the "Essence" of Man

In spite of Kant's discovery of the two wonders of the universe, "the starry heavens above and the moral law within", women and men in their complexity are the incomparable, "immortal" wonder of mortal nature. It is an understandable provincialism that we find our fellow

creatures of humanity more fascinating and mysterious, more danger-
ous and troublesome than anything else. In the great traditions of mankind, we have invented many gods in our images, who exist eternally
for the sole purpose of creating and sustaining this immense universe
so that we may have our drama and happy end. In spite and because of
our "microscopic" size in this boundless universe, we try to reduce
all things to the size of our hands or mouths. As yet, on this relatively
small globe, we have differentiated ourselves infinitely by means of
countless "names". And yet, under the condition of being cornered
together, we have participated in the common pain and bliss of living,
loving, and knowing.

Know thyself - so we have been told as the first dictum on knowledge.
We inquire into what men are and what our world is in order to know
ourselves. We try to understand humanity in order to be better men
in the spirit of Aristotle, who said in the beginning of the Nicomachean
Ethics that we inquire "not in order to know what virtue is, but in order
to become good". (1) In order to know man, we do not have to "reduce"
man to a mixture of atoms, (2) to a libidinous animal, to "nothingness",
to reason, or to a god. There is no single or simple answer which
exhausts the complexity of man, our life, and its conditions. There is
no "principle of nothing but . . ." concerning man. We are strange
creatures to whom their own "being" has persistently been a question.

We may attempt to know and explain man as long as we are aware
that our inquiry is involved with some significant aspect of man. It is
concerned with an intelligibility, not a reduction or "furcation" of the
subject matter. We may express our findings insofar as the "limited"
nature of discourse permits us; there is no alternative means of
communication required for knowledge.

In the Western history of science, the traditional approach to the
"definition" or explanation of man has been that man as a species is
distinguished from the other species of its genus by some single,
basic - if not necessarily "simple" - attribute or characteristic. In a
philosophical perspective, this approach, which goes back to Plato and
Aristotle, has presented the problem of discovering this characteristic
as the "essence" of man, and of explaining all the distinctive functions
of man in terms of it. Thus, the problem begins or ends with the discovery of the "essential" characteristic of man 1) which is common to
all men, 2) which distinguishes or differentiates men from other things,
and 3) which can be shown to be the basic factor or principle of all the

---

(1) Nicomachean Ethics, trans. by W. D. Ross, in The Basic Works of
Aristotle, ed. by R. McKeon (New York: Random House, 1941), p. 953
(II, 2:1103b. 27-9).

(2) It may be interesting to note that a human organism is composed of
the following elements, which were, in average, worth US Dollars .98
in 1936 and US Dollars 3.50 in 1969: oxygen, 65%; carbon, 18%;
hydrogen, 10%; nitrogen, 3%; calcium, 1.5%; phosphorus, 1%; and the
other elements, including gold and silver, 1.5% (AP, Feb. 27, 1969;
the news item was based on the data supplied by Prof. D. T. Forman
of Northwestern Univ.).

other characteristics of man which differentiate men from the other things. The classic, naturalistic answer, which also goes back to Plato and Aristotle, is that the "essence" of man is "nous". In modern translations based on Latin, it is "ratiocination", "raison", "reason", or "rationality" (or "vernunft"). Of course, these concepts have been construed in various ways, as suggested earlier in 1.1.

Mead's concept of rationality is a re-interpretation of the traditional concepts of reason as the "essence" of man. In his perspective of evolution, rationality is construed to be, in its present stage, a basic, enduring, and pervasive characteristic of man, the condition of a type of man's social act. It is not the "essence" of man in any traditional sense which implicates the concept of "transcendent form" or "inherent substance". Nevertheless, Mead's concept of rationality fulfills the three requirements of the above paragraph in a qualified sense.

We may try to summarize the key points on rationality in the previous Chapter 3 in a few sentences. In a situation of social act, an individual man's act is rational if its implemental mediation is functional (or, appropriate or successful). That is, the act is a) inhibited and delayed innervationally, and mediated functionally in terms of b) a selection and reconstruction of means to a given end, or c) a modification and transformation of ends in adjustment to a given means. And the implemental process, i.e., a), b), and/or c), as a whole is determined, or guided and controlled, by a symbolic process as a part of the mediation. In terms of the symbolic mediation, the individual takes d) the roles of others as e) the role of a generalized other - that is, he assumes e') a rule in d') a perspective of the others - in reference to the implemental objects. In a society where such an implemental mediation is preserved, a recurrent act is rational without any innervational delay insofar as it is f) inhibited and delayed symbolically, and mediated functionally.

To say that "man is a rational animal" (MS 92) is to mean that the teleological and intelligent functions of the human organism are determined by social mediation. Although they have provided a necessary basis of ends and means of human life, they have not been completely determinate in themselves in the social evolution of man. In a perspective of this evolution, the process of mediation implies, especially in terms of c) in the above paragraph, that man's impulses, or "human nature", can be socially modified to a large extent; in terms of b), that man's organic functions as means can be extended and elaborated by implements; in terms of e), that a large number of men can be organized as a society or on a "universal" scope, and that an individual man can participate in many different societies; in terms of d), that some men as a limited part(s) of a society can enjoy (or suffer) a functionally implemented life within the society without their own effort, if necessary for some reasons (e.g., immaturity, sickness, etc.), insofar as the other members take the roles of this limited group(s); and, in terms of f), that a good part of man's inhibitive acts can be undelayed and immediately consummated on the basis of premediation. The problem of man's irrationality lies in those inhibitive acts which are carried out immediately yet unpremediated, or mediated dysfunctionally (or unsuccessfully).

The above implications or developments of social mediation obviously distinguish man's rationality from the teleology and intelligence of other organisms, including the human organism in the biological sense. These characteristics of the organisms appear in their immediate and direct adjustment to their environments in terms of their physiological functions. In the social activities of these organisms, what is observed as mediate processes, such as bees' signals to other bees and ants' preservation of food, are also found to be determined, without inhibition and delay in each phase of their activities, by their physiological functions. The basic mechanism of inhibition and delay, which is not stimulated by the other environmental objects of an organism, would lie in the sensitivity of the organism to its own activities in the same way they stimulate the other objects. This "reflexive" mechanism, which constitutes the basis of man's symbolic mediation and rationality, is not present in the teleological and intelligent functions of the other organisms to the extent that it controls or determines their activities. Mead says:

> What I have attempted to do is to bring rationality back to a certain type of conduct, the type of conduct in which the individual puts himself in the attitude of the whole group to which he belongs. This implies that the whole group is involved in some organized activity and that in this organized activity the action of one calls for the action of all the others. What we term "reason" arises when one of the organisms takes into its own response the attitude of the other organisms involved. It is possible for the organisms so to assume the attitudes of the group that are involved in its own act within this whole cooperative process. When it does so, it is what we term "a rational being". If its conduct has such universality, it has also necessity, that is, the sort of necessity involved in the whole act - if one acts in one way the others must act in another way. Now, if the individual can take the attitude of the others and control his action by these attitudes, and control their action through his own, then we have what we term "rationality". Rationality is as large as the group which is involved; and that group could be, of course, functionally, potentially, as large as you like. It may include all beings speaking the same language (MS 334-5). (3)

Insofar as the role of a generalized other, i.e., an "attitude of the whole group", is "universal" and "necessary", in the above senses of logically open common invariancy and mutual reciprocity, it is a social rule; it is regulative for the responses of its members in their social act. Rationality, as an implemental condition of social act, is determined by the symbolic mediation in which the roles of others are taken in terms of a rule (or set of rules). In Mead's view, man's rationality is basically the concept of the social process of rule-assuming. In this sense, we understand his statements that "man is a rational being because he is a

---

(3) Cf. PA 508, MS 347 and MS 379 ff.

social being" and that "only a rational being could give universal form to his act" (MS 379-80). These statements are a re-interpretation of Kant's statement that "rational beings alone have the faculty of acting according to the conception of laws". (4)

In An Essay on Man, Cassirer stated: "The various forms of human culture are not held together by an identity in their nature but by a conformity in their fundamental task. "(5) We have accepted the given suggestion that the anthropological question we have been considering has to be answered in terms of a concept of the "fundamental task" which man realizes or performs in producing or using "various forms of . . . culture". Of course, Cassirer's explanation of this "conformity in their fundamental task" is his well known theory of "symbolic form". It is certainly beyond the scope of the present study to compare Cassirer's concept of "symbolic form" to Mead's concept of rationality. However, two comments may be made in Mead's terms.

First, although man is capable of producing and using symbols properly and improperly, it is the proper production and use, his "better" or "guiding" phase, which characterizes man. Consider the case of an implement such as a typewriter (or a government) which is characterized by the condition of its functionality, i.e., its condition when it works properly, at least at the minimum of what it is supposed to do. Analogously, man is characterized by the condition of his functionality, i.e., his condition when he acts or works - more or less - as a self-conscious, individually distinct member of a society (or societies), not merely as a biological organism. This condition of man is basically determined or realized by his proper or functional symbolic process, and it is the condition of rationality. Just as a man does not engage in symbolic process at certain times and he fails to use or produce symbols properly on certain occasions, a man is not always rational.

Second, a concept of "human culture" is certainly inadequate as a theory of man in general if it leaves largely unexplained the pervasive function of man as a homo faber, an implemental animal. In a social act, symbolic process determines the condition of rationality in the very process of determining the implemental mediation of the act. When a man goes to sleep on a bed in his house, he does not sleep on the bed as a symbolic form and in the house as a symbolic form; he sleeps on the bed as an implement and in the house as an implement. And beds, houses, and all other implements of man are a very important part of his life and culture. In a perspective of man's bio-social evolution, furthermore, it is difficult to see how the genesis and function of symbolic process can be explained unless the implemental function of symbols, symbols as implements, is accounted for.

In Mead's view, rationality is the condition of a type of man's social act. But it is not the type which man carries out exclusively in contrast to or against any act, but the type which he realizes in the very process of carrying out various acts. We may understand the case of rationality

---

(4) Fundamental Principles of the Metaphysic of Morals (trans. by T. K. Abbot), p. 30 (36 [416]).
(5) Op. cit., p. 223.

by analogy to, say, "happiness" (which has not been an explicit problem of the present study). There are happy moments of life and unhappy moments of life. As the condition of a type of "moment of life", happiness is not something which we have or pursue to have in an exclusive sense, but something which we realize in the very process of having or going through various "moments" such as those of waking up, eating, working, travelling, getting engaged, etc. In this sense, there is no exclusive type of act we carry out to be rational. In any act we carry out, we can be rational or irrational. Accordingly, rationality is a common, pervasive "endeavor" or "task" of man while irrationality is not. In recalling Cassirer's earlier noted concept of the "fundamental task" of human culture, we may understand Mead's view that rationality is the distinctive, common, and basic type of man's social act which we do not realize all the time but pursue and realize in various contexts to guide our cultural or civilized life. Thus, rationality is the guiding principle of man's civilization. (6) And, borrowing the suggestive words of Fichte, rationality is the "vocation of man" in a society of civilization.

4.2 On Truth and Rationality

Mead explains man's rationality in terms of "primitive" situations of his social act. In such a situation the act is supposedly mediated by implements, and these implements as a whole are mediated by symbols as a part of the implements. As he explains, these symbols are not necessarily assertive statements. "One points with his finger", Mead says, "or points with the glance of the eyes . . . or motion of the head . . ., by means of a vocal gesture in one language or another" (MS 97). Or, as symbols of communication, we may set a bonfire, wave a flag, or send a map. If a social act is mediated, namely, the relation of its ends and means is realized, functionally as a whole in terms of such a symbolic process as one of the means, the act is rational. Therefore, the problem of rationality permeates the social situations of man more widely that the problem of assertive statements and their truth function.

In prevalent situations of social act, such as legislating, commanding, requesting, exclaiming, and labeling (or titling), the implemental functionality (or appropriateness) of symbols cannot be properly construed in terms of the criteria of "truth" and "falsity". Nor can it be in other situations, such as arts and games (baseball, puzzles, chess, ko, etc.), in which patterns (or, forms or structures) are interpreted and used as (recurrent or repeatable) symbols. These situations cannot be understood and explained in terms of the function or condition of truth. The functions of individual men's social acts in these diverse situations

---

(6) For a criticism of the antithetical views held by certain contemporary intellectuals, see: C. Frankel, The Case for Modern Man (New York: Harper & Brothers, 1955); and The Love of Anxiety and Other Essays (New York: Dell, 1967 [orig. 1965]), especially "The Anti-Intellectualism of the Intellectuals", pp. 12-39.

require a more inclusive concept which will unify them for certain
common characteristics or conditions they have, insofar as they are
peculiarly the process and production of man's common physiological
and social developed functions.

We have suggested earlier in 1.1, by quoting Prof. Buchler's statements, that the traditional concepts of reason have been limited to the
problems of "assertive query". In an analysis of "the dictum 'Man is a
rational animal' ", (7) Prof. Ryle also argued that man's rationality in
general cannot be explained in terms of "propositional thinking", or
what is regarded as the "dual Faculty" of man, "Theoretical and
Practical Reason", in traditional philosophy. "Merely to split Reason",
Prof. Ryle stated, "into Theoretical Reason and Practical Reason is to
leave unattached lots and lots of our familiar and interesting contributions
to daily life which are peculiar to us rational animals. Ought we not, in
order to reinforce Theoretical and Practical Reason, also to invoke
artistic Reason, conversational Reason, commercial Reason, strategic
Reason and sporting Reason?"(8) It is Prof. Ryle's conclusion that
"Reason" in the traditional, intellectual sense is a "testimonial" to some
men for their special works, not an "explanation" of man's rationality
in general or of "human nature's being human nature". As a discipline
of logic and/or a priori categories, Reason constitutes merely a part of
"a battery of disciplines" - respectively different - required for those
special intellectual works in mathematics, chemistry, history, criticism
and so forth. But it is certainly not the "cause" of the basic, pervasive
"task" (or "family of tasks") of rationality which is peculiar to man in
his diverse activities.

In what follows after Prof. Buchler's statements just referred to in
the beginning of the above paragraph, he stated:

The problem of reason has been taken too often as the problem
of the limits and forms of discourse. It is the problem of how
much inquiry can accomplish, and not, unfortunately, of how
much of what can be accomplished in different forms of human
query. In such a light, it is easier to understand the misgivings
of the irrationalists. (9) For, seeing that some processes of
human experience and production have a value not owing to inquiry,
they become disillusioned with inquiry instead of accepting it as
one mode of query. Similarly, the defenders of inquiry and discourse, perceiving products of a nondiscursive character,
relegate them to a noncognitive domain or regard them extra-
rational and as the potential weapons of obscurantists, instead
of accepting them as other modes of judgment or equal mani-

---

(7) G. Ryle, A Rational Animal (London: Athelona Press [Univ. of
London] , 1962), p. 3.
(8) Op. cit., p. 7.
(9) Cf. "We have confused reason with literacy, and rationalism with a
single technology. Thus in the electric age man seems to the conventional
West to be irrational" (M. McLuhan, Understanding the Media: The
Extensions of Man, p. 30).

festations of human utterances. It is not so much that men
preoccupied with one domain are unaware of invention in other
domains, or even of properties common to the different domains:
it is the salient common properties that escape them. (10)

These "salient common properties" of "query", which provide the condition of rationality in general, are, in Mead's perspective of social
act, the functions or conditions of social mediation which is functional
(or, appropriate or successful).

In the previously cited work, Prof. Ryle also considered the question
of "some common thread that runs through all the various actions, effort,
reactions and feelings which need to be classified as peculiar to human
nature". (11) He vaguely suggested that "the perfectly general notion of
thought", "pre-propositional thoughts", (12) is the answer to the question
of this "common thread", in terms of which man's rationality in general
can be accounted. This "common thread" is explained by Mead, in
accordance with his "social behaviorism" and without presupposing
"theoretical reason" or "propositional thinking" as its required bases,
in terms of conditions of "primitive" situations in which man's social
acts are functionally mediated by implements and by "reflexive gestures"

4.3 On "Pure Reason"

It is beyond the scope of the present study to present in a perspective
of contemporary sciences what may be construed as the structure or
system of "pure reason" in the traditional, epistemological sense.
Within the framework of Mead's concept of rationality, we may merely
attempt to suggest a re-interpretation of the traditional Kantian concept
of "pure reason" as the a priori condition or limit of "judgment".
Mead says:

Kant has, in general, stated that the form must be a form of
the mind and must be antecedent. Yet we have [as] in biology
the possibility of accounting for the origin of a form [in general].
. . . The form arises out of the development of the function
(PA 630-1). (13)

The very universality . . . of . . . reason is from the be-

---

(10) J. Buchler, Nature and Judgment, p. 97.
(11) Op. cit., p. 7.
(12) Op. cit., pp. 13 & 8.
(13) In the paragraph from which this quotation is selected, Mead discusses the Kantian problem of "form" in reference to contexts of organic
processes in a phylogenic perspective. The implication of the paragraph
is quite general in reference to all contexts, including those of man's
social acts. It is only in terms of the general implication that Mead's
evolutionary account of forms in this paragraph constitutes a criticism
of Kant's views in his Critique of Pure Reason.

havioristic standpoint the result of the given individual taking
the attitudes of others toward himself, and of his finally
crystallizing all these particular attitudes into a single attitude
or standpoint which may be called that of the "generalized other".

Alternative ways of acting . . . in an indefinite number of
different particular situations - ways which are more or less
identical for an indefinite number of normal individuals - are
all that universals (however treated in logic or metaphysics)
really amount to; they are meaningless apart from the social
acts in which they are implicated and from which they derive
their significance (MS 90).

Roles of generalized others, as "forms of rationality", are functional
developments of man's social acts or experiences as implemental and
symbolic processes. They present or consist of "rules" in the general
sense explained. In the premediate field of a society, a large number of
these roles or rules is the social objects assimilated and preserved in
terms of insitutionalized and/or individually "internalized" processes
of the members of the society. In a logical abstraction, they are "ideas"
or "concepts"; or, "principles", "codes", "laws", "theories", "categories"
"themes", "patterns", and so forth. In contexts of social act, they are
re-introduced to be taken or assumed as attitudes or dispositions of
individual men which are anticipatory of transactional responses. To say
that an idea is rational is to mean that it is functional (or appropriate) as
a social object (means or ends) in implemental mediation in contexts of
social act where it is applied or operates. In this sense, rationality is
determined and constituted in contexts of social act. As indicated in the
last part of the above quotation, this conclusion is, in Mead's perspective
of social act, a re-interpretation of Kant's statement that "concepts are
empty; . . . without objective validity, senseless and meaningless, if
their necessary application to the objects of experience were not established". (14)

In reference to the experience of individual men, "reasoning" - what
is regarded as "mind" or "mental process" in the tradition of rationalism
- is re-interpreted by Mead as an individual man's "internalization" of
symbol-mediated social acts. "I know of no way", Mead says, "in which
. . . mind could arise or could have arisen, other than through the
internalization by the individual of social processes of experience and
behavior, that is, through this internalization of the conversation of
significant gestures [i.e., symbolic process], as made possible by the
individual's taking the attitudes of other individuals toward himself and
toward what is being thought about" (MS 191-2). In one sense, "reasoning"
is an internalized process of symbolic premediation. And in another
sense, it is an internalized symbolic process which implicates the role

(14) Critique of Pure Reason, trans. by N. K. Smith, p. 193 (A 155-6).
Cf. "All categories through which we can attempt to form a concept of
. . . an object allow only of empirical employment, and have no meaning
whatsoever when not applied to objects of possible experience" (op. cit.,
p. 566 [A 696]).

of a generalized other in an inclusive sense, the role of "the logical universe of discourse". This role is the foundation as well as the production of a community of "thinking men" and their "technique of experimental method", the refined, systematic method of translating one particular role to another or transforming various roles into one general role. (15)

Insofar as mind or self-consciousness is construed to be the social development and function of individual men, it does not carry its own "intrinsic" structure, such as the "innate" and/or "transcendental" structure of reason, to be imposed on social acts or experiences. In the perspective of a given society, certain basic conditions of social acts, that is, certain roles of generalized others which members of the society pervasively take, can be construed and systematized as the a priori condition of experience. And it may be regarded as constituting the structure of "pure reason". But it is not the veritas eternitas. It is a methodological (and/or methodic), logically a priori set of social, implemental rules (or roles) which are accepted provisionally as the basic, pervasive, and enduring requirements of implemental process in a perspective of the preserved premediate field of the society. It is open to revision under changes of social conditions insofar as it is not functional in implemental mediation of social acts. (16)

Mead says:

All the enduring relations have been subject to revision. There remain the logical constants, and the deductions from logical implications. To the same category belong the so-called universals or concepts. They are the elements and structure of a universe of discourse. In so far as in social conduct with others and with ourselves we indicate the characters that endure in the perspective of the group to which we belong and out of which we arise, we are indicating that which relative to our conduct is unchanged, to which, in other words, passage is irrelevant. A metaphysics which lifts these logical elements out of their experiential habitat and endows them with a subsistential being overlooks the fact that the irrelevance to passage is strictly

---

(15) Cf. MS 157, SW 311 and PA 375. And see 3.334 and Appendix A.3. The second sense of "reasoning" is significantly suggested by and supports a re-interpretation of Descartes' first intuition of "cogito, ergo sum" as "a dialogue between 'Caresius, who voices Reason itself', and 'René Descartes the Everyman' " (A. G. A. Balz, Descartes and the Modern Mind [New Haven: Yale Univ. Press, 1952], pp. 89-90; J. Hintikka, "Cogito, Ergo Sum: Inference or Performance?" Philosophical Review, 1962 (71), 3-32, reprinted in Meta-Meditations: Studies in Descartes, ed. by A. Sesonske & N. Fleming [Belmont: Wadsworth, 1965], p. 65 fn.).

(16) Mead's view is anticipatory of and supported by C. I. Lewis' "pragmatic conception of the a priori": "Our categories and definitions are peculiarly social products, reached in the light of experience which

relative to the situation in conduct within which the reflection
arises, that while we can find in different situations a method
of conversation and so of thought which proves irrelevant to the
differences in the situations, and provides a method of translation
from one perspective to another, this irrelevance belongs only
to the wider character which the problem in reflection assumes,
and never transcends the social conduct within which the method
arises (MS 90 fn.).

In a contemporary perspective, we can understand a neo-Kantian attempt
to construe, as the a priori structure of "theoretical reason", a combination or system of the Fregean logic, the Riemannian geometry, and/or
some other basic concepts of sciences, rather than that of the
Aristotelian logic, the Euclidean geometry, and the Newtonian "categories". Such a system is based on or presupposes the development of
implemental conditions of assimilation and diffusion as well as those of
discovery and invention. Furthermore, it is methodic as well as methodological in a society or societies of contemporary men. Obviously, it
cannot be explained or "justified" fully on the basis of the congenital or
"innate" capacities of man.

In a perspective of evolution, we can point out that the congenital
functions of the human species have provided the evolved, common, but
"indeterminate" or "open-ended" basis of man's diverse developments
of social mediation or culture in different societies. We may say that a
structure of rationality (and, for that matter, a structure of irrationality?)
is "innate" in respect to individual men in the sense that they are "born"
into a certain structure of prevailing roles or rules of their society (or
societies). But various structures of man's functions - including those
relatively enduring aspects of symbolic process in general and those of
assertive, theoretical discourse in particular - are, as developed implementally in the milieu of various societies, certainly not "innate" in

---

have much in common, and beaten out, like other pathways, by the
coincidence of human purposes and the exigencies of human cooperation"
("A Pragmatic Conception of the a Priori", Journal of Philosophy, 1923
[20:17], pp. 169-77; reprinted in Readings in Philosophical Analysis,
ed. by H. Feigl & W. Sellars [New York: Appleton-Century-Crofts,
1949], p. 293).

Cf. "There are occasions when Lewis points out that categories and
the concepts we use in interpreting sense experience are social products,
just as is the language we use. But he draws back at the point where
one expects and most wants a thoroughly naturalistic and pragmatic
analysis of mind, of knowing, and of language. The analysis wanted is
one in which the function of mind, or mental behavior, and categories
are exhibited as originating from and shaped under those social situations where communication is the achieved outcome of organisms
cooperating in adjusting to and controlling their environment. Such a
pragmatic account of mind and communication was developed by
George Herbert Mead" (H. S. Thayer, Meaning and Action: A Critical
History of Pragmatism, p. 231).

the traditional, metaphysical sense of man's "essence" or "nature", nor in the biological sense of "instinct".

4.4 On the Myth of Prometheus

At the very end of his Carus Lectures which were given four months before his death, Mead spoke:

> Since society has endowed us with self-consciousness, we can enter personally into the largest undertakings which the intercourse of rational selves extends before us. And because we can live with ourselves as well as with others, we can criticize ourselves, and make our own the values in which we are involved through those undertakings in which the community of all rational beings is engaged (PP 90).

We are told that Prometheus gave us the fire which has enlightened our life (psyche), and that we have acquired the art of fire-making as our enlightened vocation (ergon).

To children, a gift is what is given to them by others, their parents and other members of a society. The gift of prometheus (universal forethought or premediation) is an education in rationality (nous) which lies in the use of symbols (logos) and other implements (techne) in various contexts of society (polis). So it is this education for the vocation of man, which we have received from others, and continue further, in order to participate in and contribute to the Life of Reason.

And the rest of the Promethean historia is man's history, bound and unbound, which is as yet unfinished.

APPENDIX A

MEAD'S SOCIAL, FUNCTIONAL CONCEPT OF CONSCIOUSNESS

A.1 Problems of Consciousness in a Historical Perspective

The classical problem of mind in modern philosophy since Descartes
has been largely derived from a misconception of the theories of the
mechanical sciences of Galileo and Newton. The misconception lies in
a metaphysically motivated attempt 1) to take extended material things
to be "primary", "reality", and "in the object"; 2) to take sensible
qualities to be "secondary", "appearance", and "in the subject, mind";
and 3) to take mind to be a substance radically different and independent
from the substance of extended material things. Thus, the psychological
problem is the difficulty of explaining the evident relation of mind and
matter in the case of man.

In this historical context, both the rationalists and the empiricists
found the locus of the experience of sensible qualities, as well as of
ideas, in the individual subject or mind, and so tended to fall into the
epistemological problem of the "ego-centric predicament". Without the
rationalists' assumption that the ideas of knowledge are "innate" and
common to all subjects or minds, the empiricists were involved with
the problem of extreme subjectivism or solipsism. On the other hand,
both the rationalists and the empiricists have, as a solution of the
epistemological and psychological difficulties derived from the mind-
body dualism, turned in their respectively different ways either to 1) an
idealism which limits the knowable world to the ideas of mind, while
presupposing the unknowable world of "things in themselves", or to 2)
and idealism which regards the phenomena of mind as the totality of
reality.

In anticipation of Ryle(1) and others, Mead takes as a "philosophical"
or logical problem the dualism of mind and matter, which is behind the
modern genesis of the difficult theories of "subjective", "transcendental",
or "absolute" idealism. He sees no determining effect of the metaphysical
and epistemological difficulties derived from the dualism on the development of sciences in the hands of practicing scientists, although psychology
as a science had suffered under these difficulties, unable to free itself
from philosophy until the turn of this century.

Mead says:

From Descartes' time on it [psychology] has been a border state,

---

(1) G. Ryle, The Concept of Mind (New York: Barnes & Noble, 1965
[orig. 1949]).

lying between philosophy and the natural sciences, and has
suffered the inconveniences which attend buffer states. Descartes'
unambiguous and uncompromising division between an extended
physical world, and an unextended world of thought . . . only
avoided compromise by leaving the relations of mind and body
to the infinite power of his <u>deus ex machina</u>. The difficulties
which have attended psychology's regulation of these relations
have been only in part metaphysical. More fundamentally they
have been logical.

The natural sciences start pragmatically with a world that
is there, within which a problem has arisen, and introduce
hypothetical reconstructions only insofar as its solution
demands them. They always have their feet upon the solid
ground of unquestioned objects of observation and experiment,
where Samuel Johnson placed his in his summary refutation of
Berkeley's idealism . . . .

Psychology as a philosophical discipline carried the epistemological problem into the experience of the individual, but as a
science located the problem in a given world which its epistemological problem could not accept as given. Between the two, its
sympathies have always been with the presuppositions and method
of the natural sciences.

On the one hand, as empirical science it has sought to regard
the so-called consciousness of the individual as merely given
in the sense of the objects of the natural sciences, but as states
of consciousness were still regarded as cognitive, they had
inevitably the epistemological diathesis.

On the other hand, as experimental science it was forced to
place states of consciousness within or without the processes
it was studying. Placing them in interactionism within the
natural processes ran counter to the presuppositions of its
scientific procedure, so that the prevailing attitude has been
that of epiphenomenalism, as adaptation of Leibniz' pre-
established harmony and Spinoza's parallel attributes. They
ran as harmless conscious shadows beside the physical and
physiological processes with which science could come to
immediate terms. But this proved but an unstable compromise.
The conscious streak that accompanied the neuroses could
answer only to sensing and thinking as processes: as qualities
and significance of things, states of consciousness became
hardly tolerable reduplications of things, except in the case of
the secondary qualities. The molecular structure of things
seemed to remove these from the hypothetical objects of
physical science, and consciousness proved a welcome dumping
ground for them. This bifurcation of nature proves equally
unsatisfactory . . . . States of contact experience have no
better right to objective existence than those of distance

experience.

Psychology, however, has not been interested in these epistemological and metaphysical riddles, it has been simply
irritated by them. It has shifted its interest to the processes
where phenomenalism is most harmless, appearing as physiological psychology, as functional psychology, as dynamic
psychology . . . . The effect of this has been to give the
central nervous system a logical pre-eminence in the procedure
and textbooks of psychology which is utterly unwarranted in the
analysis of the experience of the individual. The central nervous
system has been unwittingly assimilated to the logical position
of consciousness. It occupies only an important stage in the act,
but we find ourselves locating the whole environment of the
individual in its convolutions. It is small wonder, then, that
behaviorism has been welcomed with unmistakable relief, for
it has studied the conduct of animals in necessary ignoration
of consciousness, and it has been occupied with the act as a
whole, not as a nervous arc (SW 268-70).

In the Meadean behavioristic approach to the study of mind, we still
have certain basic problems which correspond to the very closely related and yet distinct traditional problems of the mind-body dualism in
modern philosophy since Descartes: 1) the problem of the distinction
and relation of mind and body (namely, what is involved in what we
distinguish as mind and body? and how are they related, even if they
are distinguishable?); 2) the problem of objects in general (namely, how
are we going to set up a basic typology of objects?); 3) the problem of
the unity of self or the self-formation; and 4) the problem of the "ego-
centric predicament" or the individual subjectivity. Mead considers
these problems from a perspective of psychology which turns out to be
a behavioristic "social psychology". In this Appendix, his consideration
of the first and fourth problems are mainly discussed. (In Chapter 2,
the first and second problems are further considered; and in Chapter 3,
the second, third, and fourth problems are further considered.)

A.2 Three Senses of "Consciousness"

In a psychological investigation of the problem of mind or consciousness,
Mead distinguishes three different aspects or senses of the act or
experience of man which can be referred to by the ambiguous concept
of "consciousness": 1) "consciousness of" or "accessibility to certain
contents:; 2) "certain contents themselves" or "the field of experience";
and 3) "self-consciousness" or "reflective (social, symbolic) process". (2)
(In a strict logical analysis, if required, consciousness in the third
sense may be construed in two different ways analogous to the first and
second.)

---

(2) SW 271 ff, MS 30 ff, PA 73 ff, PP 4 ff, MT 392 ff, etc.

Mead says:

> When we use "consciousness" . . ., with reference to those
> conditions which are variable with the experience of the
> individual, this usage is a quite different one from that of
> rendering ourselves inaccessible to the world. In one case
> we are dealing with the situation of a person going to sleep,
> distracting his attention or centering his attention - a partial
> or complete exclusion of certain parts of a field. The other
> use is in application to the experience of the individual that
> is different from the experience of anybody else, and not only
> different in that way, but different from his own experience at
> different times (MS 30-1).

On the other hand, Mead continues:

> It is unfortunate to fuse or mix up consciousness, as we
> ordinarily use that term, and self-consciousness. Conscious-
> ness, as frequently used, simply has reference to the field of
> experience, but self-consciousness refers to the ability to call
> out in ourselves a set of definite responses which belong to the
> others of the group. Consciousness and self-consciousness are
> not the same level. A man alone has . . . access to his own
> toothache, but that is not what we mean by self-consciousness
> (MS 163).

For an example, we may consider the case of a man who kicked a stone.
Here it may be said of this situation as a paradigm of the act of human
experience: 1) that he was conscious in the sense that he saw the stone,
moved his foot, and hit the stone; 2) that he was conscious in the sense
that he expected the stone to be light, sensed his foot striking it, and
felt it hard on his toe; and 3) that he was conscious in the sense that he
knew what he was doing, namely, he thought it would not hurt his feet
and could ridicule Berkeley's idealism.

In this situation the man was conscious of certain objects, including
the stone, his feet, Berkeley's idealism, and the pain on his toe. To
say in the first sense of consciousness - if possible to say in a "reductive" or "abstract" sense without implicating further - that he was
simply conscious of these objects is to say merely that there was a
relation between the man and these objects. To speak, in the second
sense, of these objects as the contents of his consciousness is to speak
of the world of these objects in relation to him, his field of experience.
"Our constructive selection of an environment - colours, emotional
values, and the like - in terms of our physiological sensitivities", Mead
says, "is essentially what we mean by consciousness" (MS 129). And to
say in the third sense that he was conscious of himself in the situation
is to say that he was able to distinguish various factors of the situation
and to discover them related to one another in a way which rendered
the situation significant or meaningful as a unified whole. In this sense,
we mean by consciousness the social process in reference to a person.
Here it may be said that he goes further than the level of consciousness

in the first and second senses to reconstruct or redefine his own function or role in relating or responding to other objects and/or persons in the social problematic situation. "Our consciousness as such", Mead says, "is a continued meeting and solution of problems, or an attempted solution of them" (MT 410). Such an act of consciousness, or self-consciousness, is an emergence of a new self as well as that of a new environment.

In any of the three senses, consciousness is not a substance or entity which is possible in itself; it is a process of functional relations of various factors - including the sensitive, social being - of the given situation. These factors are, in a biological or psychological context, considered in reference to the individual organism or person. We may speak of consciousness as a functional relation in reference to the individual on one hand, and of the world of experience as a functional relation without reference to the individual on the other. And what is regarded as a part of the individual or a part of the environment is also entirely functional to the interest or problem we have.

In the first and second senses, consciousness - or the world of experience - is immediately there, with no problem, as selected, responded to, and/or consummated without delay. Only in the third sense do we find a problem, a cognitive problem of new self or new world, implicated in consciousness: whether certain objects of conscious-ness are exceptional or subjective; and whether they can be manipulated, consummated, or preserved. Precisely, self-consciousness emerges as a functional relation when the individual finds his situation problematic and delays his response to take the role of others properly.

A.3 Consciousness as a Social Perspective

In an historical survey of the problem of mind in the "movements of thought" in the West, Mead traces this new approach of considering consciousness as a function of the actual situation to the questions Dewey and James asked at the turn of this century. (3)

Mead says:

The . . . approach is that of Professor Dewey . . . from the standpoint of the conduct itself, which carries with it the various values which we had associated with the term "consciousness". (4) There arose at this time the question which James put so bluntly: Does consciousness exist?(5) . . . Is there any such

(3) See MT 386-404. And also his article, "The Definitions of the Psychical", Decennial Publications (Univ. of Chicago), 1903 (First Series: Vol. III), pp. 77-112; reprinted in part in SW 25-59.
(4) J. Dewey, "The Reflex Arc Concept in Psychology", Psychological Review, 1896 (3:4), pp. 357-70; reprinted in his Philosophy and Civilization (New York: Minton, Balch & Co., 1931), pp. 233-48.
(5) W. James, "Does 'Consciousness' Exist?", Journal of Philosophy, 1904 (1:18), pp. 477-91; reprinted in his Essays in Radical Empiricism

entity as consciousness in distinction from the world of our experience? Can we say that there is any such thing as consciousness which is a separate entity apart from the character of the world itself? The question, of course, is difficult to answer directly, because the term "consciousness" is an ambiguous one. We use it particularly for experiences which are represented . . . by going to sleep and waking up, going under and coming out of the anesthetic, in losing and regaining consciousness. We think of it as something which is a sort of entity, which is there, which has been under these conditions, submerged and then allowed to appear again. That use of consciousness is not essentially different from the shutting-off of any field of experience through the senses. If one, for example, turns out the lights in the room, he no longer experiences the sight of objects about him. We say he has lost consciousness of those objects. But you would not speak of him as having lost consciousness. He is simply un-able to see what is there . . . . If we closed up his eyes, shut off his nostrils, ears, mouth, shut him off from a whole series of different stimuli, even those coming to him from the surface of the body and from the visceral tract, he would probably lose consciousness, go to sleep. There, you see, the losing of consciousness does not mean the loss of a certain entity but merely the cutting-off of one's relations with experiences. Consciousness in that sense means merely a normal relation-ship between the organism and the outside objects. And what we refer to as consciousness as such is really the character of the object (MT 392-3).

And Mead goes further to construe this actual, functional interpretation of consciousness as the implication of two modern concepts, 1) the Darwinian concept of evolutionary emergence in biology and 2) the Einsteinian concept of relative objectivity in physics. Following Whitehead, (6) he generalizes the implication in his own theory of per-spective. (7) In terms of this theory, consciousness emerges as, and is intrinsically, a social (or relational) perspective, the phases of which are "objective" in reference to the given situation.
Mead says:

If we accept those two concepts of emergence and relativity
. . ., they do answer to what we term "consciousness", namely, a certain environment that exists in its relationship to the organism, and in which new characters can arise in virtue of the organism . . . . [This view] does answer to certain conscious characteristics which have been given to forms

(New York: Longmans, Green & Co., 1912), pp. 1-38.
(6) See the following footnote 8.
(7) See his article, "The Objective Reality of Perspectives", reprinted in PP 161-75 and SW 306-19. And PA 159 ff.

at certain points in evolution. On this view the characters do
not belong to organisms as such but only in the relationship of
the organism to its environment. They are characteristics of
objects in the environment of the form. The objects are
coloured, odorous, pleasant or painful, hideous or beautiful,
in their relationship to the organism . . . . In the development
of forms with environments that answer to them and that are
regulated by the forms themselves there appear or emerge
characters that are dependent on this relation between the form
and its environment. In one sense of the term, such characters
constitute the field of consciousness.

When an animal form appears, certain objects become food;
and we recognize that those objects have become food because
the animal has a certain sort of digestive apparatus . . . . We
do constantly refer to certain objects in the environment as
existing there because of the relationship between the form and
the environment. There are certain objects that are beautiful
but that would not be beautiful if there were not individuals that
have an appreciation of them. It is in that organic relation that
beauty arises. In general, then, we do recognize that there are
objective fields in the world dependent upon the relation of the
environment to certain forms.

I am suggesting the extension of that recognition to the field of
consciousness. All that I aim to point out here is that with such
a conception we have hold of what we term "consciousness", as
such; we do not have to endow the form with consciousness as a
certain spiritual substance if we utilize these conceptions, and
. . . we do utilize them when we speak of such a thing as food
emerging in the environment because of the relationship of an
object with the form. We might just as well speak of colour,
sound, and so on, in the same way (MS 330-1).

I have referred to the doctrine of relativity . . . . What I
have had particularly in mind is Whitehead's recognition(8)
. . . that if motion is to be accepted as an objective fact, we

_____

(8) As a prefatory statement to this quotation, Mead wrote in 1924: "I
have referred to the doctrine of relativity. More specifically, my
reference was to formulation of the doctrine given in Professor
Whitehead's three books, The Principles of Natural Knowledge (1919),
The Concept of Nature (1920), and The Principle of Relativity (1922)"
(SW 274-5). On the other hand, a statement of Mead's, as written in
1927, may be noted: "I do not wish to consider Professor Whitehead's
Bergsonian edition of Spinoza's underlying substance that individualizes
itself in the structure of events, nor his Platonic heaven of eternal
objects where lie the hierarchies of patterns, that are there envisaged
as possibilities and have ingression into events . . ." (SW 308-9). It
appears that Mead had no chance to comment on Whitehead's Gifford

must also accept the existence in nature of so-called consentient
sets at rest, determined by their relation to so-called percipient
events. The same events in nature appear in different consentient
sets, as these events are ordered in different time systems, and
this ordering in different time systems is dependent upon their
relations to different percipient events. Motion in nature implies
rest in nature. Rest in nature implies co-gredience, i.e., a
persistent relation of here and there with reference to some
individual, and it is this that determines the time system in
accordance with which events are ordered. If rest is a fact in
nature, we must conceive of it as stratified, to use Whitehead's
term, by the different temporal perspectives of different
individuals, though a group of individuals may have the same
perspective; we must, however, remember that this is a
stratification of nature not in a static space, but a nature
whose extension is affected with a time dimension.

It is this conception of the existence in nature of consentient
sets determined by their relations to percipient events that I
wish to generalize so that it will cover the environment in
relation to the living form, and the experienced world with
reference to the experiencing individuals. This is evidently only
possible if we conceive life as a process and not a series of
static physicochemical situations, and if we regard experience as
conduct or behavior, not a series of conscious states (SW 274-5).

One of the great contributions of relativity has been that it has
accustomed us to the recognition that the determining relationship of the individual or percipient event to the consentient set
is a fact in nature and in no sense involves subjectivity or what
Whitehead calls the bifurcation of nature. (9) If there were one
absolute spatial and temporal order of the world, the different
worlds of different individuals would seem to be experiences
which should be located within the individuals; but, in a universe
which is stratified by the selection of time order by a percipient
event, these stratifications are in nature and not in the individual,
and we are at liberty to conceive of an evolution of such experiences which has followed the evolution which we ascribe to
the forms themselves (PA 325).

In Professor Whitehead's phrase, insofar as nature is patient
of an organism, it is stratified into perspectives, whose inter-
sections constitute the creative advance of nature . . . . They
are not distorted perspectives of some perfect patterns, nor
do they lie in consciousness as selections among things whose

---

Lectures of 1927-8, Process and Reality (pub. in 1929) if he ever read
it before his death early in 1931.
(9) A. N. Whitehead, The Concept of Nature (Ann Arbor: Univ. of
Michigan Press, 1957 [orig. 1920]), Chap. II.

reality is to be found in a noumenal world. They are in their
interrelationship the nature that science knows (SW 308).

In terms of Mead's application of the view of "nature as an organization
of perspectives" to the emergent process of consciousness, it follows
that the consciousness of an individual is his perspective or view of the
actual situation to which he is in relation, and that the objects of his
consciousness are largely distant objects (a distant phase of experience),
which are objectively there within the perspective. For example, the
percept, the distant object of perception, is the distant phase of the
perspective of the individual, which emerges as the latter is in relation
to the situation and to which the act can be carried out in accordance with
the nature of the percept.
Mead says:

> The thing at a distance is there as genuinely as that which the
> hand grasps or the physical particles into which it may be
> crumbled. It is there, but it is there as a distant thing. As a
> distant thing it is the promise or threat of possible contact
> experience, but this promise or threat of contact experience
> neither abrogates its distance characters or transfers them
> to a mind to become states of consciousness, though the final
> contact is the experimental evidence of the reality of the
> promise which the object at a distance carried.

> In so far as imagery of past experience has passed into the
> perceptual object, this object may be denominated a collapsed
> act, but both elements are there in the object. Doubt or question
> transforms the contact value into a hypothesis, to be tested in
> actual conduct. In so far, the contact value becomes mental,
> but this does not render the distance values mental or justify
> the reference of them to a self as states of consciousness.

> What seems to justify this reference is the substitution of
> material particles with a content of contact experience for the
> distance experience in the physical theory of the perceptual
> situation. Physical theory states its objects in the ultimate
> form which the experimental test implies, but when it places
> underneath the colour the whorl of molecules, atoms, or
> electrons, which imagined experience would reach if it came
> into contact with the structure of the thing, it no more
> abrogates the colour at a distance than the feel of the red book
> deprives it of its redness (PA 76).

When the individual takes distant objects or events in his perspective to
be, under a certain problematic condition, in the relation of what is
called simultaneity or contemporaneity - that is, when he transforms
them as parts of a plan or hypothesis for future activity, manipulation
and consummation - consciousness in the third sense is implicated by
the perspective. Here the individual realizes the distant objects as other
than himself and reconstructs himself in the relation to them in the social

process of taking their roles. And the individual is open to the possibility of realizing those distant objects emergent in his perspective as his own subjective states of consciousness or mind.

Mead says:

> Mind as it appears in the mechanism of social conduct is . . . the establishment of simultaneity between the organism and a group of events, through the arrest of action under inhibition. . . . This arrest of action means the tendencies within the organism to act in conflicting ways in the completion of the whole act. The attitude of the organism calls out or tends to call out responses in other organisms, which responses, in the case of human gesture, the organism calls out in itself, and thus excites itself to respond to these responses. It is the identification of these responses with the distant stimuli that establishes simultaneity, that gives insides to these distant stimuli, and a self to the organism. Without such an establishment of simultaneity, these stimuli are spatio-temporally distant from the organism, and their reality lies in the future of passage. The establishment of simultaneity wrenches this future reality into a possible present, for all our presents beyond the manipulatory area are only possibilities, as respects their perceptual reality. We are acting toward the future realization of the act, as if it were present, because the organism is taking the role of the other (SW 316).

The perspective of simultaneity, or self-consciousness, as realized in social situations by the symbolic process in which the individual takes himself as an object to himself in his attempt to relate other objects to himself, is the very basis of the rationality of man. The development of such social perspectives in the "primitive" sense constitutes the objectivity of modern science as well as the complex, orderly organization of diversified society and the highly integrated career of individualized person.

A.4 The "Subjective" as a Functional Phase of Act

Mead's perspectival interpretation of consciousness has an implication on the traditional problem of the "subjective"; it provides an explication of the "subjective" as a functional phase of actual situation.

Historically, there are in modern Western philosophy three diverse motives or factors behind the Cartesian dualism and other derivative problems of mind and body: 1) the philosophical attempt to provide an independent domain for the old enterprise of Christian religion of Pope Urban and for the new enterprise of mechanical science of Galileo Galilei; 2) the philosophical attempt to take as reality what the concepts of mechanical science of Galileo and Newton posit; and 3) the common realization that certain phases of individual experience are "subjective" to oneself and inaccessible to others.

As for the first motive, we have realized that the autonomy of religion and science, if desirable and possible, does not require a metaphysical dualism, a "bifurcation of nature", and as for the second, that the concepts of physics have no inclusive privilege to the claim of reality which is largely a contextual, value problem. (10)

As for the third factor, we may briefly consider the traditional problem of the "subjective" in terms of Mead's interpretation of consciousness. We can see 1) that the phases of human act or experience which are supposedly subjective to each individual man in certain contexts do not require the substantial dualism of mind and body, and 2) that these phases are functionally variable in terms of the contexts the individual is in, since these phases in terms of consciousness in the second sense are basically a problem of physiological accessibility, and these phases in terms of consciousness in the third sense are basically a problem of provisional privacy.

In conjunction with the problem of the "subjective", the following polar concepts, most of which are mentioned by Mead, are noted:

a) "subjective"   vs. "objective"
b) "inaccessible" (to others)   vs. "accessible" (to others)
c) "private"   vs. "public"
d) "variable"   vs. "invariable"
e) "unique" or "private"   vs. "common"
f) "particular" or "individual"   vs. "universal"
g) "individual" or "personal"   vs. "social"
h) "internal"   vs. "external"
i) "mental"   vs. "physical" or "material"
j) "psychical"   vs. "physical"
k) "conscious"   vs. "unconscious"

Related to a), the polar concepts of "subjective" and "objective", the other concepts, b) to k), have different references in various but related contexts in which the mind-body problem is placed. These polar concepts, even if vaguely understood in their application to their problematic contexts, "cut" the world into two in various ways; but these various divisions in no way coincide to provide a justification of any metaphysical, substantial bifurcation of nature into mind and matter, the subject and the object, in the traditional sense. These divisions are logical distinctions and are functional in their problematic contexts.

Mead says:

In the mental processes there are two sets of objects which have in especial degree seemed to demand a mind to act as a habitat. One of these sets is that of imagery . . . . The other set of objects is that of ideas. The very nature of the idea indicates that in a very real sense it is not in the world. One's undertaking is that of fashioning the world so that it shall conform to an idea that is not there realized, and that reconstructed world is an

---

(10) Cf. J. H. Randall, Jr., Nature and Historical Experience, Chaps. 5-8; and J. Buchler, Metaphysics of Natural Complexes, Chap. 1.

environment that is confined, at least for the time being, to the
individual whose idea it is. This holds also of imagery. As
content we assume that imagery belongs to an environment
that is confined to the individual in question. In that sense it
is a private environment. It is a piece of the world into which
no one else can enter.

It is, however, an unwarranted assumption that such contents
are so substantially different from objects in the common world
of experience that they cannot belong to it . . . . A content of
imagery is normally found in the objects of the world of immediate experience, and the ideas as contents appear in per-
ceived things as their natures. It is not some substantial
character that differentiates images and ideas from the world
about; it is their accessibility . . . . Nor is inaccessibility
confined to images and ideas. Any part of the organism except
in so far as it is located in distance experience as a part of the
environment - I refer to such objects as an aching tooth or a
pleased palate - is also inaccessible to all except the individual
whose organism it is. The inaccessibility in the latter case is
plainly mechanical. If the world at large had nervous access to
the tooth such as is accorded to the suffering individual, it
would be an aching tooth to all. I see no reason to assume that,
if a similar neural access to cerebral tracts were possible, we
might not share with other identical memory-images (PA 376-7).

By way of further avoiding certain metaphysical implications,
I wish to say that it does not follow that because we have on the
one side experience which is individual, which may be perhaps
private . . ., and have on the other a common world . . ., we
have two separate levels of existence or reality which are to be
distinguished metaphysically from each other. A great deal that
appears simply as the experience of an individual, as his own
sensation or perception, become public later. Every discovery
as such begins with experiences which have to be stated in terms
of the biography of the discoverer. The man can note exceptions
and implications which other people do not see and can only
record them in terms of his own experience. He puts them in
that form in order that other persons may get a like experience,
and then he undertakes to find out what the explanation of these
strange facts is. He works out hypotheses and tests them and
they become common property thereafter. That is, there is a
close relationship between these two fields of the psychical and
the physical, the private and the public. We make distinctions
between these, recognizing that the same factor may now be
only private and yet later may become public. It is the work
of the discoverer through his observations and through his
hypotheses and experiments to be continually transforming
what is his own private experience into a universal form. The
same may be said of other fields, as in the work of the great
artist who takes his own emotions and gives them a universal

form so that others may enter into them (MS 41 fn).

It is noted in view of the above two quotations that the problem of the "subjective" rests on certain functional characters of accessibility and inaccessibility, and that these characters are different in terms of two different contexts which correspond to those of consciousness in the second and third senses. In the former, the character of accessibility is "mechanical" or physiological; and in the latter, it is temporally provisional. In reference to the problem of the "subjective", Mead explains that "the two have no necessary relationship" (MS 165) – in spite of the common feature of accessibility for oneself and inaccessibility for others. For consciousness in the second sense, the physiological character of this feature may be said to characterize the "subjective" or "private" phase of consciousness. But for consciousness in the third sense, its "subjective" or "private" phase is not determined by the physiological character of this feature but by the provisional character of what Mead calls "collapsed act", the (incipient) act of taking the role of distant objects to complete the act – within consciousness as an objective perspective.

Mead says:

Perspectives have objective existence. The obverse of this proposition is that the perspective is not subjective . . . . The logical distinction between the subjective and objective lies within the perspective. The subjective is that experience in the individual which takes the place of the object when the reality of the object, at least in some respects, lies in an uncertain future. If one used, for example, one's readiness to jump across a ditch as a rough means of estimating its breadth in place of the tape, that attitude of the individual would be subjective, not because it belongs to the individual simply but because one substitutes tentatively an attitude belonging to the individual for an existent objective character. What belongs to the individual has the same objective reality as that which belongs to his world. It is simply there. The fact that what belongs to him is largely accessible only to him, while the world is also accessible to others who exist in his social perspective, does not render the experiences of his organism subjective. They become such only when they become surrogates for an as yet unattained reality in determining his conduct.

The affective side of experience is predominantly subjective because the attitudes of which the affection is a part so largely determine our conduct in the place of the actual objective characters which are responsible for them . . . . Imagery is largely subjective because we depend upon our responses to imagery of that which is distant in space-time to determine how we would act with reference to it. Ideas are pre-eminently subjective because they are the structure of the symbols of things, and their meanings rest upon our responses by which we formulate our hypothetical plans of actions.

The relationship, then, between the individual and his world is a condition for the appearance of the relation between the objective and subjective, but it is not coincident with it. It does not exist, for example, in the perspectives of animals other than man, or in a considerable part of our own experience (PA 114-5).

It is true that certain contents of experience (particularly kinaesthetic) are accessible only to the given individual organism and not to any others; and that these private or "subjective", as opposed to public or "objective", contents of experience are usually regarded as being peculiarly and intimately connected with the individual's self, or as being in a special sense self-experiences. But this accessibility solely to the given individual organism of certain contents of its experience . . . does not alter the fact that self-consciousness involves the individual's becoming an object to himself by taking the attitudes of other individuals toward himself within an organized setting of social relationship, and that . . . apart from his social interactions with other individuals, he would not relate the private or "subjective" contents of experience to himself (MS 225).

In the context of consciousness in the third sense, the "subjective" phase presupposes the social process of self-consciousness as an objective perspective. This self-consciousness as a perspective of simultaneity in a social situation presupposes a situation in which the individual is a part, an object; but it does not presuppose the self, the very process of the formation of self-consciousness, nor the intrinsic "subjective" self. The self-consciousness is the emergent relation of the social situation in which the involved individual becomes a new self and in which a phase of the individual may be regarded as his "subjectivity".

The emergence of self - as an "objectivity" - in relation to other objects in a social situation is required for the consciousness of objects regarded as parts of the "subjective" phase of the self, as well as for the consciousness of objects distinguished as other than oneself. Otherwise, the whole process of consciousness both in the second and the third senses has to be turned into "an epistemological basis not distinguishable from Hume's or Berkeley's: to wit, that we can reduce all experience to states of individual consciousness in which form we may recognize their ultimate validity". "To do this, however", Mead says, "is to objectify the psychical state, and deprive it of the very elements that have rendered it psychical" (SW 16).

The objective structure of self-consciousness, in terms of which an individual acts within and knows the world - or in terms of which his perspective is organized - and in reference to which a phase is regarded as subjective, is based upon the social structure or common perspective of the actual situation. This structure is what Mead calls a "generalized other", which is the symbolic structure of social roles. In case the individual fails – or anticipates his failure – to select and organize the world on the basis of this common structure of society, he finds his situation problematic. He has to consider a reconstruction of the given social structure of public perspective. That is to say, he finds his self-consciousness provisionally in its "subjective" phase.

A. 5 Transactional Correlationalism ("Parallelism")

In Mead's re-interpretation of consciousness in general and the "subjective" in particular, consciousness or mind can be construed in two phases. There is on one hand the common condition under which individuals experience or are conscious, and on the other hand the phase of each individual's experience or consciousness which is private and inaccessible to others. Each of them is distinguishable in context. Their distinction and relation are important in view of psychology as a science, an attempt to control the experience of individuals. As these two phases are related, they can be correlated, that is, a "parallelistic" correlation can be established between them. And the one is determined and controlled in terms of the other on the basis of the correlation. As a simple example, the variation of the wattage of a street lamp is accompanied by a variation in the vision of passers-by. For a practical purpose, the variation can be measured in terms of the proportional decrease (or increase) of accidents in the situation. Here the suitable wattage can be selected on the basis of a correlation which has been established in a set of experimental situations.

Mead says:

A certain sort of parallelism is involved in the attempt to state the experience of the individual insofar as it is peculiar to him as an individual. What is accessible only to that individual, what takes place only in the field of his own inner life, must be stated in its relationship to the situation within which it takes place. One individual has one experience and another has another experience, and both are stated in terms of their biographies; but there is in addition that which is common to the experience of all. And our scientific statement correlates that which the individual himself experiences, and which can ultimately be stated only in terms of his experience, with the experience which belongs to everyone. That is essential in order that we may interpret what is peculiar to the individual. We are always separating that which is peculiar to our own reaction, that which we can see that other persons cannot see, from that which is common to all. We are referring what belongs to the experience just of the individual to a common language, to a common world. And when we carry out this relationship, this correlation, into what takes place physically and physiologically, we get a parallelistic psychology . . . . The psychologist is interested in getting the correlation between the conditions under which the experience takes place and that which is peculiar to the individual. He wishes to make

these statements as universal as possible, and is scientific
in that respect. He wants to state the experience of an individual just as closely as he can in terms of the field which
he can control, those conditions under which it appears
(MS 33-5).

"The term 'parallelism' has an unfortunate implication", Mead says.
"It is historically and philosophically bound up with the contrast of the
physical over . . . the psychical, with consciousness over . . . the
unconscious world. Actually, we simply state what an experience is
over . . . those conditions under which it arises. That fact lies behind
'parallelism', and to carry out the correlation one has to state both
fields in as common a language as possible" (MS 40). In consideration
of this view, it is proposed that the term "correlationalism" may be
employed in place of Mead's "parallelism".
    In this context, on the other hand, the following four distinguishable
factors of consciousness may be noted: 1) the external processes of the
environment, which are common to all individuals in a given situation;
2) the behavioral processes of each individual, which are public to
others as well as to oneself; 3) the physiological processes of each
individual, which are "indirectly" accessible to others and in some
contexts to oneself; and 4) the private or "internal" processes of each
individual, which are inaccessible - provisionally or physiologically -
to others. These factors are not of separate substantial or metaphysical
existences; they are logical distinctions of analysis, logically differentiated aspects of intrinsically related on-going processes.
    In proper contexts, it is possible in terms of their given problems
that these aspects can be distinguished, and that a correlation can be
established between two of them. For example, a correlation can be
determined between 1) and 2), or 3) and 4), with indifference to the
others - rather than between the common condition and the private experience on the basis of the earlier, general distinction. It is clear
prima facie that since these four factors are all involved in the process
of consciousness, the correlation between two of them, excluding the
others, involves a certain abstraction which may not be justified as a
general approach of psychology.
    There is a common attempt of certain physiological psychologists
and "tough-minded" philosophers to re-interpret the processes of
consciousness in terms of, or reduce them to, 3), particularly brain or
neural processes. But consciousness or mind cannot be fully explained
in terms of physiological or neural processes as long as it is construed
as a selective, functional, dynamic process based on the common or
"invariant" structures of actual situations, particularly on their social,
symbolic structures.
    Mead says:

In defending a social theory of mind we are defending a
functional, as opposed to any form of substantive or entitive,
view as to its nature. And in particular, we are opposing all
intracranial or intra-epidermal views as to its character and
locus. For it follows from our social theory of mind that the

field of mind must be co-extensive with, and include all the components of, the field of social process of experience and behavior, i.e., the matrix of social relations and interactions among individuals, which is presupposed by it, and out of which it arises or comes into being. If mind is socially constituted, then the field or locus of any given individual mind must extend as far as the social activity or apparatus of social relations which constitutes it extends; and hence that field cannot be bounded by the skin of the individual organism (MS 223 fn).

It is true that all the operations of stimuli can be traced through to the central nervous system, so we seem to be able to take the problem inside of our skins and get back to something in the organism, the central nervous system, which is representative of everything that happens outside. When we speak of a light as influencing us, we must remember it does not influence us until it strikes the retina of the eye. Sound does not exert influence until it reaches the ear, and so on, so that we can say the whole world can be stated in terms of what goes on inside of the organism itself. And we can say that what we are trying to correlate are the happenings in the central nervous system on one side and the experience of the individual on the other. But we have to recognize that we have made an arbitrary cut there. We cannot take the central nervous system by itself, nor the physical objects by themselves. The whole process is one which starts from a stimulus and involves everything that takes place. Thus, psychology correlates the difference of perceptions with the physical intensity of the stimulus. We could state the intensity of a weight we are lifting in terms of the central nervous system, but that would be a difficult way of stating it. That is not what psychology is trying to do. It is not trying to relate a set of psychoses to a set of neuroses. It is trying to state the experiences of the individual in terms of the conditions under which they arise, and such conditions can very seldom be stated in terms of neuroses. Occasionally we can follow the process into the central nervous system, but it is quite impossible to state most of the conditions in those terms (MS 38-9).

The earlier conception of the central nervous system assumed that one could locate certain faculties of the mind in certain parts of the brain, but a study of the central nervous system did not reveal any such correlation. It became evident that there were nothing but paths in the central nervous system. The cells of the brain were seen to be parts of the nervous paths provided with material for carrying on the system, but nothing was found there to carry on the preservation of an idea as such. There was nothing in the central nervous system which would enable one to locate a tract given over to abstractions. There was a time when the frontal lobe also represents nothing but paths. The paths make very complicated conduct possible, they complicate the act enormously through the mechanism of the brain; but they do not set up any structure which functionally answers to ideas. So the study of consciousness from the standpoint of the organism inevitably led men to look at consciousness itself from the point of view of action (MS 21-2).

In the cortex, that organ which in some sense answers to human intelligence, we fail to find any exclusive and unvarying control, that is, any evidence of it in the structure of the form itself. In some way we can assume that the cortex acts as a whole, but we cannot come back to certain centers and say that this is where the mind lodged in thinking and in action. There are an indefinite number of cells connected with each other, and their innervation in some sense leads to a unitary action, but what that unity is in terms of the central nervous system it is almost impossible to state. All the different parts of the cortex seem to be involved in everything that happens. All the stimuli that reach the brain are reflected into all parts of the brain, and yet we do get a unitary action. There remains, then, a problem which is by no means definitely solved: the unity of the action of the central nervous system . . . . There is nothing in the structure of the brain itself which isolated any parts of the brain as those which direct conduct as a whole. The unity is a unity of integration, though just how this integration takes place in detail we cannot say.
What I wanted to bring out is that the approach to psychological theory from the standpoint of the organism must inevitably be through an emphasis upon conduct, upon the dynamic rather than the static (MS 24).

Beyond these possible arguments against the physiological, or intra-cranial or intra-epidermal, approaches in their limited senses to the problems of consciousness, Mead admits that the basic trouble with them is that physiology on the process of consciousness is "still a dark continent" (MS 25). (11) It is evident that what takes place in the brain or in the nerves is the process "whereby we lose and regain consciousness: a process which is somewhat analogous to that of pulling down and raising a window shade" (MS 112). But as for a general approach to the problems of consciousness, all the factors involved in them must be considered and related in a way which will provide a workable means of explanation and control.
Mead says:

What, for example, is our experience that answers to clenching of the fist? Physiological psychology followed the action out through the nerves that came from the muscles of the arm and

---

(11) Cf. P. Laslett (ed.), The Physical Basis of Mind (Oxford: B. Blackwell, 1950). See 3.223, fn. 27 and 31.

hand. The experience of the act would then be the sensation of
what was going on; in consciousness as such there is an awareness of what the organ was doing; there is a parallelism between
what goes on in the organ and what takes place in consciousness.
This parallelism is, of course, not a complete parallelism.
There seems to be consciousness corresponding only to the
sensory nerves. We are conscious of some things and not conscious
of others, and attention seems to play a very great part in determining which is the case . . . . Only portions of the response
appear in consciousness as such (MS 22-3).

We are conscious always of what we have done, never of doing
it. We are always conscious directly only of sensory processes,
never of motor processes; hence we are conscious of motor
processes only through sensory processes, which are their
resultants. The contents of consciousness have, therefore, to
be correlated with or fitted into a physiological system in
dynamic terms, as processes going on (MS 22 fn.).

[Furthermore,] it is absurd to look at the mind simply from
the standpoint of the individual human organism; for, although
it has its focus there, it is essentially a social phenomenon;
even its biological functions are primarily social. The subjective experience of the individual must be brought into relation
with the natural, socio-biological activities of the brain in
order to render an acceptable account of mind possible at all;
and this can be done only if the social nature of mind is
recognized. The meagerness of individual experience in
isolation from the processes of social experience – in isolation
from its social environment – should, moreover, be apparent.
We must regard mind, then, as arising and developing within
the social process, within the empirical matrix of social interactions. We must, that is, get an inner individual experience
from the standpoint of social acts which include the experiences
of separate individuals in a social context wherein these individuals interact. The processes of experience which the human
brain makes possible are made possible only for a group of
interacting individuals: not for the individual organism in
isolation from other individual organisms.

Mind arises in the social process only when that process as
a whole enters into, or is present in, the experience of any one
of the given individuals involved in that process. When this
occurs the individual becomes self-conscious and has a mind;
he becomes aware of his relations to that process as a whole,
and to the other individuals participating in it with him; he
becomes aware of that process as modified by the reactions
and interactions of the individuals – including himself – who
are carrying it on. The evolutionary appearance of mind or
intelligence takes place when the whole social process of
experience and behavior is brought within the experience of

any one of the separate individuals implicated therein, and
when the individual's adjustment to the process is modified
and refined by the awareness or consciousness which he thus
has of it (MS 133-4).

Mead's social, dynamic interpretation of mind - and his parallelism or
correlationalism between the private phase of mind and its social
dynamics - is justified by the fact that he recognizes that the human
mind has emerged in a process of social evolution, in a living process
of human organisms in their environmental situation, which is social
and symbolic. In this transactional, dynamic process of social evolution,
mind - its contents, percepts, and images in one context and significant
symbols in another - emerges and functions as organized or unified
transactional responses (or attitudes of response), on the part of individuals, to the objects and characters in the actual situation. The
analysis of inquiry which isolates or dissects these responses does not
destroy but presupposes the actual unities or relations of on-going social
processes. Thus, the social, dynamic correlationalistic interpretation
of consciousness provides the ground for "social behaviorism", the
view that the actual situation or condition of experience is social and
that the behavioral response is the determining factor of experience in
the actual situation.

BIBLIOGRAPHY

1. Mead's works posthumously published

The Philosophy of the Present, edited, with an Introduction, by
   Arthur E. Murphy and with "Prefatory Remarks" by John Dewey
   (La Salle: Open Court Publishing Co., 1932) (The Paul Carus
   Lectures, 1930).
Mind, Self and Society - from the Standpoint of a Social Behaviorist
   edited, with an Introduction, by Charles W. Morris (Chicago: Univ.
   of Chicago Press, 1934).
"The Philosophy of John Dewey", International Journal of Ethics, 1935
   (46:1), pp. 64-81.
Movements of Thought in the Nineteenth Century, edited, with an
   Introduction, by Merritt H. Moore (Chicago: Univ. of Chicago Press,
   1936).
The Philosophy of the Act, edited, with an Introduction, by Charles
   W. Morris, in collaboration with John M. Brewster, Albert M.
   Dunham, and David L. Miller; and with "Biographical Notes" by
   Henry C. A. Mead (Chicago: Univ. of Chicago Press, 1938).
The Social Psychology of George Herbert Mead, edited, with an
   Introduction, by Anselm Strauss (Chicago: Univ. of Chicago Press,
   1956). (A slightly revised version reprinted under the new title,
   On Social Psychology: Selected Papers, 1964.)
Selected Writings, edited, with an Introduction, by Andrew J. Reck
   (Indianapolis: Bobbs-Merrill Co., 1964).
"Two Unpublished Papers": "Relative Space-Time and Simultaneity"
   and "Metaphysics", edited, with an Introduction, by David L. Miller,
   Review of Metaphysics, 1964 (17:4), pp. 511-56.
George Herbert Mead: Essays on His Social Philosophy, edited, with
   an Introduction, by John W. Petras (New York: Teachers College
   Press, 1968).
"Educational Theory: An Unpublished Paper", edited, with an Intro-
   duction, by Darnell Rucker, School and Society, 1964 (17:4), pp.
   148-52. (1)

---

(1) See Mead's paragraph fragments on aesthetic education and on
emotion and religion quoted in: Darnell Rucker, The Chicago Pragmatists,
Minneapolis: Univ. of Minnesota Press, 1969, pp. 104 & 120-4. These
fragments are derived from Mead's papers in the Archives of the University of Chicago.

2. Mead's works published during his life

1. "Herr Lasswitz on Energy and Epistemology", Psychological Review, 1894 (1:2), pp. 172-5.
2. "Die moderne Energetik in ihrer Bedeutung für Erkenntniskritik. Kurt Lasswitz . . .", Psychological Review, 1894 (1:2), pp. 210-3.
3. "A Theory of Emotions from the Physiological Standpoint", Psychological Review, 1895 (2:2), pp. 162-4.
4. "An Introduction to Comparative Psychology. C. L. Morgan . . .", Psychological Review, 1895 (2:4), pp. 399-402.
5. "Some Aspects of Greek Philosophy", University Record (Univ. of Chicago), 1896 (1:2), p. 42.
6) "The Relation of Play to Education", University Record (Univ. of Chicago), 1896 (1:8), pp. 141-5. (ES 27-34)(2)
7. "The Psychology of Socialism. By Gustave Le Bon . . .", American Journal of Sociology, 1899 (5:3), pp. 404-12.
8) "The Working Hypothesis in Social Reform", American Journal of Sociology, 1899 (5:3), pp. 367-71. (ES 125-9; in part, SW 3-5)
9) "Suggestions toward a Theory of the Philosophical Disciplines", Philosophical Review, 1900 (9:1), pp. 1-17. (SW 6-24)
10. "Recollections of Henry in Oberlin and After", in Henry Northrup Castle: Letters, edited by George and Helen Mead (London: I. W. Sands, Ltd., 1902), 807-12. (3)
11. "The Definition of the Psychical", Decennial Publications (Univ. of Chicago), 1903 (First Series: Vol. III), pp. 77-112. (Reprinted in part in SW 25-59.)
12) "The Basis for a Parents' Association", Elementary School Teacher, 1904 (4:6), pp. 337-46. (ES 63-70)
13. "Image or Sensation", Journal of Philosophy, 1904 (1:22), pp. 604-7.
14. "The Relations of Psychology and Philology", Psychological Bulletin, 1904 (1:22), pp. 375-91.
15. "Du rôle de l'individu dans le déterminisme social . . ./Le Problème du déterminisme, déterminisme biologique et déterminisme social. D. Draghicesco . . .", Psychological Bulletin, 1905 (2:12), pp. 399-405.
16) "The Teaching of Science in College", Science, 1906 (24:613), pp. 390-7. (SW 60-72)
17. "The Imagination in Wundt's Treatment of Myth and Religion", Psychological Bulletin, 1906 (3:12), pp. 393-9.
18. "Science in High School", School Review, 1906 (14:4), pp. 237-49.
19. "Editorial Notes", School Review, 1907 (15:2), pp. 160-5.
20. "The Educational Situation in the Chicago Public Schools", City Club Bulletin (Chicago), 1907 (1:11), pp. 131-8.
21. "The Newer Ideals of Peace. By Jane Addams . . .", American Journal of Sociology, 1907 (33:1), pp. 121-8.

---

(2) ")" after the number in place of "." indicates that the given article is entirely reprinted in ES, PP, SP and/or SW.
(3) A copy of this publication can be found in the libraries of Oberlin College and the University of Chicago.

22) "Concerning Animal Perception", Psychological Review, 1907 (14:6), pp. 383-90. (SW 73-81)

23. "The Relation of Imitation to the Theory of Animal Perception", Psychological Bulletin, 1907 (4:7), pp. 210-1.

24) "Editorial Notes/ . . . The Real Educational Problem", Elementary School Teacher, 1908 (8:5), pp. 281-4. (ES 24-6)

25. "Industrial Education and Trade Schools . . .", Elementary School Teacher, 1908 (8:7), pp. 402-6.

26. "Editorial Notes/The N. E. A. Resolution on Industrial Education . . .", Elementary School Teacher, 1908 (9:3), pp. 156-7.

27. "Editorial Notes/ . . . On Industrial Training . . .", Elementary School Teacher, 1908 (9:4), pp. 212-4.

28. "The Social Settlement: Its Basis and Function", University Record (Univ. of Chicago), 1908 (12:3), pp. 108-10.

29) "Educational Aspects of Trade Schools", Union Labor Advocate, 1908 (8:7), pp. 19-20. (ES 44-9)

30) "The Philosophical Basis of Ethics", International Journal of Ethics, 1908 (18:3), pp. 311-23. (SW 82-93)

31) "Editorial Notes/Moral Training in the Schools . . .", Elementary School Teacher, 1909 (9:6), pp. 327-8. (ES 71-2)

32) "Industrial Education, the Working-Man, and the School", Elementary School Teacher, 1909 (9:7), pp. 369-83. (ES 50-62)

33. "Editorial Notes/The Problem of History in the Elementary School . . .", Elementary School Teacher, 1909 (9:8), pp. 433-4.

34) "Social Psychology as Counterpart to Physiological Psychology", Psychological Bulletin, 1909 (6:12), pp. 401-8. (SW 94-104)

35) "What Social Objects Must Psychology Presuppose?", Journal of Philosophy, 1910 (7:7), pp. 174-80. (SW 105-13)

36) "The Psychology of Social Consciousness Implied in Instruction", Science, 1910 (31:801), pp. 688-93. (SW 114-22; ES 35-41)

37) "Social Consciousness and the Consciousness of Meaning", Psychological Bulletin, 1910 (7:12), pp. 397-405. (SW 123-33)

38. "Social Value. A Study in Economic Theory . . . B. M. Anderson . . .", Psychological Bulletin, 1911 (8:12), pp. 432-36.

39. "Fite's Individualism/Individualism: Four Lectures on the Significance of Consciousness for Social Relations. Warner Fite . . .", Psychological Bulletin, 1911 (8:9), pp. 324-8.

40) "The City Club's Civic Exhibit" (Remarks on the "vocational work in the public schools"), City Club Bulletin (Chicago), 1912 (5:1), p. 9. (ES 42-3)

41. "Labor Night" (Remarks on the Labor Representatives), City Club Bulletin (Chicago), 1912 (5:13), pp. 214-5.

42. A Report on Vocation Training in Chicago and in Other Cities, by a Committee of the City Club (G. H. Mead, Chairman) (Chicago: City Club of Chicago, 1912).

43) "The Mechanism of Social Consciousness", Journal of Philosophy, 1912 (9:15), pp. 401-6. (SW 134-41) (An abstract is given under the title: "The Mechanism of Social Conduct", Journal of Philosophy, 1912 [9:12], p. 355.)

44) "The Social Self", Journal of Philosophy, 1913 (10:14), pp. 374-80. (SW 142-9) (An abstract is given in Journal of Philosophy, 1913

[10:12] , pp. 324-5.)

45. "A Heckling School Board and an Educational Stateswoman", Survey, 1914 (31:15), pp. 443-4.

46) "The Psychological Bases of Internationalism", Survey, 1915 (33:23), pp. 604-7. (ES 151-61)

47) "Natural Rights and the Theory of Political Institutions", Journal of Philosophy, 1915 (12:6), pp. 141-55. (SW 150-70)

48. "Madison - the Passage of the University of Wisconsin through the State Political Agitation of 1914 . . .", Survey, 1915 (35:13), pp. 349-51 & 354-61.

49. "Smashing the Looking Glass, Rejoinder", Survey, 1916 (35:21), pp. 607 & 610.

50. "Professor Hoxie and the Community", University of Chicago Magazine, 1917 (9:3), pp. 114-7.

51. "Josiah Royce - A Personal Impression", International Journal of Ethics, 1917 (27:2), pp. 168-70.

52) "Scientific Method and Individual Thinker", Creative Intelligence: Essays in the Pragmatic Attitude (New York: H. Holt & Co., 1917), pp. 176-227. (SW 171-211)

53. "Truancy and Non-Attendance in the Chicago Public Schools. By Edith Abbott and Sophonisba P. Breckinridge . . .", Survey, July 28, 1917 (38), pp. 369-70.

54. The Conscientious Objector (Patriotism through Education Series, Pamphlet No. 33) (New York: National Security League, 1917).

55) "The Psychology of Punitive Justice", American Journal of Sociology, 1918 (23:5), pp. 577-602. (SW 212-39; ES 130-50)

56. "Retiring President's Address", City Club Bulletin (Chicago), 1920 (13:16), pp. 94-9.

57) "A Behavioristic Account of the Significant Symbol", Journal of Philosophy, 1922 (19:6), pp. 157-63. (SW 240-7)

58) "Scientific Method and the Moral Sciences", International Journal of Ethics, 1923 (33:3), pp. 229-47. (SW 248-66; ES 83-96)

59) "The Genesis of the Self and Social Control", International Journal of Ethics, 1925 (35:3), pp. 251-77. (SW 267-93; in part, PP 176-95)

60) "The Nature of Aesthetic Experience", International Journal of Ethics, 1926 (36:4), pp. 382-93. (SW 294-305; in part, PA 454-7)

61) "The Objective Reality of Perspectives", Proceedings of the Sixth International Congress of Philosophy, edited by Edgar S. Brightman (New York: Longmans, Green & Co., 1927), pp. 75-85. (PP 161-75; SW 306-19)

62) "A Pragmatic Theory of Truth", Studies in the Nature of Truth (University of California Publications in Philosophy, XI), 1929, pp. 65-88. (SW 320-44)

63) "The Nature of the Past", Essays in Honor of John Dewey, edited by John Coss (New York: H. Holt & Co., 1929), 235-42. (SW 345-54)

64. "National-Mindedness and International-Mindedness", International Journal of Ethics, 1929 (34:4), pp. 385-407. (In part, SW 355-70)

65. "Bishop Berkeley and His Message", Journal of Philosophy, 1929 (26:10), pp. 421-30.

66) "Cooley's Contribution to American Social Thought", American

Journal of Sociology, 1930 (35:5), pp. 693-706. (SP 293-307)
67) "The Philosophies of Royce, James, and Dewey in their American Setting", International Journal of Ethics, 1930 (40:2), pp. 211-31. (SW 371-91; ES 109-24)
68) "Philanthropy from the Point of View of Ethics", Intelligent Philanthropy, ed. by Ellsworth Faris, Ferris Laune, and Arthur J. Todd (Chicago: Univ. of Chicago Press, 1930), pp. 133-48. (SW 392-407; ES 97-108)
69. "Doctor [Addison] Moore's Philosophy", University Record (Univ. of Chicago), New Series, 1931 (17:1), pp. 47-9. (4)

3. Biographical or personal statements on Mead

Edward S. Ames et al., George Herbert Mead (Chicago: Univ. of Chicago Press, 1931).
Van Meter Ames, "George Herbert Mead: An Appreciation", Univ. of Chicago Magazine, 1931 (23:8), pp. 370-2.
John Dewey, "George Herbert Mead As I Knew Him", University Record (Univ. of Chicago), 1931 (17:3), pp. 173-7; mostly reprinted in Journal of Philosophy, 1931 (28:12), pp. 309-14.
James H. Tufts, "Extracts from the Address at Mead's Funeral", University Record (Univ. of Chicago), 1931 (17:3), pp. 177-8.
Henry C. A. Mead, "Biographical Notes", in The Philosophy of the Act (1938), pp. lxxv-lxxix.
David Wallace, "Reflections on the Education of George Herbert Mead", American Journal of Sociology, 1967 (72:4), pp. 396-408.

4. Reviews of Mead's works

Of PP

Paul Weiss, New Republic, Oct. 26, 1932 (72), pp. 302-3.
Victor S. Yarros, Open Court, 1932 (46:11), pp. 787-91.
E. B. McGilvary, International Journal of Ethics, 1933 (43:3), pp. 345-9.
M. C. Otto, Philosophical Review, 1934 (43:3), pp. 314-5.
James T. Farrell, Literature and Morality (Vanguard Press, 1947), pp. 177-81.

---

(4) For the unpublished materials by and about Mead, see: Edward Stevens, "Bibliographical Note: G. H. Mead," American Journal of Sociology, 1967 (72:5), 555-6. In the University of Chicago Library are found: (1) "The Papers of George Herbert Mead (1863-1931)", fourteen boxes containing students' notes of his lectures as well as the manuscripts of his published works, including MS and PA; (2) "Mead, George H., The President's Papers", a folder of papers related to Mead in his official capacity; (3) "The Papers of Henry Northrup Castle (1862-1895)", eight boxes which include fourteen letters from Mead to the Castle family (1889-1901); and (4) electrostatic copies of some 130 personal letters written by Mead.

Of MS

Bruce W. Brotherston, Journal of Religion, 1935 (15:2), pp. 232-4.
W. Rex Crawford, Annals of the American Academy of Political and
    Social Science, May 1935 (179), pp. 272-3.
Sidney Hook, Nation, Feb. 13, 1935 (140:3632), pp. 195-6.
J. R. Kantor, International Journal of Ethics, 1935 (45:4), pp. 459-61.
E. C. Lindemann, Survey, 1935 (71:9), pp. 280-1.
Arthur E. Murphy, Journal of Philosophy, 1935 (32:6), pp. 162-3.
Wilson D. Walis, International Journal of Ethics, 1935 (45:4), pp. 456-9.
Ellsworth Faris, American Journal of Sociology, 1936 (41:6), pp. 909-13.

Of MT

John Dewey, New Republic, July 22, 1936 (87), pp. 329-30. (5)
Winfred E. Garrison, Christian Century, Dec. 9, 1936 (53), pp. 1656-7.
Sidney Hook, Nation, Aug. 22, 1936 (143), pp. 220-1.
Arthur E. Murphy, Journal of Philosophy, 1936 (33:14), pp. 284-6.
L. M. Pape, Annals of the American Academy of Political and Social
    Science, Sept. 1936 (187), pp. 251-2.
Gertrude V. Rich, Saturday Review, Aug. 8, 1936 (14:15), p. 19.
Radoslav A. Tsanoff, Philosophical Review, 1937 (46:4), pp. 433-6.

Of PA

Robert Bierstedt, Saturday Review, July 2, 1938 (18:10), p. 16.
A. E. Schilpp, Christian Century, Aug. 3, 1938 (55), pp. 940-3.
Theodore Abel, American Journal of Psychology, 1939 (52:1), pp. 155-6.
Kenneth Burke, New Republic, Jan. 11, 1939 (97), pp. 292-3. (6)
H. A. Larrabee, Philosophical Review, 1939 (48:4), pp. 433-6.
Samuel M. Strong, American Journal of Sociology, 1939 (45:1), pp. 71-6.

Of SW

H. W. Schneider, Journal of the History of Philosophy, 1969 (7:1), p. 108

Of ES

Robert Atchley, Social Forces,, 1969 (47:3), pp. 371-2.
Bernice M. Fisher, History of Education Quarterly, 1969 (9:4), pp.
    497-504. (7)

Entries in Encyclopedias

T. V. Smith, Encyclopedia of the Social Sciences (New York: Macmillan,
    1930), Vol. 4, pp. 241-2.

---

(5) It is a review of both MS and MT.
(6) It is also a review of MS and MT.
(7) It is also a review of MS, SP, and SW.

David Miller, <u>Encyclopedia Americana</u> (New York: Americana Corp.,
1966), Vol. 18, pp. 473-4.
William H. Desmonde, <u>The Encyclopedia of Philosophy</u>, ed. by Paul
Edwards (New York: Macmillan, 1967), Vol. 5, pp. 231-3.
Charles W. Morris, <u>Encyclopaedia Britannica</u> (Chicago: Encyclopaedia
Britannica, Inc., 1967), Vol. 15, p. 22.
Tamotsu Shibutani, <u>International Encyclopedia of the Social Sciences</u>,
ed. by David L. Sills (New York: Macmillan, 1968), Vol. 10,
pp. 83-7.

5. <u>Articles, books, and dissertations on Mead</u>

Albright, G. L., "The Concept of Perspective in George Herbert Mead
and Jose Ortega Y Gasset", Ph. D. Dissert., New York: Columbia
Univ., 1966.
Ames, Van Meter, "Mead and Husserl on the Self", <u>Philo. and Pheno.
Research</u>, 1955 (15:3), pp. 320-31.
--, "Mead and Sartre on Man", <u>Journal of Philosophy</u>, 1956 (53:6),
pp. 205-19.
--, "Reply to Maurice Natanson's Reply", <u>Philo. and Pheno. Research</u>,
1956 (17:2), pp. 246-7.
--, "Zen to Mead", <u>Proceedings and Addresses of the American
Philosophical Association</u>, XXXIII (Yellow Springs: Antioch Press,
1960), pp. 27-43.
--, <u>Zen and American Thought</u> (Honolulu: Univ. of Hawaii Press, 1962),
pp. 236-88.
--, "Buber and Mead", <u>Antioch Review</u>, 1967 (27:2), pp. 181-91.
Bales, Robert F., "Comment on Herbert Blumer's Paper" (on G. H.
Mead), <u>American Journal of Sociology</u>, 1966 (71:5), pp. 545-7.
Bittner, C. J., "G. H. Mead's Social Concept of the Self", <u>Sociology
and Social Research</u>, 1931 (16:1), pp. 6-22.
Blau, Joseph, <u>Men and Movements in American Philosophy</u> (New York:
Prentice-Hall, 1952), pp. 262-73.
Blumer, Herbert, "Reply" (to R. F. Bales' "Comment on Herbert
Blumer's Paper"), <u>American Journal of Sociology</u>, 1966 (71:5),
pp. 547-8.
--, "Sociological Implications of the Thought of George Herbert Mead",
<u>American Journal of Sociology</u>, 1966 (71:5), pp. 534-44.
--, "Reply to Woelfel, Stone, and Farberman", <u>American Journal of
Sociology</u>, 1967 (72:4), pp. 411-2.
Bowman, Andrew L., "Meaning and Nature: G. H. Mead's Theory of
Objects", Ph. D. Dissert., New York: Columbia Univ., 1951.
Brewster, John M., "A Behavioristic Account of the Logical Function
of Universals", I & II, <u>Journal of Philosophy</u>, 1936 (33:19 & 20),
pp. 505-14 & 533-47.
Brotherston, Bruce, "The Genius of Pragmatic Empiricism", I & II,
<u>Journal of Philosophy</u>, 1943 (40:1 & 2), pp. 14-21 & 29-39.
Broyer, John A., "The Ethical Theory of George Herbert Mead",
Ph. D. Dissert., Carbondale: Southern Illinois Univ., 1967.
Burke, Richard, " G. H. Mead and the Problem of Metaphysics",

Philo. and Pheno. Research, 1962 (23:1), pp. 81-8.

Burke, Richard J., "George Herbert Mead and Harry Stack Sullivan: A Study in the Relations between Philosophy and Psychology", Ph. D. Dissert., Chicago: Univ. of Chicago, 1959.

Churchill, Jordon M., "Moral Judgment and Self-Knowledge", Ph. D. Dissert., New York: Columbia Univ., 1956, pp. 136-217.

Clayton, Alfred S., Emergent Mind and Education: A Study of G. H. Mead's Bio-social Behaviorism from an Educational Point of View (New York: Teachers College Press, 1943).

Cook, Gary A., "The Self as Moral Agent: A Study in the Philosophy of George Herbert Mead", Ph. D. Dissert., New Haven: Yale Univ., 1966.

Cottrell, L. S., Jr. and R. Gallagher, "Important Developments in American Social Psychology during the Past Decade", Sociometry, 1941 (4:2), pp. 120-34.

Coutu, Walker, "Role-playing vs. Role-taking: An Appeal for Clarification", American Sociological Review, 1951 (10:2), pp. 180-7.

Decesare, Richard, "A Comparative Evaluation of the Social Self in the Philosophy of George Herbert Mead and Gabrial Marcel", Ph. D. Dissert., Boston: Boston College, 1968.

De Laguna, Grace A., "Communication, the Act, and the Object - with Reference to Mead", Journal of Philosophy, 1946 (43:9), pp. 225-38.

Desmonde, William H., Self-Actualization: Loving and Strategic (Boston: Eagle Enterprises [Ph. D. Dissert., New York: Columbia Univ.], 1951).

--, "G. H. Mead and Freud: American Social Psychology and Psycho-analysis", Psychoanalysis (a double issue under the title Psycho-analysis and the Future), 1957 (4:4 & 5:1), pp. 31-50 & 154-6.

Doan, Frank M., "Emergence and Organized Perspectives: A Study in the Philosophy of George Herbert Mead", Ph. D. Dissert., Toronto: Univ. of Toronto, 1952.

--, "Notations on G. H. Mead's Principles of Sociality with Special Reference to Transformations", Journal of Philosophy, 1956 (53:30), pp. 607-15.

--, "Remarks on G. H. Mead's Conception of Simultaneity", Journal of Philosophy, 1958 (55:5), pp. 203-9.

El Germani, G., "Behaviorismo social de G. H. Mead", Revista International de Sociologiea, 1952 (10), pp. 353-8.

Faris, Ellsworth, "The Social Psychology of George Mead", American Journal of Sociology, 1937 (43:3), pp. 391-402.

Fen, Sing-Nan, "Present and Re-Presentation: A Discussion of Mead's Philosophy of the Present", Philosophical Review, 1951 (60:4), pp. 545-50.

Hare, Peter H., "G. H. Mead's Metaphysics of Sociality", Ph. D. Dissert., New York: Columbia Univ., 1965.

Holmes, Eugene C., "Social Philosophy and the Social Mind: A Study of the Genetic Methods of J. M. Baldwin, G. H. Mead, and J. E. Bodin", Ph. D. Dissert., New York: Columbia Univ., 1943, pp. 22-46.

Jones, Martin M., "The Categorical Concept of Emergence in the

Philosophy of George H. Mead", Ph. D. Dissert., New Orleans: Tulane Univ., 1970.

Kahn, P., "Le Symbole dans la psychologie sociale de G. H. Mead", Cahiers Internationaux de Sociologie, 1949 (6), pp. 134-49.

Karpf, Fay B., American Social Psychology, Its Origins and Development, and European Background (New York: McGraw-Hill, 1932), pp. 318-27.

Keen, Tom C., "George Herbert Mead's Social Theory of Meaning and Experience", Ph. D. Dissert., Columbus: Ohio State Univ., 1968.

Kessler, Hubert, "Basic Factors in the Growth of Mind and Self: Analysis and Reconstruction of G. H. Mead's Theory", Ph. D. Dissert Urban: Univ. of Illinois, 1940.

Kolb, William, L., "A Critical Evaluation of Mead's 'I' and 'Me' Concepts", Social Forces, 1944 (22:3), pp. 291-6.

Lee, Grace C., George Herbert Mead: Philosopher of the Social Individual (New York: King's Crown Press, 1945).

Lee, Harold N., "Mead's Doctrine of the Past" (=Tulane Studies in Philosophy, XII) (New Orleans: Tulane Univ., 1963), pp. 52-75.

Lundberg, George A., "Methodological Convergence of Mead, Lundberg, and Parsons", American Journal of Sociology, 1954 (60:2), pp. 182-4.

Majorino, Maria G., "George Herbert Mead e la psicologia sociale", Riv. Psicol. soc., 1959 (26), pp. 11-27.

McGary, John K., "Sources, Nature and Educational Implications of G. H. Mead's Theories of the Self and Society", Ph. D. Dissert., New York: New York Univ., 1943.

McKinney, David W., "Problems of the Self in the Light of the Psychopathology of Schizophrenia", Psychiatry, 1951 (14:3), pp. 331-9.

McKinney, John C., "A Comparison of the Social Psychology of G. H. Mead and J. L. Moreno", Sociometry, 1947 (10:4), pp. 338-49.

--, "Systematic Sociological Theory in the United States: An Exposition, Analysis, and Synthesis of the Methodological and Substantive Positions of G. H. Mead, Talcott Parsons, and G. A. Lundberg", Ph. D. Dissert., Lansing: Michigan State College, 1953.

--, "Methodological Convergence of Mead, Lundberg, and Parsons", American Journal of Sociology, 1954 (59:6), pp. 565-74.

--, "George H. Mead and the Philosophy of Science", Philosophy of Science, 1955 (22), pp. 264-71.

--, "The Contribution of George H. Mead to the Sociology of Knowledge", Social Forces, 1955 (34:2), pp. 144-9.

Meltzer, B. N., The Social Psychology of George Herbert Mead (Kalamazoo: Center of Sociological Research, 1964).

Miller, David L., "G. H. Mead's Conception of 'Present'", Philosophy of Science, 1943 (10:1), pp. 40-6.

--, "De Laguna's Interpretation of G. H. Mead", Journal of Philosophy, 1947 (44:6), pp. 158-62.

--, "The Nature of the Physical Object", Journal of Philosophy, 1947 (44:13), pp. 352-9.

Miyamoto, S. Frank & Sanford M. Dornbusch, "A Test of Interactionist Hypotheses of Self-Conception", American Journal of Sociology, 1956 (61:5), pp. 399-405.

Moreno, Jacob L., "Sociometry and the Social Psychology of G. H.

Mead", Sociometry, 1947 (10:4), pp. 350-3.

Morris, Charles W., "Peirce, Mead, and Pragmatism", Philosophical Review, 1938 (47:2), pp. 109-27.

--, Six Theories of Mind (Chicago: Univ. of Chicago Press, 1952), pp. 322-50.

--, "George H. Mead: A Pragmatist's Philosophy of Science", in Scientific Psychology, ed. by B. Wolman and E. Nagel (New York: Basic Books, 1965), pp. 402-8.

--, The Pragmatic Movement in American Philosophy (New York: George Braziller, 1970), passim.

Murphy, Arthur E., "Concerning Mead's The Philosophy of the Act", Journal of Philosophy, 1939 (36:4), pp. 85-103.

Natanson, Maurice, "George H. Mead's Metaphysics of Time", Journal of Philosophy, 1953 (50:25), pp. 770-82.

--, "The Concept of the Given in Peirce and Mead", Modern Schoolman, 1955 (32:2), pp. 143-57.

--, "Phenomenology from the Natural Standpoint: A Reply to Van Meter Ames", Philo. and Pheno. Research, 1956 (17:2), pp. 241-5.

--, The Social Dynamics of George H. Mead (Washington, D. C.: Public Affairs Press, 1956).

Neiman, Lionel J. and James W. Hughes, "The Problem of the Concept of Role - A Re-survey of the Literature", Social Forces, 1951 (30:2), pp. 141-9.

O'Toole, Richard E., "Experiments in George Herbert Mead's Taking the Role of the Other", Ph. D. Dissert., Eugene: Univ. of Oregon, 1963.

Percy, Walker, "Symbol, Consciousness, and Intersubjectivity", Journal of Philosophy, 1958 (55:12), pp. 631-41.

Pfuetze, Paul E., Self, Society, Existence: Human Nature and Dialogue in the Thought of George Herbert Mead and Martin Buber (New York: Harper, 1961). (Originally published under the title The Social Self [New York: Bookman Associates, 1954].)

Reck, Andrew J., "The Philosophy of G. H. Mead" (=Tulane Studies in Philosophy, XII) (New Orleans: Tulane Univ., 1963), pp. 5-31; reprinted in his book, Recent American Philosophy (New York: Pantheon Books, 1964), pp. 84-122. (A similar version is given as "Introduction" in SW.)

Reeder, Leo G., George A. Donohue, and Arthuro Biblarz, "Conceptions of Self and Others", American Journal of Sociology, 1960 (66:2), pp. 153-9.

Rosenthal, Sandra B., "A Systematic Expansion of C. I. Lewis' Conceptual Pragmatism with Reference to the Philosophies of Peirce and Mead", Ph. D. Dissert., New Orleans: Tulane Univ., 1967.

--, "Peirce, Mead, and the Logic of Concepts", Transaction of the C. S. Peirce Society, 1969 (5:3), pp. 173-87.

Rucker, Darnell, The Chicago Pragmatists (Minneapolis: Univ. of Minnesota Press, 1969), passim.

Schneider, Herbert W., A History of American Philosophy (New York: Columbia Univ. Press, 1946), passim.

Smith, T. V., "The Social Philosophy of George Herbert Mead",

American Journal of Sociology, 1931 (37:3), pp. 368-85.
--, "George Herbert Mead and the Philosophy of Philanthropy", _Social Service Review_, 1932 (6:1), pp. 39-54.
--, "The Religious Bearings of a Secular Mind - George Herbert Mead", _Journal of Religion_, 1932 (12:2), pp. 200-13.
Stevens, Edward V., "G. H. Mead on the Moral Self", Ph. D. Dissert., St. Louis: St. Louis Univ., 1965.
Stone, Gregory P. & Harvey A. Farberman, "Further Comment on the Blumer-Bales Dialogue concerning the Implications of the Thought of George Herbert Mead", _American Journal of Sociology_, 1967 (72:4), pp. 409-10.
Stryker, Sargent, "Attitude Ascription in Adult Married Offspring-Parent Relationships: A Study of the Social Psychological Theory of G. H. Mead", Ph. D. Dissert., Minneapolis: Univ. of Minnesota, 1955.
--, "The Adjustment of Married Offspring to Their Parents", _American Sociological Review_, 1955 (20:2), pp. 149-54.
--, "Role-Taking Accuracy and Adjustment", _Sociometry_, 1957 (20:4), pp. 286-96.
--, "Relationships of Married Offspring and Parent: A Test of Mead's Theory", _American Journal of Sociology_, 1956 (62:3), pp. 308-19; revised and reprinted under a new title, "Conditions of Accurate Role-taking: A Test of Mead's Theory", _Human Behavior and Social Processes_, ed. by A. M. Rose (Boston: Houghton Mifflin, 1962), pp. 41-62.
Suri, Surinder S., "The Philosophy of Mind of George Herbert Mead", Ph. D. Dissert., Evanston: Northwestern Univ., 1953.
Swanson, Guy E., "Mead and Freud: Their Relevance for Social Psychology", _Sociometry_, 1961 (24:4), pp. 319-39.
Thayer, H. S., _Meaning and Action: A Critical History of Pragmatism_, Indianapolis: Bobbs-Merrill, 1968), pp. 232-68.
Tonness, Alfred, "A Notation on the Problem of the Past - with Special Reference to G. H. Mead", _Journal of Philosophy_, 1932 (29:21), pp. 599-606.
Tremmel, W. C., _The Social Concepts of George Herbert Mead_ (Emporia: Kansas State Teachers College, 1957).
Troyer, William L., "Mead's Social and Functional Theory of Mind", _American Sociological Review_, 1946 (11:2), pp. 198-202.
Ushenko, Andrew, "Alternative Perspectives and the Invariant Space-Time", _Mind_, 1934 (43:170), pp. 199-203.
Victoroff, David, "Les idées esthétiques de G. H. Mead", _Revue d'Esthétique_, 1949 (2), pp. 142-50.
--, "Aspects originaux de la philosophie de G. H. Mead", _Revue de Métaphysique et de Morale_, 1952 (57:1), pp. 66-81.
--, "La notion d'émergence et la catégorie du social dans la philosophie de G. H. Mead", _Revue Philosophique_, 1952 (142), pp. 555-62.
--, _G. H. Mead: Sociologue et philosophe_ (Paris: Presses Universitaires de France, 1953).
Weiss, H. D., "George Herbert Mead's Personality Theory: A Comparison with That of Sigmund Freud and with Neurophysiology", Ph. D. Dissert., New Orleans: Tulane Univ., 1964.

Werkmeister, William H., A History of Philosophical Ideas in America (New York: Ronald Press, 1949), pp. 524–40.

Wilkerson, Kenneth E., "A Framework for a Theory of Rhetoric Based on the Writings of George Herbert Mead", Ph. D. Dissert., Gainesv Univ. of Florida, 1968.

Woelfel, Joseph, "Comment on the Blumer-Bales Dialogue concerning the Interpretation of Mead's Thought", American Journal of Sociology, 1967 (27:4), p. 409.

6. Other contemporary works cited and referred to

Balz, A. G. A., Descartes and the Modern World (New Haven: Yale Univ. Press, 1952).

Barrett, William, Irrational Man: A Study in Existential Philosophy (New York: Doubleday, 1958).

Bennett, Jonathan, Rationality (London: Routledge & Kegan Pual, 1964).

Berne, Eric, Games People Play (New York: Grove Press, 1964).

Bidney, David, Theoretical Anthropology (New York: Columbia Univ. Press, 1953).

Blau, Joseph, Men and Movements in American Philosophy (New York: Prentice-Hall, 1952).

Brain, R., "The Neurology of Language", Brain, 1961 (84), pp. 145–66; reprinted in Language, ed. by R. C. Oldfield & J. C. Marshall (Baltimore: Penguin Books, 1968), pp. 309–32.

Buchler, Justus, Toward a General Theory of Human Judgment (New York: Columbia Univ. Press, 1951).

--, Nature and Judgment (New York: Columbia Univ. Press, 1955).

--, The Concept of Method (New York: Columbia Univ. Press, 1961).

--, Metaphysics of Natural Complexes (New York: Columbia Univ. Press 1966).

Carroll, D. G., "Evolution of Hand Function", Maryland State Medical Journal, 1967 (16:1), pp. 99–104.

Cassirer, Ernst, An Essay on Man (New Haven: Yale Univ. Press, 1944)

--, The Myth of the State (New Haven: Yale Univ. Press, 1946).

--, The Philosophy of Symbolic Forms, trans. R. Manheim (New Haven: Yale Univ. Press, 1953-7 [orig. 1923-9]).

Chomsky, Noam, "Verbal Behavior. By B. K. Skinner . . .", Language, 1959 (35:1), pp. 26–58.

--, Cartesian Linguistics: A Chapter in the History of Rationalist Though (New York: Harper & Row, 1966).

--, "Recent Contributions to the Theory of Innate Ideas", Synthese, 1967 (17:1), pp. 2–11.

--, "Language and Mind", I & II, Columbia Forum, 1968 (11:1 & 3), pp. 5-10 & 23-25; reprinted in his Language and Mind (New York: Harcourt Brace & World, 1968), Ch. 1 & 3.

Cohen, Morris R., American Thought, ed. by F. S. Cohen (New York: Free Press, 1954).

--, Reason and Nature (New York: Free Press, 1964 [orig. 1931]).

Cooley, Charles H., Human Nature and the Social Order (New York: C. Scribner's Sons, 1902).

Danto, Arthur, "Student Morality: From Skepticism to Dogmatism", Columbia Forum, 1969 (12:3), pp. 34-8.

Debos, R., "Biological Individuality", Columbia Forum, 1969 (12:1), pp. 5-9.

Dewey, John, "The Reflex Arc Concept in Psychology", Psychological Review, 1896 (3:4), pp. 357-70; reprinted in his Philosophy and Civilization (New York: Minton, Balch & Co., 1931), pp. 233-48.

--, Reconstruction in Philosophy, (New York: Henry Holt, 1920).

--, Human Nature and Conduct, (New York: Henry Holt, 1922).

--, Logic: The Theory of Inquiry, (New York: Henry Holt, 1938).

--, Experience and Nature (New York: Dover, 1958 [orig. 1925]).

Diesing, P. Reason in Society: Five Types of Decisions and Their Social Conditions (Urbana: Univ. of Illinois Press, 1962).

Emmet, Dorothy, Rules, Roles and Relations (New York: St. Martin's, 1966).

Erlermyer-Kimling, L., & L. F. Jarvick, "Genetics and Intelligence", Science, 1963 (142), pp. 1477-9; reprinted in Intelligence and Ability, ed. by S. Wiseman (Baltimore: Penguin Books, 1967), pp. 282-6.

Frankel, Charles, The Faith of Reason: The Idea of Progress in the French Enlightenment (New York: King's Crown Press, 1948).

--, The Case for Modern Man, (New York: Harper & Brothers, 1955).

--, The Love of Anxiety and Other Essays (New York: Dell, 1967 [orig. 1965]).

--, "Justice and Rationality", in Philosophy, Science, and Method: Essays in Honor of Ernest Nagel, ed. by S. Morgenbesser, P. Suppes & M. White (New York: St. Martin's, 1969), pp. 400-14.

Freud, Sigmund, Civilization and Its Discontents, trans. by J. Riviere (New York: W. W. Norton, 1962 [orig. 1929]).

Friedrich, Carl J., ed., Rational Decision (Nomos, VII) (New York: Atherton Press, 1964).

Geiger, G. R., John Dewey in Perspective (New York: McGraw-Hill, 1964 [orig. 1958]).

Gerth, H., & C. W. Mills, Character and Social Structure: The Psychology of Social Institutions (New York: Harcourt, Brace & World, 1953).

Goodman, Nelson, "The Way the World Is", Review of Metaphysics, 1960 (14:1), pp. 48-56.

--, Fact, Fiction, and Forecast (Indianapolis: Bobbs-Merrill, 1965 [orig. 1955]).

--, "The Epistemological Argument", Synthese, 1967 (17:1), pp. 23-8.

Hare, R.M., The Language of Morals (New York: Oxford Univ. Press, 1964 [orig. 1952]).

Hintikka, J., "Cogito, Ergo Sum: Inference or Performance?", Philosophical Review, 1962 (71:1), pp. 3-32; reprinted in Meta-Meditations: Studies in Descartes, ed. by A. Sesonske & N. Fleming (Belmont: Wadsworth, 1965), pp. 50-76.

Hofstadter, Albert, "The Myth of the Whole: A Consideration of Quine's View of Knowledge", Journal of Philosophy, 1954 (50:14), pp. 397-417.

James, William, "Does 'Consciousness' Exist?", Journal of Philosophy,

1904 (1:18), pp. 477-91; reprinted in his Essays in Radical Empirici (New York: Longmans, Green & Co., 1912), pp. 1-38.

Jaspers, Karl, Reason and Existenz, trans. by W. Earle (New York: Noonday Press, 1957 [orig. 1935]).

Jones, J. Wood, The Principles of Anatomy as Seen in the Hand (Philadelphia: P. Blakiston's Sons, 1920).

Köhler, Wolfgang, Gestalt Psychology (New York: Liveright, 1947 [orig. 1929]).

--, Dynamics in Psychology (New York: Grove Press, 1960 [orig. 1940]

Langer, Susanne K., "Speculations on the Origins of Speech and Its Communicative Function", Quarterly Journal of Speech, 1960 (46), pp. 121-34; reprinted in her Philosophical Sketches (New York: New American Library, 1964 [orig. 1962]), pp. 30-52.

Laslett, P., ed., The Physical Basis of Mind (Oxford: Blackwell, 1950).

Lenneberg, E. H., "A Biological Perspective of Language", in New Directions in the Study of Language, ed. by E. H. Lenneberg (Cambridge: M. I. T. Press, 1964), pp. 65-88; reprinted in Language, ed. by R. C. Oldfield & J. C. Marshall (Baltimore: Penguin Books, 1968), pp. 32-47.

Lewis, C. I., "A Pragmatic Conception of the a Priori", Journal of Philosophy, 1923 (20:17), pp. 169-77; reprinted in Readings in Philosophical Analysis, ed. H. Feigl & W. Sellars (New York: Appleton-Century-Crofts, 1949), pp. 286-94.

--, Mind and the World Order (New York: Dover, 1956 [orig. 1929]).

Maler, P., "Developments in the Study of Animal Communication", in Darwin's Biological Work: Some Aspects Reconsidered, ed. by P. R. Bell (New York: J. Wiley & Sons, 1964 [orig. 1959]), pp. 150-206.

Malinowski, B., A Scientific Theory of Culture and Other Essays (Chapel Hill: Univ. of N. Carolina Press, 1944).

McLuhan, Marshall, Understanding Media: The Extension of Man (New York: New American Library, 1964).

Mesthene, Emmanual G., How Language Makes Us Know. Some Views About the Nature of Intelligibility (The Hague: Martinus Nijhoff, 1964

Miles, T. R., "On Defining Intelligence", British Journal of Educational Psychology, 1957 (27:3), pp. 153-65; reprinted in Intelligence and Ability, ed. by S. Wiseman (Baltimore: Penguin Books, 1968), pp. 159-76.

Mills, C. Wright, "Language, Logic, and Culture", American Sociological Review, 1939 (4:5), pp. 670-80.

Morgenbesser, Sidney, "The Realist-Instrumentalist Controversy", in Philosophy, Science, and Method: Essays in Honor of Ernest Nagel, ed. by S. Morgenbesser, P. Suppes & M. White (New York: St. Martin's, 1969), pp. 200-18.

Morris, Charles W., Six Theories of Mind (Chicago: Univ. of Chicago Press, 1932).

--, Logical Positivism, Pragmatism, and Scientific Empiricism, (Paris: Hermann et Cie, 1937).

--, Foundations of the Theory of Signs (=International Encyclopedia of Unified Science, Vol. I, No. 2) (Chicago: Univ. of Chicago Press, 1938).

--, "Science, Art, and Technology", <u>Kenyon Review</u>, 1939 (1:4), pp. 409-23.

--, "The Mechanism of Freedom", in <u>Freedom, Its Meaning</u>, ed. by R. N. Anshen (New York: Harcourt, Brace & Co.), 1940, pp. 579-89.

--, <u>The Open Self</u> (New York: Prentice-Hall, 1948).

--, <u>Signs, Language, and Behavior</u> (New York: George Braziller, 1955 [orig. 1946]).

--, <u>Paths of Life: Preface to a World Religion</u> (New York: George Braziller, 1956 [orig. 1942]).

--, <u>Varieties of Human Value</u> (Chicago: Univ. of Chicago Press, 1956).

--, <u>Signification and Significance: A Study of the Relations of Signs and Values</u> (Cambridge: The M. I. T. Press, 1964).

--, <u>The Pragmatic Movement in American Philosophy</u> (New York: George Braziller, 1970).

--, <u>Writings on the General Theory of Signs</u> (The Hague: Mouton, 1971).

Naegele, Kaspar D., "Editorial Foreword / Interaction Roles and Collectivities", in <u>Theories of Society: Foundations of Modern Sociological Theory</u>, ed. by T. Parsons <u>et al</u>. (New York: Free Press, 1961), Vol. I, pp. 147-57.

Nagel, Ernest, <u>The Structure of Science: Problems in the Logic of Scientific Explanation</u> (New York: Harcourt, Brace & World, 1961).

Napier, J., "The Evolution of the Hand", <u>Scientific American</u>, 1962 (207:6), pp. 56-62.

Nelson, R. J., "Behaviorism is False", <u>Journal of Philosophy</u>, 1969 (66:14), pp. 417-52.

Pavlov, I. P., <u>Conditioned Reflexes: An Investigation of the Physiological Activity of the Cerebral Cortex</u>, trans. & ed. by G. V. Anrep (London: Oxford Univ. Press, 1927).

Peirce, Charles Sanders, <u>Collected Papers</u>, I-VI, ed. by C. Hartshorne & P. Weiss (Cambridge: Harvard Univ. Press, 1931-5).

Piaget, Jean, <u>The Language and Thought of the Child</u>, trans. by M. Warden (New York: Harcourt, Brace & Co., 1926 [orig. 1923]).

Putnam, H., "The 'Innateness Hypothesis' and Explanatory Models in Linguistics", <u>Synthese</u>, 1967 (17:1), pp. 12-22.

Quine, W. V. O., <u>From a Logical Point of View</u> (Cambridge: Harvard Univ. Press, 1953).

--, <u>Word and Object</u> (Cambridge: M. I. T. Press, 1960).

Randall, John Herman, Jr., <u>Nature and Historical Experience</u> (New York: Columbia Univ. Press, 1958).

--, <u>Aristotle</u> (New York: Columbia Univ. Press, 1960).

--, "The Art of Language and the Linguistic Situation: a Naturalistic Analysis", <u>Journal of Philosophy</u>, 1963 (60:2), pp. 29-56.

--, "The Ontology of Paul Tillich", in <u>The Theology of Paul Tillich</u>, ed. by C. W. Kegley & R. W. Bretall (New York: Macmillan, 1964).

--, <u>The Career of Philosophy</u>, I & II (New York: Columbia Univ. Press, 1962 & 1965).

Rose, A. M., ed., <u>Human Behavior and Social Processes: an Interactionist Approach</u> (Boston: Houghton Mifflin, 1962).

Russell, Bertrand, "On Denoting", <u>Mind</u>, 1905 (14), pp. 478-93; reprinted in <u>Readings in Philosophical Analysis</u>, ed. by H. Feigl

& W. Sellars (New York: Appleton-Century-Crofts, 1949), pp. 103-1[

Ryle, Gilbert, The Concept of Mind (New York: Barnes & Noble, 1965
[orig. 1949]).

--, Dilemmas (Cambridge: Cambridge Univ. Press, 1954).

--, A Rational Animal (London: Athelona Press [Univ. of London],
1962).

Santayana, George, The Life of Reason; or, The Phases of Human
Progress (New York: Collier Books, 1962 [orig. 1905-30]).

Schneider, H. W., A History of American Philosophy (New York:
Columbia Univ. Press, 1946).

Scholl, D. A., The Organization of the Cerebral Cortex (London:
Meuthen, 1956).

--, "A Comparative Study of the Neural Packing Density in the Cerebral
Cortex", Journal of Anatomy, 1959 (93:2), pp. 1943-58.

Sebeok, Thomas A., ed., Animal Communication: Techniques of Study
and Results of Research (Bloomington: Indiana Univ. Press, 1968).

Skinner, B. F., Verbal Behavior (New York: Appleton-Century-Crofts,
1957).

Snow, C. P., The Two Cultures: and a Second Look (New York: New
American Library, 1964 [orig. 1959]).

Spearman, C. E., The Abilities of Man, their Nature and Measurement
(New York: Macmillan, 1927).

Spearman, C. E., & LL. W. Jones, Human Ability (London: Macmillan, 1950).

Sperry, R. W., "On the Neural Basis of the Conditioned Response",
British Journal of Animal Behavior, 1955 (3:2), pp. 41-4.

Stebbing, L. Susan, Philosophy and the Physicists (London: Methuen,
1937).

Strawson, P. F., "On Referring", Mind, 1950 (59), 320-44; reprinted
in Essays in Conceptual Analysis, ed. by A. Flew (London:
Macmillan, 1956), pp. 21-52.

Sturtevant, E. H., An Introduction to Linguistic Science (New Haven:
Yale Univ. Press, 1947).

Thayer, H. S., Meaning and Action: A Critical History of Pragmatism
(Indianapolis: Bobbs-Merrill, 1968).

Veatch, H. B., Rational Man: A Modern Interpretation of Aristotelian
Ethics (Bloomington: Indiana Univ. Press, 1962).

Watson, J. B., "Psychology and Behaviorism", Psychological Review,
1913 (20:2), pp. 158-77.

--, Behavior, An Introduction to Comparative Psychology (New York:
Henry Holt, 1914).

--, Psychology from the Standpoint of a Behaviorist (Philadelphia:
Lippincott, 1919).

--, Behaviorism (New York: W. W. Norton, 1925).

Whitehead, A. N., The Concept of Nature (Ann Arbor: Univ. of Michigan
Press, 1957 [orig. 1920]).

--, The Function of Reason (Boston: Beacon Press, 1958 [orig. 1929]).

Wiseman, S., "Introduction", in Intelligence and Ability, ed. by S.
Wiseman (Baltimore: Penguin Books, 1967), pp. 7-15.

Wittgenstein, Ludwig, Philosophical Investigations, trans. by G. E. M.
Anscombe (New York: Macmillan, 1953).

INDEX OF NAMES